Toward
a Psychology
of Awakening

Toward
a Psychology
of Awakening

 Buddhism, Psychotherapy,
and the Path of Personal
and Spiritual Transformation

John Welwood

SHAMBHALA

Boston & London

2002

Shambhala Publications, Inc.
Horticultural Hall
300 Massachusetts Avenue
Boston, Massachusetts 02115
www.shambhala.com

Grateful acknowledgment is made to Robert Bly for permission
to reprint portions of his translation of Goethe's "The Holy
Longing." Reprinted from *News of the Universe: Poems of Twofold
Consciousness*, edited by Robert Bly. Sierra Club Books, 1986.
Copyright © 1984 by Robert Bly.

16   15   14   13   12   11   10   9

Printed in the United States of America

⊗ This edition is printed on acid-free paper that meets
the American National Standards Institute z39.48 Standard.
♻ This book was printed on 30% postconsumer recycled paper.
For more information please visit www.shambhala.com.
Distributed in the United States by Random House, Inc., and
in Canada by Random House of Canada Ltd

Library of Congress Cataloging-in-Publication Data

Welwood, John, 1943–
Toward a psychology of awakening: Buddhism,
psychotherapy, and the path of personal and spiritual
transformation/ John Welwood.
p.   cm.
ISBN 978-1-57062-540-4 (cloth)
ISBN 978-1-57062-823-8 (pbk.)
1. Buddhism—Psychology.   2. Psychotherapy—Religious
aspects—Buddhism.   3. Spiritual life—Buddhism.   I. Title.
BQ4570.P76 W45   2000
294.3'375—dc21   99-046050

I would like to dedicate this book
to my first real mentor,

EUGENE GENDLIN,

who helped me discover
and appreciate
the subtle beauty and mystery
of inner experiencing.

Contents

PART THREE
THE AWAKENING POWER OF RELATIONSHIP

Toward
a Psychology
of Awakening

Introduction

✤ DEEP WITHIN THE HUMAN SPIRIT, now largely sev-
ered from its ancient moorings, there is a search unfolding—for a new
vision of why we are here and what we may become. Perhaps it is only
now, in postmodern times, when we have unprecedented access to all
the world's spiritual traditions, as well as more than a century of Western psychology to draw on, that we can forge a larger understanding
of the human journey that addresses all the different facets of our
nature. The new vision we are needing is one that brings together two
different halves of our nature, which have been cultivated in different
ways on opposite sides of the globe. While the traditional spiritual
cultures of the East have specialized in illuminating the timeless, *suprapersonal* ground of being—the "heaven" side of human nature—
Western psychology has focused on the earthly half—the *personal* and
the *interpersonal*. We need a new vision that embraces all three domains of human existence—the suprapersonal, the personal, and the
interpersonal—which no single tradition, East or West, has ever fully
addressed within a single overall framework of understanding and
practice.

Spiritual practice, when cut off from the rich feeling-textures of
personal life, can become dry and remote, just as personal life becomes
narrow and confining when cut off from the fresh breezes of spiritual
realization. Now that our world has become so disconnected from
larger spiritual values and purpose, we need to find new ways of integrating spiritual wisdom into our personal lives if we are to meet the
great challenges we face heading into the new millennium. The
emerging dialogue between the ancient spiritual traditions of the East
and the modern therapeutic psychology of the West holds great promise in this regard.

By helping us explore the relationship between the personal and spiritual sides of our nature, this East/West dialogue can bring into focus the vital connections between mind, heart, body, soul, and spirit, so that we may recognize them as inseparable facets of a single, living whole. And on a practical level, it may also help us develop a more integrated approach to spiritual growth, health and well-being, relationship and human community.

The convergence of East and West raises particularly interesting questions in the psychological arena. How might psychotherapy and spiritual practice work as allies in helping people awaken to who they genuinely are? What can the spiritual traditions of the East tell us about the source of psychological balance? What implications does meditative awareness have for psychological health and for the development of dynamic, transformative interpersonal relationships? What new possibilities emerge when psychological work takes place in a spiritual context? And how might Western psychological insights and methods actually contribute to spiritual development? How can Buddhism and other ancient spiritual traditions most effectively address our psychologically-minded culture, where individual development is such a central value? What is the relationship between individuation—the development of soul—and spiritual liberation—total release from the limiting boundaries of self? How is it possible to integrate the personal/psychological and the suprapersonal/universal sides of our nature?

These are some of the issues addressed in this book, which is divided into three sections. The first explores basic issues and questions about the relationship between contemplative spirituality and Western psychology. The second addresses the practical implications of this encounter for psychological health and healing. And the third explores major implications for relationship and community.

My inspiration to explore the interface of Eastern and Western psychology first arose in 1963, when, as a young man in my twenties in Paris, I found myself staring into the black hole of Western materialism without the slightest idea of how to fashion a meaningful life for myself. While I appreciated the ritual and music of the church I grew up in, Christianity, at least as it was taught to me, did not provide an experiential practice that allowed me to access the living spirit. My discovery of Zen in the early 1960s opened up a totally appealing and revolutionary new perspective: that each of us can discover our own true nature, which lies directly within, realize it experientially, and thus awaken to a richer and deeper way of being.

Recognizing this kind of awakening as the real purpose of human existence gave me a direction where before I had none. Discovering Alan Watts's book *Psychotherapy East and West* took me a step further, by presenting the idea that Western psychotherapy could be a potential force for awakening, especially for Westerners. Inspired to find out how I might contribute to this search for a Western path of awakening, I decided to enter the field of clinical psychology and become a psychotherapist. I had found my life's work.

Yet I quickly became disillusioned by graduate school at the University of Chicago, where the emphasis was on conventional academic psychology, with its narrow, limited view of human nature and potential. As grace would have it, however, I found a real mentor there—Eugene Gendlin, an existentially oriented philosopher and psychotherapist who was in the process of developing the Focusing method, an innovative way of helping people tune into their inner experiencing and discover clear directions for change and growth in what first appears to be an unclear felt sense. Gendlin opened up the whole world of inner experiencing for me. He was the first person I had ever met who spoke directly about the actual process of felt experience—how it works, how it moves, how it unfolds and leads to sudden, unexpected breakthroughs.

Unlike my other professors, Gendlin described the inner psychological landscape in human and poetic, rather than clinical terms. By revealing the rich, multilevel process of inner experiencing to me, he handed me the key that helped me make sense of the whole therapeutic undertaking. Therapy was not, in the end, about diagnosis, procedures, or cures, but about developing a new kind of living relationship with one's experiencing. In meeting and learning from him, I found my life beginning to change from black-and-white to technicolor. For that I will always be grateful to him.

Throughout graduate school I pursued my own inquiry into a

question that intrigued me, energized me, and called to me like no other: the relationship between the awakening spoken of in Zen—the breakthrough into larger, universal truth—and the personal changes that occur in therapy. In looking for a way to work on myself and understand my life more fully, I became increasingly interested in Buddhism. My early encounters with the Tibetan teacher Chögyam Trungpa Rinpoche were particularly compelling.

Trungpa was steeped in the Mahamudra and Dzogchen schools of Tantric Buddhism—traditions that are based on a profound realization of the luminous, expansive, wakeful nature of consciousness. I had never met such an unusual, inscrutable, and thoroughly provocative and intriguing human being before. I remember once walking into a room for an interview with him and being astounded by the vast space that seemed to radiate from him in all directions. It felt as though the roof and walls of the room had been blown out. Never having experienced anything like that before, I found it tremendously magnetic.

Trungpa was uncompromising in his insistence that it was essential to do this strange thing: sitting on a cushion for hours on end. I used to think, "Why would anyone want to do that?" It seemed so much more interesting to read and talk about spiritual philosophy than to just sit there and not do anything. I thought, "Maybe thousands of years ago they had to do that sort of thing, but surely there must be some more high-tech method today." Yet as I began to practice meditation, it opened up my world in a whole new way. We are born with this incredible instrument called a mind, which can tune in heaven and hell and everything in between, but no one ever gives us operating instructions on how to use it or what to do with it. Meditation provided a way of actively seeing into the nature and activity of this mind. Gradually, despite all my initial resistance, I developed a profound respect for the practice of sitting meditation that has remained with me ever since.

After practicing meditation for many years, however, I found that there were certain areas of my life that it had not touched. As beautiful and stirring as I found the Buddhist teachings to be, I began to realize that I could not simply import them wholesale into my Western psyche. I would go on retreats and have wonderful realizations and openings that I was unable to integrate into my everyday functioning. My spiritual practice also seemed to reinforce in me a certain detachment from the interpersonal arena. Eventually, certain crises in my intimate relationships made it clear to me that I had work to do on my psychological issues.

Up to that time I had been operating under a romantic fantasy of enlightenment, culled from the old Zen stories I'd read—that somehow in a moment of realization all the old patterns would fall away and I would walk away a new man. That seemed such a nobler way to find freedom than doing battle in the therapeutic trenches. So when I finally began my own therapeutic work in earnest, I was truly surprised to discover what a powerful tool psychological inquiry could be, and how, in its own way, it too provided a path into deeper understanding of myself.

Although I had dearly hoped that meditation and spiritual practice would be the answer for all my ills, my experience did not bear this out. I found that psychological and spiritual work were both necessary, and that neither by itself seemed sufficient for helping me handle my life. Eventually I learned to honor them both as having different yet equally important gifts to offer.

Looking around at my fellow spiritual practitioners, I saw many of them avoiding dealing with their personal issues, and felt that many of them could benefit from psychological work as well. In fact, the spiritual community I was in underwent a major blowup because one of the leaders, despite all his spiritual realization, refused to face his own narcissism and grandiosity, acting it out in destructive ways instead. And I saw that covert psychological dynamics played a large part in most of the crises that many spiritual communities were undergoing at that time. Witnessing this contradiction—where spiritual teachers and students who clearly had developed a certain level of genuine spiritual insight and awareness nonetheless remained stuck in unwholesome personality patterns—was both troubling and revealing. It was becoming clear to me that psychological work had something important to offer to spiritual seekers, at least in the West.

Soon after completing my doctoral work, I discovered the fledgling

Journal of Transpersonal Psychology, where others who were also interested in exploring the interface between psychology and spirituality had begun to publish. I became one of the earliest regular and most frequent contributors to that journal and then went on in 1979 to publish my first book, *The Meeting of the Ways: Explorations in East/ West Psychology*.

Then I turned to writing a book on the spiritual dimension of intimate relationships, which I felt a strong need to understand more deeply. This work turned out to be a tremendous challenge, on every level of my being. With all it put me through, writing that book—*Journey of the Heart*—was the hardest thing I'd ever done. A few years into the project, I came to a crossroads where I realized I had to choose between completing the book or shifting my work back toward its original focus on the intersection of psychotherapy and meditative practice. Mostly for personal reasons, I chose to continue the work on relationship. Little did I realize it would take me fifteen years in all to complete.

Now that I have published three books on the subject of relationship, *Toward a Psychology of Awakening* represents a return to the roots of that work, and to my first love: the interface of Eastern and Western psychology. This book stakes out this new field of inquiry—what I call the psychology of awakening—and is the first in a series of future books devoted to this area.

What then is the *psychology of awakening*? This term is meant to bridge and bring together two previously separate domains: individual and interpersonal psychology, as studied in the West, and the path of awakening, as articulated by many great spiritual lineages, especially the meditative traditions of the East. Western psychology has mostly neglected the spiritual domain, to its detriment, while the contemplative paths have lacked an adequate understanding of psychological dynamics, which inevitably play a major part in the process of spiritual development. As long as these dynamics are not recognized, they affect the spiritual practitioner and the spiritual path in covert ways that can exert a distorting influence on the whole undertaking. So, in certain ways, *awakening needs psychology just as much as psychology needs awakening*.

A comprehensive psychology of awakening would explore the relationship between the suprapersonal, the personal, and the interpersonal. My particular approach to the psychology of awakening emphasizes *practice* in these three domains—meditation for the suprapersonal dimension, psychological work for the personal, and conscious relationship practice for the interpersonal—and how these three can work together and enhance one another. Each of these practices also has ramifications for the other two domains. Meditation can have a profound influence on how we treat ourselves and others. Psychological work can promote spiritual deepening as well as greater interpersonal sensitivity. And conscious relationship work can help us both awaken from our conditioned patterns and become a more authentic person.

The psychology of awakening points in two main directions and raises two sets of questions, each of which opens up a new area of inquiry, never before addressed by the existing psychological and spiritual traditions.

One set of questions has to do with the psychological ramifications of the spiritual path. For example, what happens to people psychologically when they start to recognize or turn toward their larger nature? What psychological issues and challenges are likely to come up and need to be addressed? As awareness starts to move beyond the boundaries of the conditioned personality structure, this expansion inevitably challenges that structure, flushing out old, subconscious, reactive patterns that often emerge with a vengeance. Traditional religions used to describe these obstacles and attacks along the path in terms of demons or devils. But from a modern perspective, they can also be understood and worked with psychologically—as subconscious aspects of one's conditioned personality structure that often break through into consciousness only when that structure is thoroughly challenged by the process of awakening to one's larger nature. If these psychological issues are not addressed, they often cause distortions in people's spiritual development. So it is not enough just to have spiritual realizations. It is also essential to deconstruct the subconscious emotional and mental patterns that are held in the body and the mind, and that prevent people from fully embodying a larger way of being in their lives.

A second set of questions has to do with how psychologically oriented personal work and interpersonal practice could also support, serve, and further our movement toward awakening. Most people in our culture who turn toward the spiritual life also suffer from some kind of psychological wounding, but their spiritual practice often does not address or help them understand or deal with their woundedness. Yet how can we hope to embody genuine spiritual realization—overcoming self-hatred, aggression, emotional reactivity, narcissistic egocentricity, and a host of other defensive patterns—if we have not first understood and come to terms with the psychological dynamics underlying these phenomena? And since our relations with others are the ultimate litmus test of our spiritual development, how can we create more conscious relationships, which could also serve, support, and nurture our larger spiritual journey?

Thus we need to understand how working with conditioned fears, beliefs, and defensive relational patterns from the past can serve as a stepping-stone that can further our movement toward spiritual liberation. This kind of psychological clearing is central to the process of individuation—the development of the genuine individual, who can embody and express the larger dimensions of being in his or her *person*. In addition to learning how to open and surrender to the divine or ultimate, we also need to understand how the maturation of the genuine individual, at least for Westerners, can help us integrate our spiritual realization into the whole fabric of our personal life and interpersonal relations. Another way to say this is that in addition to *waking up* to our ultimate spiritual nature, we also need to *grow up*—to ripen into a mature, fully developed person.

All the chapters in this book arose out of personal questions I encountered in the course of my own practice in Western psychotherapy and Buddhist meditation. And each is an attempt to build a bridge between the different paths of psychological and spiritual work. My method is primarily phenomenological: I start from experience and stay close to experience, rather than trying to construct a grand synthetic theory.

In their different ways, each chapter addresses the central concern that many Westerners on a spiritual path are grappling with today: the relationship between personal, individual experience and impersonal, universal truth, between psychological and contemplative ways of working with ourselves, between individuation and spiritual liberation. And this concern is part of a larger question: What unique challenges does the path of awakening pose for a modern Westerner? This is the unifying focus and theme of the book, which is a loosely structured set of forays, explorations, and inquiries into this territory.

Because my primary concern is with the process of human transformation, rather than with the technical details of any given tradition, I have chosen to discuss East and West, psychotherapy, meditation, and Buddhist psychology in broad terms, without focusing on the different schools and perspectives within these traditions. I have also taken the liberty of presenting Buddhist thought in a contemporary, somewhat psychological vein, rather than in strictly traditional terms. My main concern here is not so much the Buddhist tradition per se, but rather the question of how to forge a psychology and path of awakening that addresses the unique challenges of our times and circumstances. Similarly, when discussing psychotherapy in this book, my main focus is not so much on therapy per se as on how psychological ways of working with our experience can help the genuine individual to ripen in a way that complements and furthers spiritual development.

At the same time, I do not wish to psychologize Buddhism—to make it into a set of mental health techniques or therapeutic principles—or to spiritualize psychology, elevating it into a substitute for spiritual work. Psychological and spiritual work, psychotherapy and meditation, may overlap, but they are different domains, with very different purposes: self-integration and self-transcendence. My purpose in this book is to look at the relationship between these two paths.[1]

This book represents a thirty-year journey and draws on my major writings on the psychology of awakening, most of which I have published in earlier versions in various magazines and journals over the past three decades. In bringing this material together here, I have extensively revised and updated each chapter to reflect my current thinking and writing style. I believe that these chapters, taken together, present a coherent, multifaceted approach to psychospiritual development.

The reader will find that I return to certain central issues and themes—the nature of meditation, transmutation, coemergence, unconditional presence, the interplay of form and emptiness, the complementarity of psychological and spiritual work—in different ways in various chapters. I have let these recurrences stand in the belief that the different ways and contexts in which I discuss these themes will help the reader see their significance and applicability more broadly. Although I have arranged the chapters to be read in a particular order, it is also fine to read this book by starting with what interests you most and skipping around.

This book weaves together theory and practice. Readers primarily interested in practice may want to concentrate more on parts 2 and 3. While the chapters in part 1 are more theory-oriented, there is practical material in each of them as well. Chapters 8 and 14, which conclude parts 1 and 2 respectively, are the most recent and most comprehensive in the book and thus merit special attention. Readers with little interest in the theory of consciousness may want to skip chapters 4–6 altogether, as these are the most heavily theoretical in the entire book. I have gathered the notes and references into separate sections at the end, so as not to clutter the main text.

May this book be of benefit to those who seek to bring together in their lives the three realms of human existence—the personal, the interpersonal, and the great expanse of being that lies beyond the person altogether. I have recast a Buddhist invocation to express the basic aspiration behind this book:

> *Ah! Your very being is the perfect teacher.*
> *Recognizing your nature, take this to heart.*
> *For all those who have not realized this,*
> *Arouse compassion,*
> *To help them find this pure and holy space.*

PART ONE

Integrating Psychology *and* Spirituality

Introduction

✤ WHAT IS THE RELATIONSHIP between psychological and spiritual work, between personal growth and spiritual development? How can we work on becoming a mature, authentic person, while still recognizing that we are something that goes beyond personhood altogether? These questions take us to the very heart of what it means to be human.

Spiritual practice involves exploring who and what we ultimately are—our true, essential nature, shared alike by all human beings. The direct, experiential realization of true nature has been a particular specialty of the Eastern contemplative traditions. Eastern teachings emphasize living from our deepest nature, turning the mind around so that it can see into its very essence, rather than constantly facing outward, focusing on tasks and objects to grasp and manipulate. Recognizing the essential nature of our awareness as an open, wakeful, luminous, and compassionate presence allows us to relate to our life in a much richer and more powerful way. This realization is what allows us to liberate ourselves from the chains of past conditioning, known in the East as karma.

From this perspective, since well-being, happiness, and freedom are intrinsic—that is, contained within our essential nature—the most important task in life is to realize this true nature. While the illumined yogis and saints of the East represent some of the strongest testimony to the power of this vast, nonpersonal dimension of being, it is also fully accessible to anyone, East or West.

While the wisdom of the East has illuminated the ultimate nature of being—beyond the world, beyond the individual person, beyond human relationship, and beyond human history—the wisdom of the West has taken a very different tack. The Western wisdom traditions teach that we are here not just to realize our divine nature but to embody that nature in human form. If the East has focused on the vertical, timeless dimension, the West has focused on the horizontal—the individual's life as it unfolds in time.

The West has also given birth to a revolutionary, intoxicating idea that has taken the world by storm: the sanctity of the individual. Individuals are here not just to fulfill traditional agendas handed down by family, society, and conventional religion, but to discover their unique gift and fully embody that gift in their lives. This is the principle of individuation, which is not such a priority in the East. The Western idea of the individual has also helped liberate the capacity to ask questions and freely investigate the nature of things without allegiance to rigid orthodoxies, giving rise to the scientific method. This in turn has led to the development of Western psychology.

Western psychology focuses on the conditioned mind and illuminates it every bit as brilliantly as the East illuminates unconditioned awareness. Western psychology allows us to understand, for the first time, the individual psyche—how it develops and becomes conflicted, and how it replays inner conflicts, defensive patterns, and interpersonal dynamics from early childhood in adult life. From this perspective, psychological healing comes about through understanding, clarifying, and working with these developmental dynamics.

East and West have thus spawned two distinct types of psychology, based on totally different methods and pointing in totally different directions.[1] Eastern contemplative psychology, based on meditative practice, presents teachings about how to achieve direct knowledge of the essential nature of reality, which lies beyond the scope of the conventional conceptual mind. Western therapeutic psychology, based on clinical practice and conceptual analysis, allows us to trace specific causes and conditions influencing our behavior, mind-states, and self-structure as a whole. Yet though the Eastern emphasis—on nonpersonal awareness and direct realization of truth—and the Western emphasis—on individual psychology and conceptual understanding—may seem contradictory, we can also appreciate them as complementary. Both are essential for a full realization of the potentials inherent in human existence.

Indeed, beyond the differences of geography, race, and culture, *East and West ultimately represent two different aspects of ourselves.* In this sense, they are like the relationship between breathing out and breathing in. The Eastern emphasis on letting go of fixation on form, individual characteristics, and history is like breathing out, while the Western emphasis on coming into form, individuation, and personal creativity is like breathing in. And just as breathing in culminates in breathing out, so breathing out culminates in breathing in. Each side, without the other, represents only half of the equation.

East and West each harbor at their core essential realizations that together can help the world forge, out of the two ways human consciousness has evolved on opposite sides of the globe, a larger appreciation of the human journey. To discover our human wholeness, which is surely essential for the survival and evolution of humanity and the planet, we need to bring the two sides of our nature—absolute and relative, suprapersonal and personal, heaven and earth—together at last. This is precisely the great promise and potential of a new, integrative psychology of awakening. And this is the work that the chapters in this first part of the book begin to address.

The first chapter was where I originally coined the term *spiritual bypassing* in 1984, to describe a common tendency I discovered among Western spiritual seekers to use spiritual ideas and practices to avoid dealing with their emotional unfinished business. This chapter describes inner transformational work in terms of three main principles—heaven (letting go), earth (grounding), and human (awakening the heart)—and shows how psychological and spiritual practice work with these principles in their different ways.

Chapter 2 translates into psychological terms the principle of coemergence, taken from the Tibetan Buddhist tradition, which sees imprisonment and freedom, confusion and sanity arising together as two sides of one reality. Drawing on this principle, this chapter shows how all the seemingly neurotic elements of our personality have a larger meaning, intention, or intelligence hidden within them. Discovering this can help us work with our conditioned personality as a path that leads forward, rather than as a pathology that keeps us stuck in the past. The key lies in regarding our personality structure not as a problem or an enemy—something to fix, condemn, or eradicate—but rather as a stage of development that provides a stepping-stone for further evolution.

Chapter 3, on ego strength and egolessness, explores a seminal difference between Eastern and Western psychology—their view of the nature and role of the central self-conscious ego. This chapter clarifies the differences between Eastern and Western views of ego, while also looking at where they could agree. It concludes with a Buddhist view of ego development, exploring the relationship between ego and egolessness as contracted and relaxed awareness.

Chapter 4 is the first in a sequence of three chapters, representing the earliest material in this book, that explore the nature and dynamics of consciousness in an East/West framework. Readers who are not interested in theory of consciousness may want to skip these three chapters. These chapters present a phenomenological approach to mind, showing how we experience reality on three different levels: through the surface, conceptual mind; through subtler body-mind knowing; and at the deepest level, through unconditioned, nonconceptual awareness.[2] What follows is a brief overview of these three levels of consciousness, which chapters 4–6 explore in different ways.

At the surface level, mind uses the tools of focal attention and concept to fix its sights on one object after another. The surface conceptual mind perceives solid forms, thinks definite thoughts, and registers familiar emotions. This is the level of mind where ego operates— through forming self-concepts, setting up a basic division between self and other, and pursuing control and mastery in worldly functioning.

Underneath the conceptual mind is a wider kind of body-mind sensing/knowing that operates in a subtler, background way. This subtle body-mind contains both personal and transpersonal elements. We can recognize this level of body-mind through a diffuse type of attention that can tune into subtle feeling and intuition, energy flow, and a sense of interrelatedness with all of creation. The body-mind, as a dynamic field of energy, is inherently attuned to the larger patterns and flows of the universe. Out of this attunement emerge sudden and surprising insights, creative inspirations and discoveries, and larger, transpersonal qualities, such as clarity, compassion, joy, or spontaneity.

At the deepest level, meditation practice reveals mind to be an open, nonconceptual awareness, which is the ultimate source of all our particular experiences. If surface mind is like whitecaps and body-mind is like waves, then the deeper, unconditioned essence of mind is like the ocean itself, which makes possible and infuses all the activity happening on its surface. The waves and whitecaps represent becoming—our changing, evolving nature—while the ocean itself is Being, our changeless nature.

A simple way to glimpse the nature of this deeper nature is to ask yourself as you read this, "Who is taking in these words? Who is experiencing all of this right now?" Without trying to *think* of an answer, if you look directly into the experiencer, the experiencing consciousness itself, what you find is a silent presence that has no shape, location, or form. This nameless, formless presence—in, around, behind, and between all our particular thoughts and experiences—is what the great spiritual traditions regard as our true nature, or ultimate ground, also known as the essential self or holy spirit. This is not an experience among experiences. Instead, as a radical depth of presence and transparency, it is the ground of all experience, and it is impossible to grasp with the conceptual mind.

All three levels of mind are always at play in our ongoing experience. Since we constantly swim in the ocean of silent, nonconceptual awareness, it is normally too near, too transparent, and too obvious to notice unless we bring special meditative attention to it. It is much easier, however, to notice our felt sense of bodily presence. If you focus on this, you enter the subtler dimension of body-mind. Paying attention to how you are in your body right now, you may notice feeling-qualities that can be articulated—as, for instance, "tension" or "lightness." In naming these qualities, you move into surface thinking mind, which is now interacting with the wider body-mind. You could also articulate your feeling still further, making it more and more specific as, for instance, "wishing the author would hurry up and make his point," "I don't agree with what he is saying," or "I'm tired and need some sleep."

These three levels of mind, then, lead to three orders of truth. Thinking mind, left to its own devices, produces *conceptual,* logical, and scientific truths. When thinking mind interacts with felt experience, this gives birth to grounded, *experiential* truths. And finally, the truth arrived at through realization of the deep nature of mind is living, *contemplative* truth, which reveals a deeper order of being beyond both thinking mind and felt experience.

As I initially explored these three levels of truth, I realized that they also roughly corresponded to the Buddhist notion of the three *kaya*s or bodies of the Buddha—three ways in which reality manifests to a human being.[3] The most apparent level of reality is the *nirmanakaya,* the level of differentiated form, where surface mind operates. Yet the objects of surface mind—behaviors, words, and thoughts—arise out of and express a more subtle level of reality, the *sambhogakaya*—where we function as a dynamic field of energy. At this level, I am not just my fleshly body, not just my thoughts, not just my feelings, and not just my bounded ego, but a larger energy field, which is intimately interconnected with the world and can therefore tap into subtler ways of knowing and being. This level is a bridge between the form-oriented functioning of surface mind and the formless quality of nonconceptual awareness.

The energy play of the body-mind in turn arises from the *dharmakaya,* the ultimate ground of human existence—pure unconditioned awareness. In Buddhist psychology, this formless ground of being is variously called mind-as-such, big mind, no-mind, unborn mind, or mind-essence. It is the ground of silence underlying and contained in sound, the ground of stillness underlying and contained in movement, the ground of nonconceptuality underlying and hidden within all thinking and feeling. As the unconditioned ground of being implicit in all becoming, it is the basis for the development of wisdom, enlightenment, true liberation, and reconciliation with life and death.

Recognizing these three levels is essential if we are to develop an integrative psychology of awakening that can address the whole range of human experience.[4] Western psychology has mainly focused on the workings of the surface mind—how it is conditioned by beliefs, culture, interpersonal imprints, childhood events. Eastern psychologies have mostly focused on the subtle energetic fields of the body-mind and the larger dimension of nonconceptual awareness. Clearly, a psychology of awakening must recognize and take account of all three levels.[5]

Chapter 4 looks at the workings of these three levels of mind in terms of the interplay of form and emptiness in the stream of consciousness. Chapter 5 presents a new way of understanding unconscious process—not as a separate, unknowable dimension of mind, but as the holistic background ways in which the human organism interrelates with reality. And chapter 6 explores the three levels in terms of our living experience of psychological space. These three chapters also discuss implications of this understanding for psychological health, creativity, human relationship, and spiritual realization.

Chapter 7 addresses the gradual process of unfolding that leads to personality change in psychotherapy and explores how this differs from the sudden realization that happens on the spiritual path. The experiential process that leads to progressive realizations, through making explicit what was already implicit in the body-mind, is what I call *horizontal unfolding*. Yet there is also a more radical kind of *vertical* emergence where a new depth of being suddenly breaks through, radically shifting the context in which we previously operated. Just as horizontal unfolding is a central part of psychological work, vertical emergence is a core feature of spiritual realization.

Chapter 8 is a more recent piece of writing that distills my understanding of where psychological and spiritual work intersect and where they part ways. In this chapter I lay out a whole progression of ways of relating to our experience, from alienation to pure nondual presence. I particularly focus on the relation between the dualistic mode of therapeutic self-reflection—where there is an observer standing back and studying the patterns of what is observed—and the nondual immediacy of pure presence, as revealed in advanced meditative realization. Although these two ways of relating to our experience feel very different, this chapter shows how they represent complementary stages in the larger dialectic of awakening.

1

Between Heaven and Earth

Principles of Inner Work

✤ As a PSYCHOTHERAPIST and meditation practitioner, I am continually faced with questions about the relationship between psychological and spiritual work—in my own experience, as well as with clients, students, and friends. Over the course of thirty years of considering these questions, I have gone back and forth between two different perspectives—sometimes regarding the psychological inquiry into self as diametrically opposed, even antagonistic, to the spiritual aim of going beyond self, and at other times seeing it as an extremely useful complement to spiritual work. This is a complex issue that we will consider in detail throughout this book. We can begin with a basic consideration of the essential challenges of inner work common to these two paths, and the different directions they take in addressing them.

Spiritual Bypassing

Starting in the 1970s I began to perceive a disturbing tendency among many members of spiritual communities. Although many spiritual practitioners were doing good work on themselves, I noticed a widespread tendency to use spiritual practice to bypass or avoid dealing with certain personal or emotional "unfinished business." This desire to find release from the earthly structures that seem to entrap us—the structures of karma, conditioning, body, form, matter, personality—

has been a central motive in the spiritual search for thousands of years. So there is often a tendency to use spiritual practice to try to rise above our emotional and personal issues—all those messy, unresolved matters that weigh us down. I call this tendency to avoid or prematurely transcend basic human needs, feelings, and developmental tasks *spiritual bypassing.*

Spiritual bypassing is particularly tempting for people who are having difficulty navigating life's developmental challenges, especially in a time and culture like ours, where what were once ordinary landmarks of adulthood—earning a livelihood through dignified work, raising a family, keeping a marriage together, belonging to a meaningful community—have become increasingly elusive for large segments of the population. While still struggling to find themselves, many people are introduced to spiritual teachings and practices that urge them to give themselves up. As a result, they wind up using spiritual practices to create a new "spiritual" identity, which is actually an old dysfunctional identity—based on avoidance of unresolved psychological issues—repackaged in a new guise.

In this way, involvement in spiritual teachings and practices can become a way to rationalize and reinforce old defenses. For example, those who need to see themselves as special will often emphasize the specialness of their spiritual insight and practice, or their special relation to their teacher, to shore up a sense of self-importance. Many of the "perils of the path"—such as spiritual materialism (using spiritual ideas for personal gain), narcissism, inflation (delusions of grandiosity), or groupthink (uncritical acceptance of group ideology)—result from trying to use spirituality to shore up developmental deficiencies.

Grasping, Rejecting, Desensitizing

Many spiritual traditions speak of three basic tendencies that keep us tied to the wheel of suffering: the tendency to *reject* what is difficult or painful; the tendency to *grasp* onto something solid for comfort and security; and the tendency to *desensitize* ourselves so that we don't have to feel the whole problem of pleasure and pain, loss and gain at all.

Spiritual bypassing is a symptom of the first tendency—to turn away from what is difficult or unpleasant, such as the vicissitudes of a weak ego: if you do not feel strong enough to deal with the difficulties of this world, then you find ways to transcend your personal feelings altogether. This is a major potential pitfall of the spiritual path, especially for modern Westerners. The attempt to avoid facing the unresolved issues of the conditioned personality only keeps us caught in their grip.

The second tendency—to grasp and fixate—is often one of psychotherapy's subtler pitfalls. Some people find it so fascinating to delve into their feelings, archetypes, dreams, and relationships that they become endlessly absorbed in working on all their psychological material. Treating this kind of self-examination as the ultimate journey can turn it into an egocentric dead end. As Freud once remarked, we can never drain the swamp. Endlessly focusing on our inner states or conflicts in the personality structure can become a subtle trap that prevents us from seeing beyond the personality altogether.

The third tendency—to simply desensitize ourselves to both our personal experience and our spiritual calling—is the most common of all in our society. There is a part in most of us that would rather take it easy, sink into some groove, and get through life with as little effort or challenge as possible. This leads to our common Western addictions—to television, spectator sports, consumerism, or alcohol and drugs—as ways to numb out and avoid facing the rawness of being fully alive.

Heaven, Earth, and Man

These three major pitfalls—spiritual bypassing, egocentric self-absorption, and desensitized distraction—can be counteracted by tapping certain essential resources that are contained in three dimensions of the human condition, known in traditional Chinese philosophy as heaven, earth, and man (human).

In the simplest terms, we are beings who stand upright on the earth, with our feet on the ground and head raised up to the open sky.

Because our feet are rooted to the ground, there is no other choice than to be right here, right where we are. This means that we have to fully respect the world and ourselves on this horizontal plane—something that spiritual bypassing fails to do. This is the earth principle.

At the same time, our head is oriented toward the open sky above and all around, where we are able to see far-off things: horizons, stars and suns and planets, and the vast context of space surrounding the earth. Gazing in wonder and curiosity at the world around us, we can see beyond our immediate self-interest and survival concerns. Despite the apparent meaningfulness and importance of our earthly cares, if we go up a hundred feet, what is happening down here begins to lose some of its significance. If we go up even farther, as the astronauts did, all of this becomes but a tiny speck. When we move vertically—and our consciousness can always do this—we find endless space as far as we can go. Human consciousness is not just of this earth. Our lives take shape against the background of infinite space. This is the heaven principle.

The basic human stance—straight back, with upright head and shoulders, firmly rooted to the earth below—exposes the whole front of the body to the world. Four-legged animals are careful to protect their vulnerable front. The porcupine's quills keep predators away from its soft belly. But as human beings we walk around with our belly and heart—our two main feeling centers—completely exposed to the world. To feel is to respond with the body to the world around us. Basic feeling is happening all the time, whether or not we pay attention to it. Because we sit or stand between heaven and earth with our front exposed, the world and other people can enter and touch us. This is the third, specifically human element of the heaven-earth-man triad.

Not honoring any one of these three dimensions leads to a distorted, imbalanced life. If we focus only on our immediate existential and survival concerns, we will get bogged down, stuck in the mud, glued to the earth. Yet if we don't take enough account of our earthly needs, we become disconnected, lost in the stars, head in the clouds. And if we try to avoid the rawness and tenderness of the heart, we will become trapped in our character armor, which we initially developed to protect our vulnerable feeling centers. Instead of the armadillo's shell or the porcupine's quills, we grow ego defenses. To be fully human is to forge bridges between earth and sky, form and emptiness, matter and spirit. And our humanness expresses itself in a depth and tenderness of feeling or *heart* that arises at the intersection of these poles.

Now we can consider three types of inner work that can help us cultivate and balance these three dimensions of our nature.

Grounding and Coming into Form: The Earth Principle

The essential purpose of spiritual practice is to liberate us from attachment to a narrow, conditioned self-structure, so that we realize we are something much larger. In order to reap the full benefits of such practice, however, we first need to have a workable self-structure. This means being grounded in earthly form.

Yet all too often in our fast-paced, urban-technological society we never learn to be grounded in our own experience. With the breakdown of close-knit families and communities, children are increasingly shaped and influenced by the neurosis in their nuclear family and in their culture at large. As a result, many people spend most of their lives unconsciously reenacting distorted patterns established in childhood. Recognizing, working with, and growing out of these unconscious patterns is the groundwork for developing an authentic individuality that is not compulsively driven by conditioned tendencies from the past—limiting self-images, denied needs, self-punishment, childhood scripts, dysfunctional interpersonal patterns, fears of loving and losing love. This is primarily psychological rather than spiritual work.

Fully inhabiting the body, working with our psychological patterns, coming into our true form—this is the work of grounding, the earth principle in action. At its best, psychotherapy can help us be more fully embodied, more grounded in ourselves. This kind of work can also be quite humbling. It involves what Robert Bly calls the "awful descent into the wound." The core wound we all suffer from is the disconnection from our own being. This inner disconnection originally took place in childhood as we contracted in fearful reaction to an environment that did not fully see, welcome, or accept us. When practiced in a spiritual context, psychotherapy can be a form of soulwork, helping us find a deeper meaning in our suffering: our particular pain and neurosis show us exactly where we have shut down, and thus where we also need to unfold as individuals. *Soul* in this sense is a direction of inwardness, a deep experiencing of individual meaning, purpose, aliveness.

Different psychological approaches work with grounding in different ways. Many systems share an understanding that real change manifests through energy shifts in the body, rather than through talk or intellectual insight alone. For instance, in the Focusing method developed by Eugene Gendlin, it is essential to move out of the thinking mind into the lived body, connect with a bodily felt sense of whatever one is working on, and let that body sense find a voice, a way of unfolding. Other approaches such as Gestalt psychology or bioenergetics also help the body open up and respond in new ways.

Spiritual practice also involves grounding or movement downward. In the Eastern traditions, coming down to earth may involve connecting with the center of gravity in the body below the navel, called *hara* in Japanese or the lower *tan tien* in Chinese. Practices such as aikido or tai chi chuan ground a person in this way. The sitting posture in meditation also has a grounding effect, as does the emphasis on work, precise attention to detail, and mindfulness of body in the Zen tradition ("chopping wood, carrying water"). However, although grounding practices often have an important supportive role in a complete spiritual path, they are not the main focus of spiritual work.

Letting Go: The Heaven Principle

If soulwork involves coming down to earth, working with structure, and coming into form, the essence of spiritual work involves learning to surrender and let go of all investment in form. Perhaps we have done a tremendous amount of psychological work, working through our major neuroses, scripts, and emotional entanglements. Yet even if we are what humanistic psychologists call "fully functioning" or "self-actualizing," we still hold on to ourselves in many subtle ways. It is hard to just let ourselves be, without grasping onto some structure, some agenda, some goal or activity. We become nervous when we encounter empty space, when there is a gap in a conversation, when we don't know what to say, when we are in a waiting room and there are no magazines on the table.

When we let ourselves open to that space, as in sitting meditation, we come to see the subtlety and pervasiveness of holding on to the central fixation of "me, myself, and I." Spiritual work brings to light and helps us release this attachment to limited notions of who we are, so that we may realize our larger nature, which lies beyond all form, structure, or thought. If psychotherapy is like pruning and fertilizing a tree so it can grow up and bear fruit, spiritual practice is more radical medicine. It goes to the roots—the root clinging to a limited concept of self, which prevents us from relaxing and sinking deeper into the larger ground of being.

Buddhist practice, for instance, works with freeing ourselves from five universal tendencies that cause suffering, called the root *klesha*s or poisons: grasping, aggression, ignorance, jealousy, and pride. As long as we are stuck in a limited understanding of who we are, these *klesha*s will continue to arise, regardless of how much psychotherapy we have done.

A traditional Tibetan analogy describes three levels of spiritual practice, in terms of how they work with the root *klesha*s, which are compared to a poisonous plant. The first level of working with these poisonous tendencies is to replace them with virtuous tendencies. This is like uprooting the plant. The limitation of this approach is that in the uprooting you may also lose the connection with the earth in which the plant is rooted. Trying to avoid negative feelings and emotions through heavenly transcendence—rising above, trying to purify oneself through denying the lower impulses—can lead to spiritual bypassing and inner division.

A second level of practice is to develop an antidote to the poisons instead of uprooting the plant. In Mahayana Buddhism, for instance, the antidote to the poisonous activity of the *klesha*s is the discovery of *sunyata,* or emptiness—the open dimension of being that dissolves the tendency to become attached to anything. However, this may leave us with a subtle preference for emptiness over form, which can also leave us inwardly divided.

The third way, according to this analogy, is to develop immunity to the poison through judiciously eating leaves of the plant. This is the way of Tantric or Vajrayana Buddhism, which transmutes the poisons into *amrita*—what we might call the juice of life, the nectar of our true nature. Of course, a great deal of training and preparation is necessary for this kind of transmutation, so that we can actually assimilate the poison. This is the function of basic meditation training. By learning to open to the poisons of the mind and recognizing how they are all self-created fixations, arising out of our disconnection from our own true nature, we no longer fall under their power. This third way unlocks the vital energy contained in the poisons—energy that can help us maintain our connection with the earth, our passion, and everyday life. When we are no longer compelled to reject our neurotic tendencies, we have more compassion and understanding for how they affect other people as well. And this allows us to work with others more directly and skillfully.

Awakening the Heart: The Human Principle

The interplay of earth and heaven, coming into form and letting go of form, gives rise to a third principle of inner work—awakening the heart, which corresponds in Chinese thought to the man (human) principle. Awakening the heart involves stepping out of our character armor in order to let reality and other people into us. An open heart is also the source of courage (a word that derives from the French word for heart, *coeur*). Courage involves facing the world squarely and letting your heart be touched, forever opening to life, come what may.

Psychological work can go a long way toward opening the heart, yet fully awakening the heart requires the more total letting go discovered through spiritual realization. Without the vast spaciousness of the heaven principle we might be able to let others in but then not be able to let them go or let them be. Letting go also involves a sense of humor, which arises when we step out of being stuck in a structure. When we laugh, we have just stepped out of a structure. Without a sense of space, humor, and letting go, the heart could become too syrupy, sentimental, heavy, or attached.

Awakening the heart also requires being grounded, because without our connection to earth, there could be no compassion. If we can only let go but cannot take hold, if our only concern is with space or spirit, then we may never be able to fully commit ourselves to work with our own circumstances or with other sentient beings. True compassion develops out of our struggle with the world of form, limitation, personality, karma. If we are only oriented toward spirit, we could become impatient with the stuckness we find in ourselves and other people.

Working with Suffering

A complete path of inner development that addresses both our personal psychology and our deeper spiritual nature must involve all three principles—grounding, letting go, and awakening the heart—which counteract the obstacles of spiritual bypassing, egocentric self-involvement, and numbing distraction. The core element of such a path would be an awareness practice such as meditation, which helps connect us with all three principles. Along with that, a method of psychological inquiry is extremely helpful for addressing the unconscious patterns and emotional complexes that interfere with living more authentically, with groundedness, openness, and heart.

In my work as a psychotherapist I have found that I must continually stay in touch with heaven, earth, and heart, all three. To begin with, I have to listen to and respect the client's real problems, which belong to the realm of form, earth. If I don't do that, there is no connection between the two of us. Yet if I focus only on form, on the problems, then I lose a sense of the open mind, open heart, open space surrounding them. Psychological work then becomes too literal-minded and serious, losing its magic, its creative spark. When I started doing therapy right after graduate school, I had too small a vision of human nature and took the content of the problems too seriously. Later, after developing a larger sense of vast, open awareness through meditation, I found that I did not become burned out or bogged down by my client's problems, and my responses came from a much deeper place.

One of meditation's great gifts was to help me distinguish between immediate experience and mental interpretations of that experience. This in turn allowed me to be more open to my client's suffering, without taking the heaviness of their problems so seriously. It is never burdensome to follow someone's genuine experiencing. Only the mental fixations—the stories, beliefs, and judgments about our experience—become burdensome, never someone's living experiencing itself. In the end I don't give all that much attention to the content of people's problems, because I am listening more to the being who is struggling with the problem. Thus, the heaven principle—providing space, letting go of holding on to form—can also play an important part in psychological work, even though it is not as central here as in spiritual work. In this way, riding the experiential process—respecting the other's feelings while continually tapping into a larger sense of openness underlying them and meeting the other in his or her immediacy and rawness—becomes meditation in action.

With the help of meditation practice, I have been able to find delight in the work of therapy even when staying with clients in the midst of great suffering. Even pain and neurosis contain their own colors and have their own strange beauty. I have always found intelligence within the heart of every psychological conflict, and I can usually find ways to appreciate people's character armor—how it serves to protect them, and what a skillful creation it is in its own way, just like the porcupine's quills or the armadillo's shell.

Since human development and transformation arise out of the interplay of earth and heaven, bounded and unbounded, the essential practice, common to both psychotherapy and meditation, is to bring our larger awareness to bear on our frozen karmic structures. Often this larger awareness is obscured—either buried beneath our problems, emotions, reactions, or else detached, dissociated, floating above them. So it is essential first to cultivate awareness and then to bring it to bear on the places where we are contracted and stuck. This allows us to taste the poisons of confused mind and transmute them.

I once had a dream that portrayed the interplay between earth and heaven at the core of human life. I was in a huge tent with a high roof in which a lot of activity and celebration was going on. Although I was involved in the activity inside the tent, I was also simultaneously aware of the magical quality of space in the tent surrounding us and supporting our celebration.

This is our nature as human beings: our lives unfold within earthly structures and frameworks that are permeated and surrounded by vast reaches of open space. In my dream, the structure of the tent was necessary to keep out the rain and protect the life within. Therapy and grounding work focus on form or structure—which is like helping the tent stand up firmly or patching the leaks. Yet whatever structures we build are never entirely solid but always ventilated by emptiness, the open dimension of being—like the tent's sides, open all around. While psychological work helps us come into form, spiritual work emphasizes what is beyond form, the boundless. In the end, cultivating openness to this larger space surrounding all our structures is what allows the fresh breezes of change and renewal to keep circulating through our lives.

2

Personality

Path or Pathology?

✦ WHO DO WE *think* we are? This is the central question at the heart of both psychological and spiritual development. Who we take ourselves to be, and how we defend this identity, is the primary factor that will determine our degree of psychological well-being and spiritual realization.

Oddly enough, we have little say about our personality, for by the time we start to notice its existence and its patterns—usually in our teenage years—it is already fairly well established. How then to relate to this shape that we have grown into? Should we treat our conditioned personality as a flaw that stands in the way of our spiritual development—and thus, in this ultimate sense, as a pathology? Or could it be, as some esoteric traditions hint, that our personality is not just an arbitrary error, but might instead serve as an essential stepping-stone on the path of our spiritual unfolding?

If we could discover larger qualities of being and intelligence hidden within our most rigid or neurotic personality patterns, then we would not have to get rid of the personality in order to reach some "higher" spiritual dimension beyond it. Instead, working with the tight, constricted places in our personality structure could itself reveal everything we need on the path of self-realization. Like sanding wood so that the true grain reveals itself, the journey of awakening would involve transforming our personality so that it became a transparent vehicle, which the deeper qualities of our essential being could shine through.

Therapeutic Aggression

Tara was a client of mine who had suffered extreme lack of emotional contact and nurturing as a child and, as a result, adopted a tough, independent stance that proclaimed, in essence: "I don't need anybody. I can take care of myself." This identity had allowed her to survive the lack of love in her home. Later in life, however, her exaggerated independence became dysfunctional, as all personality patterns do at some point. It had become a way of continuing to deprive herself, a major obstacle to receiving love and caring, and a source of great suffering.

In her late twenties, Tara had joined a spiritual commune whose methodology was to break down its members' egos, which were regarded as barriers to spiritual realization. The community practiced a collective form of spiritual bypassing, by trying to implant an ideal "spiritual" identity in its members while denigrating personal needs and concerns. So the leaders of the community adopted an aggressive slash-and-burn approach toward Tara's independent stance. She went along with this, convinced that her old personality patterns were blocking her spiritual advancement. In stripping away her toughness, however, she also lost touch with her power, will, and sense of purpose. When the commune finally dissolved, she was incapacitated for dealing with ordinary life and had to spend many years recovering.

In fashioning a tough, independent identity to survive her family circumstances, Tara had drawn on an intrinsic capacity of her nature—strength. Where another person might have reacted to her family by collapsing into depression or withdrawal, she had been able to summon the resources to overcome great deprivation. Although her identity eventually became limiting and constricting, nevertheless it contained at its core her essential strength, which was one of her most striking qualities. So when she submitted to the commune's attack on her personality, she lost touch with her own power and will as well.

Trying to bring about transformation through waging an assault on the conditioned personality is a mistake that a number of spiritual teachers and therapists have made. Sometimes this kind of "therapeutic aggression" is quite blatant, as in Tara's case. And sometimes it manifests in more subtle forms of persuasion, where the basic message is that you would be a better person if you were someone different from the one you are. Yet attacks on their personality only rob people of the basic material that provides impetus for the journey of awakening.

It is as though awakening needs the personality, as fire needs fuel, to feed on. The personality is a frozen form of our true nature. So whenever some aspect of our personality thaws out, this provides a certain illumination and liberates a certain energy. And each newly liberated unit of energy and illumination in turn provides further heat to thaw the frozen self-structure.

Attacking the personality only cuts people off from the larger intelligence that is bound up in the personality structure. This kind of assault also stirs up fear and resistance that impede forward movement, often reducing people to a state of helplessness or dependency. Coercive attempts to dismantle the personality only heighten the inner division, conflict, and strain that are hallmarks of the ego. If personality is to become path rather than harden into pathology, we need to learn to work with ourselves as we are, without aggression or blame. This means creating conditions that encourage the personality structure to break open from within, revealing essential qualities of our being that are hidden within it. Just as the Tibetan meditation master Chögyam Trungpa once pointed out, "When you clean your teapot, then the teapot wakes you up," so we could say that when you work on your personality structure, your personality wakes you up.

To work with her personality structure as path, Tara had to inquire into her exaggerated independence, try to understand it, and relate to it more directly, rather than trying to change or prematurely transcend it. As she started to do this in therapy, she gradually realized that her toughness had been a way of trying to take care of herself. Underneath the hardness was an extreme sense of vulnerability, along with an uncertainty that she was worth being cared for. This discovery gave her a direction: she needed to learn to understand and care for herself in her vulnerable places and treat herself in a more loving way. Opening to herself in this way created a base of inner support that helped her recover her strength, as well as acknowledge her softer side, both to herself and to others.

Identity Formation

We are all born with access to certain innate qualities of being that precede and become woven into the fabric of our personality structure. Different traditions speak of these in different ways. Yogic and alchemical systems might describe them in terms of elements such as earth, fire, water, and air. Sufism describes capacities for will, peace, knowledge, compassion, joy, and strength associated with different centers in the body and colors: white, black, green, yellow, red. Mahayana Buddhism speaks of certain quintessential human qualities—or "perfections"—that exist embryonically in our nature but that can also be cultivated: generosity, patience, exertion, mindful presence, compassion, discriminating insight, discipline, power, and wisdom. Tibetan Buddhism speaks of five basic wisdom energies—equanimity, mirrorlike clarity, capacity for effective action, spaciousness, and discrimination—that are also connected with various colors and elements. These are egoless human qualities that nobody owns, yet which naturally seem to manifest in different intensities and configurations in different individuals.

To understand how our personality draws on these qualities or capacities of our being, we need to consider the situation of infants, who in their complete vulnerability have a rather tenuous connection with existence. We all face the question of existence versus nonexistence from the moment we are born. Lack of love or caring represents a powerful threat of nonexistence because it places the child's physical or psychological survival and integrity at risk.

No matter what our childhood history, we all inevitably encounter what Buddhism describes as the three marks of existence: the difficult realities of pain, impermanence, and the lack of a solid, definite sense of who we are. We are different from other animals in that there is no fixed prescription for how to be human, and little clear guidance about how to know or be ourselves. This means that our life is inevitably marked by fear of our potential nonexistence. This fear of nonexistence gives rise to our ongoing *identity project*—the attempt to make ourselves into something solid, substantial, and real.

In addition, most of us encounter real or perceived threats to our well-being, security, and survival in childhood. Since children lack the capacity for self-reflection—for objectively seeing and knowing themselves, for holding their experience in awareness—they need adults to provide holding and reflecting for them. But when children do not feel seen, recognized, loved, or welcomed by their family or society, it is like looking in a mirror and seeing no one there. A sense of deficiency and dread arises: "Maybe the truth is that *I am not.*"

In response to this threat of nonexistence, children try to defend and affirm themselves by creating some form of stable self-existence. They develop an identity structure, based on self-images and stories that identify who they are. "Who am I? *I am me.*" This identity is a cluster of self-representations, initially formed through our interactions with others. Whether our story is positive or negative—"I'm special," "I'm beyond needing love," "I'm no good," or even "I'm nobody"—we hold on to this self-identity for dear life. We will cling to a negative self-identity, even if it is choking us, because it gives us a sense of existence—"I am something, rather than nothing."

Children show tremendous ingenuity in turning threats to their existence into a stable identity that relieves anxiety by giving them a solid sense of existence. The intelligent impulse behind our identity project is the desire to overcome our fear of being deficient, to know ourselves, to value ourselves, and to feel that we are real. For example, one client of mine, Dan, coped with severe deprivation in childhood by making an identity out of deprivation itself: he felt most fully himself when feeling empty, hungry, deprived. Maintaining this state of inner deprivation was his identity project. It was originally a brilliant strategy for maintaining sanity in a situation that threatened to overwhelm him.

As an adult, however, Dan's attachment to deprivation made it hard to receive nourishment from life and other people. He felt uncomfortable with women who actively loved him, for this threatened him with loss of himself. And he felt uncomfortable having much money because this threatened the sense of lack at the core of his identity. His personal style had become a trap, a frozen mode of being in the world that cut him off from the fullness of his true nature and the fullness of his relationship to all that is. In a similar way, every personal identity starts out as a brilliant survival strategy, constructed out of a person's native resources. But it eventually turns into a compulsive identity project, which becomes a source of inner conflict and an obstacle to further growth.

Even though Dan's identity had outlived its usefulness and was now working against him, it was helpful for him to appreciate the purpose it had served. In creating a sense of existence out of the feeling of nonexistence, he had literally managed to make something out of nothing. *He was something because he was nothing!* This brilliant strategy showed great ingenuity and creativity—capacities that he also expressed through his art. His drawings were quite spare, consisting of a few simple lines floating in a background of open, uncluttered space. His work was influenced by Zen and its aesthetic of emptiness. His intimate rapport with emptiness was a real strength, allowing him to make do with very little. However, it also had a neurotic twist. He mistakenly equated Zen emptiness with his own sense of inner lack, and would use Buddhist logic to justify and perpetuate his sense of impoverishment.

Coemergence

The Mahamudra lineage of Tibetan Buddhism sees the awakened mind and the confused mind as two sides of the same reality. From this perspective, neurosis and sanity, imprisonment and freedom, existence and nonexistence, pathology and path are said to *coemerge*, arising together as two interwoven sides of one whole cloth. An image from this tradition that portrays coemergence is that of the silkworm binding itself in its own silk. The silk represents the beautiful, rich resources that are intrinsic to our being. We draw on these resources to form a personality structure that at first protects us from the vicissitudes of life but later incarcerates us.

Several case vignettes will serve to illustrate further how a larger intelligence lies hidden within pathological strategies and symptoms:

- A man had developed the identity of a psychological cripple, with the story line, "I can't do it, I'm not capable," as a way of deflecting attacks from his mother, who would not allow him his own autonomy. In therapy, just as he would get close to important material, a "fog" would arise in his mind, and he would say, "I can't do this . . . This is beyond me." This fog arose only in moments when he was on the verge of getting in touch with something that might allow him to move beyond his cripple identity. When he finally recognized that this strategy was a highly intelligent move, designed to protect him from attack, rather than evidence of real incompetence, the fog disappeared and allowed him to start working on this old identity more directly. His masquerade had been a brilliant one that had kept himself and everyone else fooled.

- A woman had developed a strategy of pleasing others and felt tremendous anxiety when she was not doing so. Yet in this strategy there was also a real wish to help, which had first developed as a way of trying to bring light to the unhappy members of her family. Indeed, she had a great light within her. The problem was that she had identified with being the torchbearer and had come to believe that if she were not bringing light to the world, then she was in danger of being destroyed.

- A woman who had developed a pervasive habit of lying had a hard time believing in herself because she felt like a fraud. She had begun to lie in childhood as a way of making herself look good and thus protecting herself from her parents' critical attacks. Since she knew herself to be good inside and could not understand why they couldn't see that, lying became her way of trying to get them to see that she *was* good.

- A man suffered from depression because he felt that life was hopeless. Yet when he investigated this depression, he discovered a well of sadness, which was connected to growing up in a disconnected, dysfunctional family. Feeling sad as a child had actually helped him feel more alive, more real than his family, and was thus a way of differentiating himself from them and finding himself. The problem was that he had come to identify with his sadness, thinking that was who he was. And this was the source of his depression. Through realizing that his sadness had merely been a doorway into soulfulness, depth, and sensitivity to life, he began to realize that he could have those qualities without having to identify himself as an outsider who was doomed to feel alienated all his life.

What is often confusing is that our inner resources have become so interwoven with our defensive strategies that we do not know how to sort out the gold from the dross within ourselves. Yet the Tantric teaching of coemergence suggests a way to do this. If every defensive pattern contains hidden intelligence and resources, this means that we do not have to reject the defensive personality. Instead, we need to crack it open, so that we can discover and gain access to the intelligence and resources that lie hidden within it.

Identity Crisis and Existential Choice

Sooner or later the personality strategy we adopted in childhood to survive our family circumstances becomes an obstacle to our further unfolding. And this inevitably leads to some kind of identity crisis, forcing us to look more consciously at what we have been doing to ourselves. In this way, identity crisis often marks the beginning of a path of unlocking the intelligence, sanity, and other powerful inner resources that have been locked up in our conditioned personality.

How we negotiate such identity crises will determine the direction of our lives. Even though we might recognize that our old personality structure constricts the larger life within us, how can we let go of what has given us a secure sense of existence? "Who am I if not this familiar identity? How will I cope, feel safe, or survive without it?" Insofar as our identity is originally built as a defense against nonexistence, the prospect of letting it go brings us face to face with primal fears of death and the unknown. In any process of growth, psychological or spiritual, we always reach this existential choice point, where we must decide whether we really want to move forward into the unknown. "If I give up my old, familiar ways, who will I be, and what will become of me?"

There are three main choices at this point. The first two tend to reinforce pathology, while the third gives us a path.

We could decide not to rock the boat, not to risk moving forward into the unknown, even though our old identity pattern has outlived its usefulness. For instance, clients in therapy will often start to rationalize their neurotic pattern: "Well, things are not really all that bad. My way of being may cause some problems, but at least it's a known quantity." Yet when people choose to turn back from a freedom they have glimpsed lying ahead, this weaves them more tightly into their cocoon. Their identity becomes more pathological, because they are now deliberately using it to hide from the larger possibilities of their being.

A second choice is to attack or punish ourselves for the personality we have become, or to strive with all our might to live up to a lofty ideal of who we should be. Yet trying to avoid the unknown by substituting a new, more "spiritual" identity for the old one does not provide a genuine path.

A third possibility involves opening to our experience and facing and working with ourselves as we are, instead of aggressively trying to make ourselves into something different. This requires developing the capacity to stay present in the midst of pain, fear, and the whole range of experience we go through. Through this kind of presence we start to tap the power of our being, which can act on the personality constrictions that have been obscuring it.

Working with Ourselves as We Are

How can we go about converting the fears and fixations of our personality into stepping-stones on the path of awakening? Before real change is possible, we first have to see, feel, and understand *what is*—as distinct from our familiar version of reality. This is not easy. We are blinded by hopes and fears, habitual ways of feeling and perceiving, cherished beliefs and opinions. So the first step in turning personality into path is developing a commitment to seeing ourselves as we are, no matter how much we might dread what we'll discover.

An awareness practice, such as meditation or inner contemplative inquiry, is helpful for developing the capacity to witness what we are doing without becoming caught up in judging it as good or bad. Through sitting quietly with ourselves, we see how we are constantly trying to maintain our identity, how our thoughts act as a kind of glue that holds our identity structure together. As we witness the compulsive self-maintaining grip of the mind, without judging or blaming it, our sustained awareness can act as a gentle solvent that begins to dissolve the glue of the personality structure. As the structure loosens, larger qualities of our being that have been covered up by it begin to be revealed.

Of course, we often don't like what we discover when we see ourselves as we are. We come up against the pain of our karma—the tangled pattern of actions and reactions, accumulated conditioning, habit, unconsciousness, and fear. As one spiritual wag put it, "Self-knowledge is always bad news," at least initially.

At this point it is not enough just to acknowledge what is; we need to make a fuller relationship with it. This means opening our heart to the situation we are in—feeling it, facing it squarely, and letting it touch us. This does not mean having to like what we find. If we hate certain parts of ourselves, we can also acknowledge and work with our self-hatred, as part of what is. Whatever arises, we can learn to face it directly and inquire more deeply into it.

Bringing awareness to the pain of our stuckness in our patterns often activates a sorrow from deep within—what I call a "purifying sadness." This is a soul sadness. It is a direct recognition of the price we have paid for remaining stuck in our narrow patterns while turning away from our larger nature. If felt and listened to, this sorrow reveals a deep longing and will to wake up, tell the truth, be real, and do what needs to be done to be more fully alive. Befriending our experience—by making space for what is, along with all our feelings about it—is what facilitates that movement. It allows the desire for change to arise as a natural expression of caring for ourselves—as a *holy longing*—rather than as a crusade against our failings.

Transmuting Neurosis

As the larger intelligence of our being starts to come forward, certain peripheral aspects of our personality start to fall away on their own. More entrenched features, however, still have too much psychic energy invested in them to give up that easily. What is called for here is not a crusade against them but a more gentle transmutation, which comes about through understanding the nature of the obstacle more deeply. Padmasambhava, who brought Buddhism to Tibet, provides an example of how to proceed. Instead of declaring war on the old demons of the shamanistic pre-Buddhist culture, he converted them into protectors of the Dharma. In a similar vein, recognizing the deeper intelligence in our own demons helps us redirect their obstruction in a more life-positive direction.

For example, one male client of mine found it hard to overcome an old oppositional identity that had outlived its usefulness. The scriptline of this basic stance was: "I don't want to and you can't make me." When he was a child, this stance had important survival value as a defense against a mother who was controlling and invasive. His basic "no" contained strength and intelligence in it: it was his way of trying to preserve his integrity by refusing to be consumed by a domineering mother. Unfortunately, it also caused tremendous anxiety and inner constriction, greatly limiting his capacity to connect with other people.

For much of his adult life he had tried unsuccessfully to get rid of his negativity and "think positively." The problem was that he felt strongest and most himself when asserting his no, so that in rejecting his no, he also lost his vitality and power. His image of the naysayer in himself was of a monster in his belly (where he felt most tense), whose job was to tighten the valves of his "inner plumbing" so that he would never feel overwhelmed by Other—by emotional nourishment, love, or emotional stimulation from the world.

His family had provided no modeling of true strength or power. The tightening in his gut was his way of trying to develop what the Japanese call *hara*—the grounded strength in the belly that was a missing element in his family. As he came to understand the essential purpose of this inner tightening—to protect himself, preserve his integrity, and develop a strength no one had ever modeled for him—he no longer needed to kick this monster out.

By consciously aligning himself with the basic purpose in his no, he discovered it as a friend whose energy could be rechanneled in more life-positive ways. For instance, instead of just saying no to the world by shutting down his energy channels, he found that he could draw on the powerful energy of his no to confront challenging situations head on, instead of just feeling overwhelmed by them. In this way, as he connected with the genuine, life-affirming energy in his no, he gained access to his genuine, life-affirming yes as well.

This example illustrates how even the things inside us that seem most terrible or unworkable contain a deeper intent that needs to be unlocked and redirected in a life-affirming way. Hidden within every wound we always find a particular blessing. If we blame ourselves for our personality patterns, we cannot access the gift contained within them and thus only impoverish ourselves further. Whatever we are struggling with, whatever seems most neurotic, can become an important stepping-stone on our way. Whatever problem, question, or confusion we have, whatever seems impossible in our lives—if we go toward it, see it, feel it, make a relationship with it, use it—*becomes our path*.

It is easy to become discouraged by life's challenges, to ask, "Why is it so difficult to be human, why do I have to go through this, why am I not more enlightened?" In our despair we fail to appreciate the *path quality* of human evolution. Enlightenment is not some ideal goal, perfect state of mind, or spiritual realm on high, but a journey that takes place on this earth. It is the process of waking up to all of what we are and making a complete relationship with that.

Because we begin life in a totally vulnerable state, we have to construct a personality shell to protect ourselves; because our awareness is so wide open, and as children we cannot yet understand or deal with that, we first have to make ourselves into a solid, bounded entity in order to feel that we really exist. All our personality defenses are completely understandable, and all have their own intelligence. They also provide us with a path. Feeling the weight and constrictions of the conditioned personality is what motivates us to seek our larger nature. The problem is not our personality but our refusal to keep growing beyond it—which leaves us suffering from a case of arrested development.

Tantric Buddhism uses the metaphor of a snake uncoiling in midair to describe the process of awakening. The coils of our neurosis have raw, wild energy tangled up in them. To uncoil these tangles, so that we do not remain ensnared, we do not have to kill the snake, or even sublimate its energy into more socially approved forms. Instead, by simply allowing it to do what it naturally wants to do—to unwind—we can tap its power and aliveness. What allows the coiled snake of the mind to unwind is awareness and gentle compassion. Compassion does not try to suppress the snake's wildness, but rather draws on the energies tied up in our neuroses to propel us forward on our path. And this path—of liberating the qualities of our being, proclaiming and celebrating them, and using them to help ourselves and other people—is never-ending.

3
Ego Strength and Egolessness

*The ego feeling we are aware of now is . . . only a shrunken vestige
of a far more extensive feeling—a feeling which embraced the
universe and expressed an inseparable connection of the ego with the
external world.*

—SIGMUND FREUD

THE DIAMETRICALLY OPPOSITE NOTIONS of ego
strength and egolessness epitomize the seminal difference between the
psychologies of West and East. Western psychotherapy emphasizes
the need for a strong ego, defined in terms of impulse control, self-
esteem, and competence in worldly functioning. Eastern contemplative psychologies, by contrast, regard the ego—the separate, bounded,
defensive self that appears to be in charge of the psyche—as ultimately
unreal and unnecessary. Eastern psychology looks beyond the notion
of a strong ego toward a larger quality of being that is egoless, or free
of the constraints of the bounded self-sense. Just as spiritual seekers
with only a superficial knowledge of Western psychology often misun-
derstand the therapeutic goal of ego strength, so most Western psychologists would regard the notion of egolessness as an invitation to
psychosis.

Are these two notions of ego strength and egolessness irrevocably
opposed? Or is it possible to strip away the superficial differences between Eastern and Western psychology and forge a common ground
of understanding? This is a matter of vital importance, for it raises
essential questions about the direction and aim of human life. What
then is ego, and how exactly is it a problem? Is it possible for a West-

erner to function in the modern world without being under the driving influence of an ego? And what would that mean?

The Nature and Function of Ego

When it comes to clear or consistent definitions of the terms *ego* and
self, Western psychology is a jumble of imprecise notions and conflicting ideas, in which theoretical constructs are mixed up with experientially based notions in confusing ways. Even psychoanalysts who share
similar theoretical orientations use the terms *ego* and *self* in a wide
range of different ways. To add to the confusion, *ego* is often used as a
translation of terms from Eastern psychology that differ in meaning
and connotation from the psychoanalytic ego.

Psychoanalysts often speak of two domains of the ego: the functional—its capacity to organize and manage both internal functioning
of the psyche as well as external functioning in the world—and the
self-representational—its capacity to synthesize a consistent self-
concept out of various images of itself. Ego defined as an organizing
or synthesizing activity is not something we directly experience. It is
purely a theoretical construct that serves a useful explanatory function.

Nonetheless, it is possible to have some experience of ego as a kind
of energetic constellation in the body-mind. Mystics and seers, for
instance, can often perceive ego activity directly, as a core of tension
or contraction in the body that is thick, tight, and opaque. In everyday
life, we are also familiar with a part of us that is geared toward worldly
functioning. And we have a consistent sense of *I-ness*.

Yet if we look more closely, we find that the familiar I consists
mostly of thoughts or images. Mostly what we mean when we refer to
I is what the great Indian sage Ramana Maharshi called the *I-thought*.
Our experience of ourselves is not fresh, immediate, or direct, but is
filtered instead through concepts or images of who we are.

Buddhist psychology considers the fixation on this I-thought, as a
center around which human life revolves, to be extremely problematic.
When the conceptualized I, based on identifications and conditioned
beliefs, becomes the command center of the psyche—the knower, the

observer, the controller, the doer—this cuts us off from the more authentic knowing and acting that arises from our true nature. Meditation experience reveals a vast expanse of being and awareness that is egoless, that is, not owned or controlled by this bounded, controlling sense of self. The core of the Buddha's teaching is that meditation provides a way to uncover the jewel of our authentic nature by cutting through the habitual concepts of self that obscure it like a film of dust.

The Functional, Managerial Ego

A psychology of awakening, which recognizes the larger realm of egoless awareness, could recognize the functional ego as a transitional mental structure that serves a useful purpose in human development. It is an interim caretaker, a managerial function created by the mind for the purpose of navigating in the world. Initially, this allows children to survive, function, and develop during their early years when they cannot yet fully recognize or draw on the power of their larger being. Ego, then, is a control structure we develop for purposes of survival and protection. The *I* thinks it is in control, and this belief provides a necessary sense of stability and security for the developing child.

Ego therefore serves a useful developmental purpose as a kind of business manager or agent that learns and masters the ways of the world. The tragedy of the ego, however, is that we start to believe that this manager—this frontal self that interfaces with the world—is who we are. This is like the manager of a business pretending to be the owner. This pretense creates confusion about who we really are.

There is a certain poignancy to this. As an imitation of our true nature, ego is a way of *trying to be*. If we lack the true strength to deal with difficult circumstances, we *try* to be strong—by tensing and tightening. Lacking true confidence, we try to get ahead or be on top—by forcing and pushing. Lacking direct knowledge of our value, we try to be lovable—by compromising ourselves, trying to save our parents, or pleasing people. All of these can be useful adaptations in childhood, for they provide some semblance of real inner resources we are not yet fully in touch with.

According to Buddhism, ignorance is the root of suffering. Yet as the Indian sage Sri Aurobindo taught, ignorance is merely incomplete knowledge. In this sense, ego is a form of incomplete knowledge—an attempt to know ourselves as real and capable, rather than deficient. It is incomplete because it operates only on the surface of our nature, as an outer facade, and is not grounded in the true reality of our being. This is a poignant situation because the ego, the managerial self, is trying hard to do the right thing, without ever really succeeding.

Therefore criticizing the ego is like condemning a child for not being an adult. Our personality is simply a stage on the path. Instead of indulging in ego-bashing, a more helpful approach is to appreciate how ego tries its best and have some compassion for its ultimate failure.

Indeed, if we define ego strength as the capacity to function effectively in the world, without being debilitated by inner conflict, certainly no Eastern teacher would have any argument with that. The Buddhist notion of egolessness is not meant to counteract ego strength in that sense. Practically speaking, most spiritual teachers would agree that a grounded sense of confidence is an important basis for spiritual practice, which aims at letting go of self-fixation altogether.

Yet at some point in adult development, we may start to recognize that ego's effortful striving does not really work. We discover the painful truth: the Wizard of Oz who's pretending to control things behind the scenes has no real power to deliver the goods—the mastery or satisfaction it claims to be capable of achieving. As the Russian teacher Gurdjieff used to say, *I* cannot *do* anything. Just as digestion and the blood's circulation happen on their own, so genuine action, decision, understanding, and feeling arise, in truth, from a larger grace and intelligence that lies outside the ego's grasp. At some point in our development, it is time to let go of the fabricated control structure that once served us so well.

So from a larger spiritual perspective, the central ego-self around which most people's lives revolve is at best an early stage of development, rather than an ultimate, indispensable organizing principle of consciousness. To reify the ego as a necessary, enduring structure of the psyche—as Western psychology does—only solidifies its central position in our lives and impedes our capacity to move beyond it. If the small managerial self runs our life, this is not because ego is indispensable but because we have not found a larger principle to guide us. Ego is a pretender to the throne; it sits in the seat of the real sovereign, which is our true nature, our larger being.

Once we no longer believe in ego as a permanent structure necessary for the balanced functioning of the psyche or for efficient action in the world, we can start to recognize how capacities for balance, harmony, integration, power, and skillful action are resources inherent in our larger nature. As these larger capacities of being are uncovered, they can take over functions that the controlling ego-self formerly managed. Then it becomes possible to function in the world in a way that will not cut us off from our being.

The Self-Representational Ego

The second domain of ego—the continuity of a known, familiar sense of self, the belief that "I am consistently me"—raises a more subtle and difficult question: If ego is not ultimately real, how is it that I continue to feel that I am the same *me?* Buddhist psychology explains the relative consistency of the sense of self in terms of karma, the transmission of tendencies from one mind-moment to the next. Each grasping mind-moment carries forward a previous moment of grasping and passes it on to a successive moment. The father of American psychology, William James, echoes this notion of karma in his analysis of how thoughts inherit and transmit a chain of seeming ownership:

Each pulse of cognitive consciousness, each thought, dies away and is replaced by another. . . . Each later thought, knowing and including thus the thoughts which went before, is the final receptacle . . . of all that they contain and own. Each thought is thus born an owner, and dies owned, transmitting whatever it realized as its self to its own later proprietor . . . like the log carried first by William and Henry, then by William, Henry and John, then by John and Peter, and so on. All real units of experience overlap. Each thought dies away and is replaced by another, saying, "Thou art mine and part of the same self with me."

Thus, who I think I am now is always determined by who I thought I was a moment ago. Ramana Maharshi described this illusory continuity of ego in a strikingly similar way as James:

This ghostly ego . . . comes into existence by grasping a form; grasping a form it endures; leaving one form it grasps another form. . . . Ego is like that caterpillar which leaves its hold only after catching another.

In this way, the thought process is what continually recreates the sense of a continuous, consistent self. Most of our thinking, indeed, revolves around and confirms the central I-thought.

Western and Eastern psychology do share an important area of agreement regarding the nature of the ego identity: they both see it as a construction, fabricated through the power of conditioning. According to Western developmental psychology, newborn infants lack a sense of self and develop it only gradually through interactions with their caretakers. Children construct their sense of self through internalizing and identifying with aspects of their parents and how their parents relate to them. This ego identity is formed out of *self-representations*—images of oneself that in turn belong to larger, transactional self/other imprints called *object relations*.

Although Eastern psychology does not take account of child development, it too sees the egoic identity as a construction of the mind, formed through conditioning, or karma. Thus defining ego as the *fabricated* or *constructed self* is something that Eastern and Western psychology could agree on. Both sides would concur with Ernest Becker's statement that the child's defensive ego allows "him to feel that he *controls* his life and his death . . . that he has a unique and self-fashioned identity, that he is *somebody*." The key difference is that Eastern thought sees this *somebody* as ultimately unreal and dispensable, while Western psychologists tend to grant it permanent status, regarding it as substantive, enduring, and indispensable.

Yet how can a constructed sense of self, built out of self-concepts, be real or have any genuine, lasting power? This is a question that Western psychology has never confronted. The psychologist J. F. Masterson displays this confusion when he defines the *real self* as "all our self-images plus the ability to relate them to each other and recognize them as forming a single, unique individual." A Buddhist might say to Masterson: "How could a *real* self consist of images? What is real about a collection of self-representations, since these are only mental concepts? This sounds like a house of cards to me." Precisely because the egoic self is a mental fabrication, contemplative psychologies regard it as having no inherent reality.

If there is a true self beyond ego, it would have to be a reality that can be directly known and recognized, without recourse to images—an I beyond I, as it were. Ramana Maharshi called this "the pure 'I' . . . the pure being . . . free from thought-illusion." The limitation of Western psychology is that it fails to look beyond the conventional ego or self toward this larger dimension of being.

Although C. G. Jung spoke of a transcendent Self behind the ego, Jung's Self could never be directly realized, but only revealed through images—archetypal images, in this case. And while Jung recognized a spiritual principle in the psyche, like most Western psychologists he could not allow for egoless awareness as a developmental step beyond ego. He could only see it as a step backward, leading toward a more primitive state of mind dominated by the unconscious, at the expense of mature, differentiated consciousness. In his words: "Consciousness is inconceivable without an ego. If there is no ego, there is nobody to be conscious of anything. The ego is therefore indispensable to the conscious process. The Eastern mind, however, has no difficulty conceiving a consciousness without an ego. . . . [A]n egoless mental condition can only be unconscious to us, for the simple reason that there would be nobody to witness it."

Ego as Grasping

To understand the meaning and importance of egolessness in Buddhist psychology, we need to consider its view of ego more closely. If

Western psychology defines ego primarily as a *structure*, built on self-representations and self/other imprints (object relations), Buddhist psychology focuses instead on ego as an *activity*—a recurring tendency to make oneself into something solid and defined, and to grasp onto anything that maintains this identity, while rejecting anything that threatens it. One Tibetan term that is often translated as *ego* literally means "grasping at self" (*dak-dzin*), or "holding on to the 'I' I think myself to be." It is this activity of grasping that turns any experience—from chasing worldly status to subtler forms of holding on to ideas, feelings, or even spiritual experiences—into ego activity.

Ego in the Buddhist sense, then, is the ongoing activity of holding oneself separate, making oneself into something solid and definite, and identifying with this split-off fragment of the experiential field. Continually maintaining this identity project perpetuates a division between self and other that prevents us from recognizing ourselves as seamlessly woven into the larger field of reality. And the more we hold ourselves separate from the world, from our own experience, and from the naked power of life itself, regarding these as *other*, the more we fall prey to inner struggle, dissatisfaction, anxiety, and alienation.

A Buddhist View of Ego Development

Western psychology studies the development of ego (as a structure) horizontally, in terms of a sequence of stages spanning a number of years in childhood. By contrast, Buddhist psychology looks at the egoic self in a more vertical, immediate way—as the activity of recreating and reinforcing our concept of self over and over again at every moment. If we made a cross-sectional diagram of ego activity, we would see five layered tendencies at work, known as the *skandha*s, operating within and shaping our experience of reality.[1]

The sense of a separate self initially arises out of contracting against the boundless openness of being in order to establish some measure of security and control. This contraction establishes *me* as something bounded, definite, substantial, and separate, and sets up a split between self and not-self. This is the first *skandha*, known as *form* or the "birth of ignorance." From the perspective of developmental psychology, the first *skandha* would correspond to the stage when the child's consciousness cathects, or identifies with, the body. Out of this, the belief that "I am this body" arises, along with its attendant sense of boundedness and separation.

Once the *I* has separated out from the larger expanse of reality, it checks to see whether the not-self standing over against it is friendly, threatening, or neutral. This is the *skandha* of *feeling*—feeling out situations to see if they are for us or against us. In this way, our relation to reality becomes shaped by the categories of pleasure and pain, hope and fear, like and dislike. We like people, situations, and experiences that confirm our identity or make us feel more solid and secure, and we dislike anything that threatens our bounded identity. The split between self and not-self that emerges in the first *skandha* now also takes place *within* the self. We like the good (adequate, lovable, competent) self we hope we are, and we dislike the bad (inadequate, unlovable, deficient, unworthy) self we fear that we may be.

The third *skandha*, termed *perception* or *impulse*, involves adopting a stance—of passion, aggression, or ignorance—toward situations, based on whether we perceive them as friendly, threatening, or neutral. *Passion* here means the activity of chasing, grasping, seducing, possessing, incorporating, or clinging to situations that confirm our identity. Some people try to confirm themselves through chasing after pleasure, others through holding on to pain ("I suffer, therefore I am"). *Aggression* involves attacking or rejecting whatever threatens our identity project—our attempt to establish ourselves as solid, real, and valid. We must continually ward off anything that might invalidate us or imply that we are bad or inadequate. And *ignorance* involves apathy and indifference toward situations that are not interesting because they neither confirm nor threaten us.[2]

The fourth *skandha*, known as *conceptualization*, represents a further step toward solidifying our identity. We generate elaborate beliefs and interpretations about reality based on our patterns of hope and fear. These stories and beliefs about self and world further reinforce and crystallize our strategies of grasping, aversion, and indifference. They keep us imprisoned and isolated in a narrow, self-perpetuating conceptual world.

These four tendencies are like cascading rivulets that all come to fruition in the fifth *skandha*, the ongoing *stream of consciousness*. If you look at what propels the endless torrent of your thoughts and feelings, you will inevitably find the first four *skandhas*—contraction and solidification, hope and fear, grasping and rejecting, and the continual reconstellating of familiar self-concepts—in operation. Most of our mental activity is an attempt to prove that we exist, that we are something solid, and that we are okay. Ego maintains itself through the endless self-talk of the busy mind, which covers up any gaps or open spaces in the mindstream.

If we were to sketch this cross-section of ego, the five *skandhas* might appear like layers of a cake. This layered texture can actually be discovered through careful attention to the play of the mind. When we start to meditate, what we usually notice first is the top layer—the relentless chatter of the busy mind, with its chaotic flux of thoughts and impressions. With continued practice, we start to uncover the underlying layers of the ego mind driving our thoughts: concepts of self and other, the continual tendency to grasp and reject, the continual churning of hope and fear underlying that, and on the bottom layer, the tension and contraction involved in trying to maintain and preserve a separate self-identity.

William James described the flux of thought underlying what he called the "central self" in a similar way:

> Now can we tell more precisely in what the feeling of the central active self consists? . . . First of all, I am aware of a constant play of furtherances and hindrances in my thinking. . . . Among the matters I think of, some range themselves on the side of the thought's interests [passion], whilst others play an unfriendly part thereto [aggression]. The mutual inconsistencies and agreements, reinforcement and obstructions . . . produce . . . incessant reactions of my spontaneity upon them, welcoming or opposing, appropriating or disowning, striving with or against, saying yes or no. This palpitating inward life is, in me, that central nucleus [of the self].

James takes a further step in the Buddhist direction by recognizing that beneath these mental dynamics, no substantial self can be found:

> But when I . . . grapple with particulars, coming to the closest possible quarters with the facts, it is difficult for me to detect in the activity any purely spiritual element at all [i.e., any central self]. Whenever my introspective glance succeeds in turning around quickly enough to catch one of these manifestations . . . in the act, all it can ever feel distinctly is some bodily process, for the most part taking place within the head.

Ego and Egolessness

Although the egoic activity of contracting, grasping, and identifying is relentless, it is not solid or continuous like a barnacle on a rock. Rather, grasping and contraction come and go, like a fist alternately clenching and relaxing. If a fist remained clenched all the time, it would cease to be a hand and would become a different sort of limb. Just as a fist is the activity of clenching an open hand, so the ego is the solidifying of open, nongrasping awareness, which is inherently *egoless*. Ego continually arises out of and subsides back into egolessness, like a fist tensing and relaxing again.

If ego is awareness in a contracted state and egolessness is awareness in a relaxed state, it is clear that ego cannot exist without egolessness, which is its ground. Therefore, theologian Harvey Cox was mistaken in asserting, "There is no basis whatever in our Western experience for understanding what the Buddhists mean by egolessness." Everyone has little glimpses of egolessness in the gaps and spaces between thoughts, which usually go unnoticed. Ego is dying and being reborn at every moment. We continually have to let go of what we have already thought, accomplished, known, experienced, become. A sense of panic underlies these births and deaths, which stimulates further grasping and clenching. Existential anxiety arises as a sense of impending death, a dawning realization that the *I* is nothing solid, that it has no true support and is continually threatened by the possibility of dissolving back into the egoless ground of being from which it arose. Ego contains at its very core *a panic about egolessness*, an anxious reaction to the unconditional openness that underlies each moment of consciousness.

Identifying with a self-concept is an attempt to give ourselves some shape, some hold on things, some security. Experience may change, but at least, so we hope, the experiencer endures. But in fending off its continual impending dissolution into openness, the experiencer gets in the way of its own experience, becoming an obscuration that prevents direct contact with our true nature, with others, and with the larger sweep of life.

Understanding egolessness as the open hand out of which the clenched fist of ego forms helps us see that it poses no real threat to our existence or effective functioning in the world. A fist may be useful for some purposes, but in the long run we can do a lot more with an open hand. And in the end, it is only egoless awareness that allows us to face and accept death in all its forms. Recognizing ego death as an integral, recurring aspect of life makes it possible to overcome our fear of letting go. When we are not so driven to prove, justify, defend, or immortalize our bounded self, we can breathe more deeply, appreciate death as a renewing element within the larger circle of life, and embrace reality in all the forms in which it presents itself.

Thus the fear of many psychoanalysts—that egolessness sounds like a forerunner of psychosis, paralysis, or decompensation—is unfounded.[3] For egoless awareness does not mean losing sight of the conventional boundaries of where this mind/body leaves off and other mind/bodies begin. Rather, these conventional self-boundaries are seen as just that—conventional constructions—rather than as absolute demarcations that fence off a solidly existing, separate territory.

The continual activity of grasping onto an ego identity is essentially narcissistic, for it keeps us occupied with propping up an image of ourselves. Even Freud recognized the narcissism inherent in the ego when he wrote, "The development of the ego consists in a departure from primal narcissism and results in a vigorous attempt to recover it." So if we truly want to move beyond narcissistic self-involvement, we must work on overcoming our identification with whatever we imagine ourselves to be—any image of ourselves as something solid, separate, or defined. The less involved we are with images of who we are, the more we will be able to recognize our deep bond with all sentient beings, as different expressions of the mystery that also pervades our inmost nature.

4

The Play of the Mind

Form, Emptiness, and Beyond

Form is emptiness, emptiness itself is form; emptiness is no other than form, form is no other than emptiness.

—HEART SUTRA

In every crescendo of sensation, in every effort to recall, in every progress towards the satisfaction of desire, this succession of an emptiness and fullness that have reference to each other and are one flesh is the essence of the phenomenon.

—WILLIAM JAMES

*In the gap between thoughts
nonconceptual wisdom shines continuously.*

—MILAREPA

❀ IT IS EASY TO IMAGINE that life is just happening to us, as though we had no part in directing the three-dimensional movie going on all around us. Yet according to Buddhist contemplative psychology, and some Western psychological theories as well, our experience of reality—how we see things, what they mean to us, how we feel and respond to them—is largely constructed by the mind. This is actually good news. For if suffering is created by the mind, this means that the mind can also undo the suffering it has created.

If we are to live more consciously, or know ourselves more fully, or wake up from the nightmare of our personal or collective past, it is essential to look at the nature of our mind—how it shapes our reality and how it might also set us free. As one Tibetan Tantric text points out, "The mind is that which creates both imprisonment and liberation, confusion and awakening, so it is essential to know this king which generates all our experience."

Western philosophy has studied the mind mainly through conceptual thought and rational analysis; as a result, it has granted thinking, even "thinking about thinking," the highest status. Modern depth psychology has gone beyond this traditional understanding by giving greater importance to what eludes thought—subconscious feelings, wishes, impulses, images. Yet modern psychology's view of mind remains limited because, in characteristic Western fashion, it focuses on the *contents* of mind, while neglecting mind as an experiential *process*.

William James was an early critic of psychology's tendency to overemphasize the contents of the mind while ignoring the flowing stream of consciousness itself—which for him was like saying that "a river consists of nothing but pailsful, spoonsful, quartpotsful, barrelsful, and other molded forms of water. Even were the pails and the pots all actually standing in the stream, still between them the free water would continue to *flow*." In directing attention toward the flow of consciousness, the free water that cannot be confined to its molded forms, James comes close to the Buddhist understanding of everyday mind as a *mindstream*, a continuous flow of moment-to-moment experiencing.

Buddhist psychology goes one step further, however. Beyond the static Western focus on contents of mind and the more dynamic view of the mindstream as a flow of experiencing, it recognizes a still larger dimension of mind—the presence of nonconceptual awareness, or *nonthought*, as it is sometimes called. In contrast to the forms that consciousness takes—thought, feeling, perception—the larger nature of consciousness has no shape or form. Therefore, it is often described as *emptiness*. If the contents of mind are like pails and buckets floating in a stream, and the mindstream is like the dynamic flowing of the water, pure awareness is like the water itself in its essential wetness. Sometimes the water is still, sometimes it is turbulent; yet it always remains as it is, wet, fluid, watery. In the same way, pure awareness is never confined or disrupted by any mind-state. Therefore, it is the source of liberation and true equanimity.

When we start to observe the play of the mind, what we most readily notice are the contents of consciousness—the ongoing, overlapping sequence of perceptions, thoughts, feelings. As we develop a subtler, finer, more sustained kind of witnessing, through a discipline such as meditation, we discover in addition to these *differentiated mind-moments* another aspect of the mindstream that usually remains hidden: inarticulate gaps or spaces appearing between our discrete thoughts, feelings, and perceptions. These spaces between the pailsful and bucketsful of water floating in the stream are hard to see at first and impossible to remember because they have no definite form or shape we can grasp onto. Yet if we do not try to grasp them, these *undifferentiated mind-moments* can provide a glimpse of the larger reality that lies beyond the mindstream: the pure ground of nonconceptual awareness that encompasses and also surpasses all the activities of mind.

Thus the play of the mind includes three elements: differentiated and undifferentiated mind-moments, and the larger background awareness in which the interplay between these two takes place. In the Tibetan Mahamudra tradition, these three elements are known as movement, stillness, and awareness. The alternation between movement and stillness—differentiated and undifferentiated mind-moments—makes up the flowing stream of consciousness that is the foreground level of mind. And through the relative stillness of the silent spaces between thoughts we find a doorway into the essence of mind itself, the larger background awareness that is present in both movement and stillness, without bias toward either.[1] This larger awareness is self-existing. It cannot be fabricated or manufactured because it is always present, whether we notice it or not.

Form and Emptiness in the Stream of Consciousness

Our most common experience of nonthought or emptiness is the appearance of little gaps between our thoughts—gaps that are continually occurring, though normally overlooked. For instance, after speaking a sentence, there is a natural pause, marked by a punctuation mark when written out, which allows a split-second return to undifferentiated awareness. Or between the words of the sentence itself, there may be halts and gaps (often covered verbally by "hm" or "ah") that allow split-second attention to a preverbal sense of what we wish to say.

As one of the first Western explorers of consciousness, William James was particularly interested in these undifferentiated moments in the mindstream—which he called the "transitive parts," in contrast to the more substantial moments of formal thought and perception. He also understood the impossibility of using focal attention to try to observe these diffuse transitional spaces that occur between more substantive mind-moments: "Now it is very difficult, introspectively, to see the transitive parts for what they really are. If they are but flights to a conclusion, stopping them to look at them before the conclusion is reached is really annihilating them. . . . The attempt at introspective analysis in these cases is in fact like seizing a spinning top to catch its motion, or trying to turn up the gas quickly enough to see how the darkness looks."

The difficulty of apprehending these undifferentiated moments through focal attention has led Western psychology to disregard them altogether, an error that James called the psychologist's fallacy: "If to hold fast and observe the transitive parts of thought's stream be so hard, then the great blunder to which all schools are liable must be the failure to register them, and the undue emphasizing of the more substantive parts of the stream."

The mind's tendency to grasp onto solid forms is like a bird in flight always looking for the next branch to land on. And this narrow focus prevents us from appreciating what it is like to sail through space, to experience what one Hasidic master called the "between-stage"—a primal state of potentiality that gives birth to new possibilities. Continually looking for a belief, attitude, identity, or emotional reaction to hold on to for dear life, we fail to recognize the interplay of form and emptiness in the mindstream—out of which all creativity arises.

Beauty itself is a function of this interplay. Things stand out as beautiful only in relation to the space surrounding them. The most lovely antiques mean nothing in a cluttered room. A sudden clap of thunder is awesome not just because of the sound, but because of the silence it has interrupted, as James points out: "Into the awareness of the thunder itself the awareness of the previous silence creeps and continues; for what we hear when the thunder crashes is not thunder *pure*, but thunder-breaking-upon-silence-and-contrasting-with-it. . . . The *feeling* of the thunder *is* also a feeling of the silence as just gone."

Feelings within the stream of consciousness also take on their specific character by virtue of the spaces surrounding them. Genuine feeling, unlike reactive emotions, generally arises in spaces of stillness and contemplation. For example, a sense of sadness following a moment of quiet reflection may convey a deeply poignant truth, unlike the sorrow arising from a busy state of mind filled with self-accusatory thoughts.

Similarly in music, the contour, meaning, and beauty of a melody derive from the intervals between the notes. Recognizing this, the great pianist Artur Schnabel once wrote, "The notes I handle no better than many pianists. But the pauses between the notes—ah, that is where the art resides." A single tone by itself has little meaning, and as soon as two tones are sounded they are instantly related by the shape of the space or interval between them. The interval of a third conveys a totally different feeling than does a fifth. When sounding these intervals, the notes themselves are of secondary importance, for any pair of notes the same interval apart will sound rather similar.

Thus music provides an interesting analogy for the interplay between form and emptiness within the larger ecology of mind. *Form is emptiness:* the melody is actually a pattern of intervals between the tones. Although a melody is usually thought of as a sequence of notes, it is equally, if not more so, a sequence of spaces that the tones simply serve to mark off. And *emptiness is form:* nonetheless, this pattern of intervals does make up a definite, unique melodic progression that can be sung and remembered. And the ground of both the tones and the intervals is the larger silence that encompasses the melody and allows it to stand out and be heard.

Our usual addiction to the grasping tendency of mind causes us to overlook the spaces around thoughts, the felt penumbra that gives our experience its subtle beauty and meaning. Neglecting these fluid spaces within the mindstream contributes to a general tendency to overidentify with the contents of our mind, and to assume that we are the originator and custodian of them. The troublesome equation "I = my thoughts about reality" creates a narrowed sense of self, along with an anxiety about our thoughts as territory we have to defend.

Felt Meaning

So far we have explored emptiness as a sequence of gaps in the mind-stream that provide a surrounding space or penumbra that lets our experience stand out as what it is. But if we look more deeply into one of these undifferentiated mind-moments, we can also discover a rich and diffuse pre-articulate experiential intricacy, which we sense implicitly before giving it any explicit expression. Before I put these words onto paper, for instance, there is what Gendlin calls a *felt sense* of what I am wanting to say—how I am prereflectively sensing the direction I am moving in before I articulate it in words.

As you are reading this, you also have some overall sense of what I am saying, even if you cannot exactly articulate it. This is what carries you along from word to word, sentence to sentence, paragraph to paragraph, and allows you to keep making sense of what I am saying.

A felt sense is what you would inwardly refer to if someone were to ask you, "How are you feeling right now?" In order to answer precisely, you have to look past the automatic answers that spring to the tongue and sense inwardly an amorphous "something" that is at first fuzzy or inchoate. Perhaps your eyes roll to the side, you pause, sigh, mumble, or sit down to reflect on this preverbal felt sense. As you begin to connect with how you feel, this vague something takes shape and there is a sense of recognition, "Yes, that's what it is." Returning to focal attention, you could then articulate or elaborate various aspects of what you sense, such as "I'm feeling tired and frustrated and somewhat wary, but not entirely hopeless."

As Gendlin has shown, most of our action and speech is guided by this underlying implicit, pre-articulate experiencing. Thought, imagery, and action are different ways in which we formulate and express these pre-articulate senses, which are relatively empty compared to the forms they may take.

So when the "mind goes empty" or we meet an "empty gaze," what is often occurring is some inward reference to a rich background of undifferentiated felt meaning. According to James, "A good third of our psychic life consists in these rapid premonitory perspective views of schemes of thought not yet articulate." And so, as he puts it, "the feeling of an absence" is not the same as "the absence of a feeling." Deep within moments of relative emptiness we discover the *diffuse richness* of our felt involvement with life.

In order to articulate a pre-articulate felt sense, we need to relax our usual dependence on focal attention and shift to a more diffuse attention that allows a holistic scanning of experiential intricacy. Creative thinking, action, and decision-making, spiritual or psychotherapeutic insight, and artistic expression all arise out of this holistic scanning of what we sense but do not yet formally know. As Mozart remarked of the process of composing music, "Best of all is the hearing of it all at once."

Absolute Emptiness: The Larger Ground of Awareness

Gaps in the mindstream—spaces between thoughts, moments of quiet, and diffuse felt senses—represent a *relative* kind of emptiness. These gaps are relatively formless in comparison to the more graspable forms of thought, perception, or emotion. Yet the stillness in these gaps is only relative because it is easily disrupted or displaced by the next moment of activity that occurs in the mindstream. This type of stillness is simply an experience among experiences—what the Tibetans call *nyam* (temporary experience).

Beyond the *relative emptiness* that we discover in these gaps in the mindstream lies the much larger *absolute emptiness* of nonconceptual awareness, which Buddhism regards as the very essence of mind. This nonconceptual awareness is an absolute stillness or emptiness whose space and silence actually pervade, and thus cannot be displaced by, whatever goes on in the mind. Meditation practice can help us find this larger stillness in movement, this larger silence within sound, this nonthought within the very activity of thinking.

Without sustained and disciplined inner attention, it is almost impossible to discover, enter, or abide in this absolute ground of steady awareness. For as long as we skim along the surface of consciousness, our moments of stillness are quickly disrupted by the activity of thought, feeling, and perception. Meditation practice provides a direct way to tune into this larger dimension of nonconceptual awareness. As one Tibetan text describes this discovery, "Sometimes in meditation there is a gap in normal consciousness, a sudden complete openness. . . . It is a glimpse of reality, a sudden flash which occurs at first infrequently, and then gradually more and more often. It may not be a particularly shattering or explosive experience at all, just a moment of great simplicity."

Meditation is designed to help us move beyond the surface contents of the mind. Underneath the mind's surface activity—the vivid whitecaps of thought and emotion as well as the subtler flows of felt sensing—the ocean of awareness remains perfectly at rest, regardless of what is happening on its surface. As long as we are caught up in the waves of thought and feeling, they appear solid and overwhelming. But if we can find the presence of awareness within our thoughts and feelings, they lose their formal solidity and release their fixations. In the words of the Tibetan teacher Tarthang Tulku, "Stay in the thoughts. Just be there. . . . You become the center of the thought. But there is not really any center. . . . Yet at the same time, there is . . . complete openness. . . . If we can do this, any thought becomes meditation." In this way, meditation reveals the absolute stillness within both the mind's turbulence and its relative calm.

Here then is the deeper sense in which form is emptiness: the essence of all thought and all experience is complete openness and clarity. In this sense, Buddhist psychology provides an understanding of mind that resembles quantum physics' view of matter. In quantum field theories, "the classical contrast between the solid particles and

the space surrounding them is completely overcome." Just as sub-
atomic particles are intense condensations of a larger energy field, so
thoughts are momentary condensations of awareness. Just as matter
and space are but two aspects of a single unified field, so thought
and the spaces between thoughts are two aspects of the larger field of
awareness, which Zen master Suzuki Roshi described as *big mind*. If
small mind is the ongoing grasping and fixating activity of focal attention, big mind is the background of this whole play—pure presence
and nonconceptual awareness.

Figure 1 illustrates the relationship between the three aspects of
mind discussed here. The dots are like differentiated mind-moments,
which stand out as separate events because of the spaces between
them. Although these spaces appear to be nothing in comparison to
the dots, they nonetheless provide the context that allows the dots to
stand out as what they are and that joins them together. The spaces
between the dots also provide entry points into the background, the
white space of the page, which represents the larger ground of pure
awareness in which the interplay of form and emptiness takes place.

FIGURE 1. *The Three Aspects of Mind*

Big Mind

The big mind of pure awareness is a no-man's-land—a free, open reality without reference points, property boundaries, or trail markers.
Although it cannot be grasped as an object by focal attention, it is not
merely an article of faith. Quite the contrary; in the words of a Tibetan text, "The nothingness in question is actually experienceable."

Unfortunately, when the untutored mind regards it as a mere blankness or nothingness, the jewellike radiance of this pure awareness becomes obscured. As Dzogchen teacher Tenzin Wangyal points out, "The gap between two thoughts *is* essence. But if in that gap there is a lack of presence, it becomes ignorance and we experience only a lack of awareness, almost an unconsciousness. If there is presence in the gap, then we experience the dharmakaya [the ultimate]." The essence of meditation could be described quite simply, in Tenzin Wangyal's words, as "presence in the gap"—as an act of nondual, unitive knowing that reveals the ground of being in what at first appears to be nothing at all. As another Tibetan text explains, "The foundation of sentient beings is without roots. . . . And this rootlessness is the root of enlightenment." Only in the groundless ground of being can the dance of reality unfold in all its luminous clarity.

5

Meditation and the Unconscious

The great error of modern psychology has been to speak of the unconscious as though it were some kind of unknowable. . . . But insofar as the unconscious is the body . . . the unconscious can be known and studied. . . . And insofar as it is . . . [a] timeless principle, the unconscious can be finally realized in an act of unitive knowledge.

—ALDOUS HUXLEY

For Zen the main point is that the entire structure of being, including its unconscious aspect, must be radically broken through. . . . The aim of Zen is the breaking-up of the dualistic structure of consciousness-and-unconsciousness.

—RICHARD DeMARTINO

✦ MEDITATION HAS YET to be accurately portrayed or understood by Western psychology. C. G. Jung made an early attempt to make sense of meditation, interpreting it in the light of his concept of the collective unconscious. However, Jung's view is generally unsatisfactory to meditation practitioners, who find the dualistic model of an unconscious mind, set off from consciousness, inaccurate for describing their experience.

Western depth psychology has generally conceived of meditation as a means, like dreams, for accessing the unconscious. Wolfgang Kretschmer, for instance, writes, "Dreams are similar to meditation, except meditation gains the reaction of the unconscious by a systematic technique which is faster than depending on dreams." Jung, referring to Buddhist meditation, saw it as a direct route into the unconscious: "Meditation does not center upon anything. Not being centered, it would be rather like a dissolution of consciousness and hence a direct approach to the unconscious condition. . . . Meditation . . . seems to be a sort of Royal Road to the unconscious."

Yet what does it mean to say that meditation is a royal road to the unconscious? Jung's view of meditation as a dissolution of consciousness goes counter to the experience most meditators have—that meditation actually heightens and sharpens consciousness.

Depth psychology is certainly correct in suggesting that meditation can provide access to dimensions of our mind that we have not been fully conscious of before. But for most meditators, meditation is a royal road to nondualistic experience, rather than to a subterranean unconscious mind. Meditation reveals awareness as a unified field, where strict divisions between subject and object, inner and outer, or conscious and unconscious simply do not exist. If we are to understand meditation in Western psychological terms, we need a whole new understanding of unconscious process.[1]

The Traditional Model of the Unconscious

The unconscious has served as an important explanatory concept in Western psychology, helping to account for what happens in psychopathology, dreams, and altered states of consciousness. Yet since discussions of the unconscious are mostly speculative, it is often not clear exactly what this term actually refers to. One researcher pointed out that Western psychologists have used the term *unconscious* as an explanatory concept in at least sixteen different senses. The unconscious has become a catchall concept that appears to explain phenomena for which there is no other explanation, while often not explaining much at all, since its exact experiential meaning remains obscure.

In revising traditional notions of the unconscious, we do not have to deny that some kind of unconscious process occurs in such phenomena as selective perception and forgetting, slips of the tongue, laughter, habitual reactions, neurotic symptoms, and dreams. Clearly these phenomena point to a way in which the body-mind organism as a whole functions outside the narrow range of ordinary focal attention. It is the notion of *the* unconscious as a separate mental realm with its own contents that needs to be reevaluated, especially for a psychology of awakening.

Freud himself realized that his early topographical notion of the unconscious as a separate region was problematic, and he tried replacing it with the idea of unconsciousness as a dynamic property of the id-ego-superego interplay. Yet despite Freud's willingness to keep revising his theory, he never clearly distinguished the dynamic model of the unconscious from the topographic one.[2]

Jung, whose work is more friendly to transpersonal experience, was unfortunately less meticulous than Freud about the theoretical problems involved in the concept of the unconscious. He tended to make statements like the following, which ascribe an autonomous agency to the unconscious: "The unconscious perceives, has purposes and intuitions, feels and thinks as does the conscious mind." Consequently, Jungians still talk as though the unconscious is a psychic system with "a mind of its own," a container with a distinct set of contents that are like those of consciousness, except that they remain below the threshold of awareness.

In interpreting certain kinds of experience as reified "unconscious contents" (instincts, repressed material, archetypes), the depth psychology model perpetuates the Cartesian notion of mind as "something distinct and apart, a place or a realm that can be inhabited by such entities as ideas."[3] And for some Jungians, such as Esther Harding, this dark realm apart becomes a projection screen for Victorian fears of vital forces, as she reveals when she writes, "Beneath the decent facade of consciousness with its disciplined moral order and its good intentions lurk the crude, instinctive forces of life, like monsters of the deep." This dualistic approach defines mind as a separate system of internal events, and the greater part of mind, which is unconscious, as inherently dark, unknowable, *other*. This creates a dualism within a dualism, leaving human beings essentially alienated from themselves and from reality.[4]

The Depth-Psychology Interpretation of Meditation

Like classical physics, the traditional notion of the unconscious can serve a useful function, within certain limits; in particular, it has been useful for making sense of psychopathology. Yet it completely breaks down when it tries to explain meditation and nondualistic experience—which are analogous to the macro- and microscopic data that forced modern physics to develop relativity and quantum theory.

Although Jung made a valiant effort to understand meditation, the limitations of his model of the unconscious, along with his lack of direct experience with the practice itself, doomed him to failure. Like many Western theorists, Jung conceived of meditation as a withdrawal from life into an inner world, betraying what he called the "introverted prejudice" of the East. He saw meditation as bringing one nearer "to the state of unconsciousness with its qualities of oneness, indefiniteness, and timelessness." This led him to conclude that meditation was a kind of surrender to the unconscious—a dangerous indulgence that could work against being in the world. When meditation is conceived as an introverted probing of unconscious contents, it appears to be a dangerous occupation or else a form of narcissism.

Jung's view of meditation as a dissolution of consciousness, an introverted withdrawal, a descent into the indefinite regions of a separate unconscious mind, betrays the dualistic assumptions inherent in his thought. Jung's assumption of the real existence of a separate unconscious mind also required a belief in the real existence of the ego as a counterweight. The ego was what allowed consciousness to function, representing the main line of defense against the possibility of being overwhelmed by unconscious contents. In his words, "I cannot imagine a conscious mental state that does not relate to an ego."

From a Buddhist perspective, such dualistic divisions an inner world separate from outer reality, the unconscious as a separate mental realm, or the ego as a necessary defense against unconscious contents—are concepts that only reinforce the self/other split, which is the basis of the confused state of mind known as *samsara*. According to Chögyam Trungpa, the defensive nature of ego arises in reaction to our perception of some solid, imposing reality set over against us:

> Where there is . . . the concept of something that is separate from oneself, then we tend to think that because there is something outside, there must be something here as well. The external phenomenon sometimes becomes such an overwhelming thing and seems to have all sorts of seductive and aggressive qualities, so we erect a kind of defense against it. . . . And this creates a kind of gigantic bubble in us which consists of nothing but air and water, or, in this case, fear and the reflection of the external thing. So this huge bubble prevents any fresh air from coming in, and that is "I"—the ego. So in that sense there is the existence of ego, but it is in fact illusory.

Once we conceive of the unconscious as something *other*, separate from consciousness, then it is easy to regard it as having "seductive and aggressive qualities" threatening an ego that must be defended against these provocations. Indeed, Jung advised Westerners against practicing meditation for this very reason: the seductiveness of ego loss could precipitate a dangerous uprush from the unconscious. Thus, Jung could not comprehend how the meditative experience of egoless perception could offer a clear and precise way of being and living in the world. Instead, he could only understand the notion of awakened mind in terms of the inner realm of the unconscious: "Our concept of the collective unconscious would be the European equivalent of *buddhi*, the enlightened mind."

Jung's interpretation of meditation as a royal road to the unconscious contrasts sharply with that of Buddhist teachers, who describe meditative awareness as clear, transparent perception, free of conceptual filters, rather than as an act of going inward: "The practice of meditation does not require an inward concentration. . . . In fact without out the external world, the world of apparent phenomena, meditation would be almost impossible to practice, for the individual and the external world are not separate, but merely co-exist together." And the aim of meditation is not to develop vague trancelike states; rather, it is to sharpen awareness, to see things as they are: "When you wake up fully, you see everything clearly. You are not distracted because you see everything as it is." "Meditation [involves] relating with the conflicts of our life situations, like using a stone to sharpen a knife, the situation being the stone."

When the Eastern texts say that enlightened mind cannot be described, Jung equates *indescribable* with *unknowable*, assuming that they must be referring to the unconscious. And so the sharpened perception of enlightened mind becomes dulled, in his perspective, into a vague abstraction:

> The statement that "the various names given to it [enlightened Mind] are innumerable" proves that the Mind must be something as vague and indefinite as the philosopher's stone. A substance that can be described in "innumerable" ways must be expected to display as many qualities or facets. If these are really "innumerable," they cannot be counted, and it follows that the substance is well-nigh indescribable and unknowable. It can never be realized completely. This is certainly true of the unconscious, and a further proof that the Mind is the Eastern equivalent of our concept of the unconscious, more particularly of the collective unconscious.

What Jung does not realize is that meditation can provide a direct, precise recognition of the ultimate nature of consciousness, which can be described in innumerable ways. This is like taking pictures of Mt. Fuji from every possible angle, yet none of the pictures, nor even the whole series, can ever capture the living majesty of the mountain. Jung misinterprets this to mean that Mt. Fuji can never be seen or known clearly and directly, simply because it can be described from so many different perspectives.

It is clear, then, that the nondualistic awareness accessed through meditation is not comprehensible within a theory of mind based on dualistic assumptions. A new understanding of unconscious process is necessary in order to see how it is possible for meditation to put us in direct touch with "things as they are."

Toward a New Understanding of Unconscious Process

The new model of unconscious process that I propose is based on the assumption that human experience is an interactive way of organizing or relating to reality (to the physical world, other people, life, and Being itself), rather than some kind of inner, purely mental phenomenon. In this light, conscious and unconscious are not two separate regions of a psyche, but rather two different modes in which the body-mind organism structures relatedness. Unconscious process is *a holistic mode of organizing experience and responding to reality* that operates outside the normal span of focal attention. This mode of functioning takes account of larger fields of interconnectedness without breaking them into linear, sequential units. What is unconscious, then, are the holistic ways in which the body-mind organism experiences its interconnectedness with reality, prior to the articulations of reflective thought.

This holistic body-mind processing displays an intelligence that is nonreflective and nonintellectual. It operates in the background of the experiential field, whose foreground consists of the workings of *focal attention*, which pinpoints discrete objects of thought, feeling, and perception. Unconscious process may be nonlinear, but it is not inherently dark or unknowable. It is only unknowable through focal attention, which would necessarily distort its nature by breaking its larger fields of interconnectedness into serial, discrete elements.

There is another kind of attention—a *diffuse attention*—that allows a whole field to be experienced all at once, without linear analysis. While diffuse attention plays an important, often unrecognized role in ordinary awareness, it reaches its fullest expression in meditation and nondualistic experience, where the focus of attention broadens out for longer periods of time, and the conventional subject/object division dissolves in a larger field of awareness.

The Dynamics of Figure and Ground

Since unconscious process operates as the background of the experiential field, appreciating how it works requires an understanding of figure/ground dynamics. Four features of the figure/ground interrelationship are particularly relevant here:

1. *Figure and ground are continually shifting features of the experiential field.* Whatever comes into the foreground of consciousness, as figure, subsequently functions as part of the background whole (hence unconsciously). For example, everything I know and have seen about a particular person now functions as the global background that allows me to notice something new about him today. This new quality stands out as figure for a while, and then too becomes part of the ground, allowing further qualities to stand out. In this way, many kinds of information and relatedness function holistically in the background of consciousness, without our being aware of them in an explicit way. Thus, the body-mind organism knows, as we say, "unconsciously," more than focal attention can ever articulate. This accounts for how what was once conscious now functions unconsciously (as ground), and how from this ground, which functions in a pre-articulate holistic way, a new figure may suddenly appear. When it appears, it may seem as though it had been there all along, "in the unconscious." It was not there like a discrete content in a container, however, but as an implicit element within a larger background field of organism/environment interrelatedness.

2. *The ground is implicit in the figure.* That is, the figure assumes, and has meaning only in relation to, its ground. To use a cognitive example, if I differentiate the concept *dog* into collies, beagles, and boxers, then *dog* becomes the cognitive background that remains implicit in my study of collies. In this sense the unconscious ground is not a separate principle, but is present implicitly in whatever focal attention is perceiving.

3. *While focal attention continually differentiates figures, we also have access to a diffuse attention that can apprehend a whole experiential field without differentiating it into figure and ground.* Diffuse attention is necessary for contacting and knowing pre-articulate portions of the background experiential field.

4. *The term* ground *as used here has a double meaning—it refers both to*

what is in the background and to what serves as the ground that underlies, encompasses, and makes possible present experiencing. Insofar as this ground is not solid or fixed but a shifting, organic flux, it is a "groundless ground."

What follows is a phenomenological description of four progressively wider, interpenetrating levels of the normally unconscious background of experience. The word *levels* has no topological meaning here, but refers instead to "fields within fields" or "grounds within grounds." Each of these fields shapes how we relate to reality and allows for a certain kind of knowing. The wider background fields shape everyday consciousness in a global, all-encompassing way, while the more "frontal" fields allow for more differentiated kinds of knowing.

The unconscious ground can be differentiated into four levels: the *situational ground* of felt meaning—our implicit felt sense of the immediate situation we are in; the *personal ground*—how patterns of past experience and accumulated meaning implicitly shape our present consciousness, behavior, and worldview; the *transpersonal ground*—the ways in which the body-mind organism is attuned to larger, universal qualities of existence; and the *open ground*—pure, immediate presence to reality prior to identification with the body-mind organism.

The Situational Ground: Felt Meaning

The most accessible ground of our experience is what Eugene Gendlin has called *felt meaning*, the way in which every situation we are in always has implicit meaning for us, which we can actually sense in our body. A felt sense is how we feel our relatedness to particular situations. For example, if you happen to meet someone you know passing on the street, before you can *think* of what that person means to you, your body already has a felt response to meeting him, such as delight or apprehension. People often have a hard time accessing their bodily felt responses but can usually learn to do so through relaxing focal attention and attending more diffusely to bodily sensations. This relatively accessible background corresponds to, and is an experiential rendering of, the traditional concept of the *preconscious*.

Felt meaning normally functions as the immediate situational background against which focal attention differentiates particular objects of interest. As Gendlin has shown, most of our speech and action is guided implicitly by background felt meanings, which provide a continuity and context for our present transactions with the world:

> What we go through is much more than what we "have" [explicitly].
> ... Going through a simple act involves an enormous number of familiarities, learnings, senses for the situation, understandings of life and people, as well as the many specifics of the given situation. All this goes into just saying "hello" in a fitting way to a not very close friend. We go through, we are all this, but we "have" only a few focal bits of it. The feel of doing anything involves our sense of the whole situation at any moment, despite our not focally reflecting on it as such.

During meditation, with no fixed object to focus on, attention naturally starts to diffuse, and aspects of the situational ground emerge in the form of thoughts and feelings about one's life or immediate circumstances. We may remember things that have been forgotten, find ourselves mulling over decisions or problems in our life, or notice our responses to other meditators sitting in the same room. If we do not follow these thoughts and feelings, their fascination diminishes. Given enough time, we begin to get bored with, and move beyond, this "subconscious gossip," as Trungpa calls it.

The Personal Ground

The personal ground is somewhat less accessible than the situational ground. It is the background way in which personal meanings, associations, and interpersonal patterns formed during the individual's history presently shape consciousness and perception. In Merleau-Ponty's terms, there is a "sedimentation" of layers of meaning that make up one's habitual style of relating to the world. The personal ground also corresponds to Stanislav Grof's "systems of condensed experience" (COEX), which may vividly emerge during psychedelic drug sessions. But instead of seeing these as contents stored in an unconscious mind, we can understand them as strands of a whole background tapestry of meaning that subtly influences and shapes our present experience. Specific methods that cultivate diffuse attention, such as hypnosis, psychotherapeutic introspection, or drugs, make this ground more accessible to conscious investigation.

Focal attention by its very nature screens out wholes in favor of differentiated parts. This narrow focus, reinforced by the tendency to perceive in fixed, habitual ways, creates distortions in the experiential field that the organism tries to correct for through behavioral, imaginative, and emotional expression (dreams, fantasy, bizarre symptoms). For Jung, this corrective tendency, which plays a central role in psychopathology, is an aspect of the *shadow*, the compensatory function of the unconscious.

The shadow too can be understood as an instance of the holistic structuring processes of the organism, rather than as the workings of a separate unconscious mind. Focal attention selectively emphasizes certain aspects of the experiential field while ignoring others, thereby casting into the shadows these unattended parts of the field. The shadow is the mirror reversal of what focal attention has emphasized. Overemphasizing any part at the expense of the whole sets an opposite tendency in motion, as part of a larger equilibrium process. Thus, we can understand "messages from the unconscious" as the body-mind organism trying to bring forward aspects of the experiential field that have been selectively ignored.

During meditation, the personal ground (both its habitual tendencies and its shadow aspects) emerges in the form of memories, fantasies, projections, or emotional upheaval. Not being engaged in our ordinary activities, we can see more clearly the lenses—our beliefs, tendencies, strategies, and self-deceptions—that shape our personal sense of reality. The diffuse attention of meditation invites what has been swept under the rug to emerge and be acknowledged, often leading to important insights. Meditation in this sense is a vehicle for self-knowledge, as it allows us to observe and disidentify with whole patterns of conditioning. As the Buddhist teacher Dhiravamsa puts it,

"By observing our thoughts and emotions, we are able to see that each of them is conditioned by something else. . . . You see what kind of person you are, what your particular weaknesses, qualities, and characteristics are . . . without having to be told by anyone, without being tested, interpreted, or diagnosed. You can be your own analyst by looking into yourself, seeing yourself every moment."

The Transpersonal Ground

The next wider level of ground expresses an even deeper interconnectedness between organism and world, extending beyond the confines of purely personal experience. This transpersonal ground is comprised of deep structures of responding and relating to reality that are intrinsic to our human makeup. Here we discover all the most universally valued qualities of human nature—compassion, generosity, humor, courage, gentleness, strength, and so on. These capacities are expressions of our basic responsiveness to reality. Each of them represents an appropriate way of responding to a different facet of reality. In some situations only humor will do, while other situations call for generosity, patience, or courage. Humor is a way of playing with what is, taking it lightly rather than making it solid and heavy, while strength allows us to cut through obstacles.

These *soul qualities* are universal seed potentials that are part of our human heritage, and that individuals cultivate and actualize in their different ways. They are not our personal creation. The transpersonal ground is an in-between zone where, in Ken Wilber's words, we "are not conscious of our identity with the All and yet neither is our identity confined to the boundaries of the individual organism."

From this perspective, archetypes can be understood as basic human modes of interconnectedness with reality, rather than as instinctually based contents of a collective unconscious. The mother archetype, for instance, derives from the basic human experience of holding and being held. At first we experience this holding as physical—in the mother's arms. But infants are also in need of a larger "holding environment" to help them learn how to hold and handle their own experience. In the Eastern traditions, a mandala is a highly evolved form of holding container—a facilitating structure that allows experience to unfold and evolve in the direction of deeper truth. On the archetypal level, there is a connection between mother, mandala, and ground—which are some of the ways in which the archetypal principle of holding environment operates.

Archetypal principles always take on individual meanings and forms of expression, which are partly determined by a person's life history, social context, and immediate situation. For instance, the personal meaning of holding might be different for someone who experienced lack of holding in childhood (distrust, fear of falling) than for someone who experienced invasive or aggressive holding (fear of commitment, fear of belonging). Similarly, how given individuals express or emphasize compassion, humor, or generosity will of course vary, depending on their personal characteristics and cultural context. Yet the general experience of compassion is universal; all human beings recognize it in some form.

The transpersonal ground usually functions far in the background of consciousness, covered up by our focus on more readily grasped situational and personal concerns. Yet sometimes it breaks through into consciousness in the form of sudden insights, inventions, creative inspiration, visions, intuitive breakthroughs, and psychic phenomena—all of which arise out of our fundamental connectedness with reality. Creative insight develops through feeling out and synthesizing larger networks of relatedness, in ways that are impossible for focal attention. This organismic resolution of problems is also an essential factor in psychotherapy and physical healing. In meditation, this basic sense of connectedness may be felt as a state of well-being, feeling settled and at one with life.

Transpersonal interrelatedness may also be experienced directly in the ecstatic oneness of nature mysticism. As the mystic Thomas Traherne celebrates this oneness, "You never enjoy the world aright till the sea itself floweth in your veins, till you are clothed with the heavens and crowned with the stars; and perceive yourself to be the sole heir of the whole world . . . till you more feel it than your private estate, and are more present in the hemisphere, considering the glories and beauties there, than in your own house."

The transpersonal ground seems to correspond roughly to what some schools of Buddhism refer to as the *alaya-vijnana*. The Yogachara school sees the *alaya* as a transitional consciousness that lies between totally open, unconditioned awareness and individuated, personal consciousness. It is "the first phase in the process of self-differentiation. . . . It is not the absolute consciousness since . . . consciousness has already started bifurcating. . . . The alaya is the first phenomenalization of the Absolute." It is here—in identifying with the subtle responsiveness of the mind/body totality—that the sense of a separate self starts to develop. In D. T. Suzuki's words, "Though it is pure and immaculate in its original nature, [*alaya*] allows itself to be affected by *manas*, the principle of individuation. And thus affected, the dualism of subject and object is created in it."

The Open Ground

While the transpersonal ground can be experienced as a sense of oneness between self and world, it still involves a subtle identification with the body-mind organism. Beyond the *oneness* of the transpersonal ground lies the *zero-ness* of the open ground, which indicates an even deeper interpenetration with reality.

This widest ground of experience is a pure, immediate interrelational presence before it becomes differentiated into subject-object relationship perception. Experientially, the open ground can be felt as the sense of pure being that underlies all our differentiated experiences. As Trungpa describes this, "Our most fundamental state of mind . . . is such that there is basic openness, basic freedom, a spacious quality; and we have now and have always had this openness. It is natural being which just is."

Split-second flashes of this open ground—also described in Buddhism as primordial awareness, original mind, or no-mind—are happening all the time before events become interpreted in a particular way. This kind of presence is so transparent and all-encompassing that it usually recedes into the background of the experiential field, while the differentiated objects of attention—thoughts, emotions, perceptions—occupy the focus of attention. Yet it can be discovered in every fresh moment of awareness, before our thought cloaks it in concepts. As the psychologist Matte Blanco describes this:

> The findings of introspection suggest that there is, in fact, a very fleeting instant of *prise de conscience*, or "becoming aware," . . . when sensation is in consciousness in a naked state, not clothed in either explicit or implicit propositions, not even rudimentary ones. But an essential feature of this phenomenon is that it is fleeting. As soon as it arises in consciousness, sensation is caught by thoughts, wrapped by them.

Or as Trungpa describes it:

> When we see an object, in the first instant there is a sudden perception which has no logic or conceptualization to it at all; we just perceive the thing in the open ground. Then immediately we . . . begin to rush about trying to add something to it, either trying to find a name for it or trying to find pigeon-holes in which we could locate and categorize it. Gradually things develop from there.

We continually recreate our conceptual versions of reality through this instantaneous, automatic wrapping of naked awareness in thought and interpretation schemes that are imbued with personal meanings and associations. For instance, as I listen to a bird singing, my attention may be captivated by feelings the song arouses in me or by thoughts and associations that arise in response to it. What I normally do not notice is the sheer clarity of presence that is the ground and pure essence of this experience. Nonetheless, it is possible to notice this larger transparency through split-second gaps that appear in the normally dense fabric of mind. First thing in the morning, right after waking up, before thinking begins to take over, is a prime time to glimpse this open, spacious ground of awareness.

In meditation, awareness of the open ground breaks through as we wear out the projects and distractions of thought and emotion. Suddenly there appears a gap in the stream of thought, a flash of clarity and openness. It is neither particularly mystical or esoteric, nor any kind of introverted self-consciousness, but a clear perception of direct reality, or *suchness*.

From a Buddhist perspective, ignorance is the failure to recognize this larger ground of pure awareness underlying all the objects of consciousness, while treating the latter as objective reality. This pure awareness is our original nature, and meditation is the major way to let it emerge from the background position to which it has been relegated. In Zen *satori*, the emergence of the basic ground can have a sudden and dramatic quality—as the "bottom of the bucket breaking through" to the thoroughly clear, ever-present awareness in which the subject/object and conscious/unconscious dichotomies disappear, and things stand out clearly as what they are.

This fundamental ground of pure awareness is an unconditional presence that can become faceted, shaped, or elaborated without losing its expansive openness. From this perspective, awareness begins with pure openness; it first becomes differentiated at the transpersonal level, then individualized at the personal level, and finally particularized at the situational level. Although awareness becomes more and more faceted, further and further shaped at each more differentiated level of consciousness, its open, unconditioned nature is ever present, even in the most fixated states of mind. This open ground, though beyond the grasp of focal attention (and in this sense "unconscious"), is not a mysterious psychic region but is perfectly knowable, both in fleeting glimpses and in sudden awakening. It is a deep level of mind/world interpenetration that goes far beyond conceptualization and thought. By tapping into this wider attunement, meditation allows for a more direct, precise relationship with what is. At this level of open awareness, "the meditator develops new depths of insight through direct communication with the phenomenal world. Conceptualized mind is not involved in the perception and so we are able to see with great precision, as though a veil had been removed from our eyes."

The open ground is always present. At any moment, especially if one sharpens one's attention through meditation, one may glimpse this ineffable, nonspecifiable, omnipotential open awareness that underlies specific mind-states.

Summary and Conclusions

In sum, this brief phenomenology of unconscious process as a network of fields within fields allows us to understand the conscious/unconscious polarity as two aspects of the organism's interconnectedness with reality. This approach allows us to correct the misinterpretations of meditation fostered by the dualistic depth psychology model of the unconscious.

The Jungians tend to see mind as a psychic container with various contents, leading them to interpret spiritual awakening in terms of "an extraordinarily significant and numinous content [that] enters consciousness," resulting in a "new viewpoint." But this way of speaking obscures the nature of contemplative experience, which is a radical passing beyond all "viewpoints." Awakening is not additive, in the sense of unconscious contents breaking through into consciousness, but if anything, subtractive, in that it removes preoccupation with *all* contents of mind. In experiences of awakening, as Herbert Guenther points out, "attention is on the field rather than on its contents."

Depth psychology portrays the unconscious as *other*—alien, unknowable, even threatening. And so meditation is conceived as potentially dangerous, in that it may subject the ego to "the disintegrating powers of the unconscious." Such confusions led the Zen teacher Hisamatsu Shin-ichi, after a conversation with Jung, to delineate the difference between the open ground (which he calls "no-mind") and the Jungian unconscious:

> The unconscious of psychoanalysis is quite different from the no-mind of Zen. In the unconscious . . . are the *a posteriori* personal unconscious and the *a priori* collective unconscious. They are both unknown to the ego. But the no-mind of Zen is, on the contrary, not only known, but most clearly known. . . . More exactly, it is clearly "self awakening to itself" without separation between the knower and the known. No-mind is a state of mind always clearly aware.

The psychoanalytic model regards the inner demands of the unconscious and the outer demands of the world as two opposing worlds, with the ego situated in between. This leads to the view that meditation is an inner withdrawal, away from relating with reality. The confusion here stems from the dualistic conception of inner and outer, where "inner" is assumed to mean "inside the body-mind organism." However, we can also understand inner and outer differently. *Inner* reality docs not have to refer to a realm of the psyche inside the organism. Rather, what is inner is the essential organizing principle that shapes the outer reality of constituent elements. In music, melodic movement is inner, while the individual tones are outer; in behavior, intention and purpose are inner, while action is outer; in sex, making love is inner, while sexual technique is outer. As the inmost reality of human consciousness, the open ground is what allows the endless flow of moments to unfold and have meaning. It is not an unconscious mind situated somewhere inside the organism.

If what is normally unconscious is our interconnectedness with all things, this also has important implications for the understanding of neurosis, defense mechanisms, and psychopathology in general. From this perspective, what makes the ego anxious is not threatening unconscious contents so much as the groundless, open nature of our being. We can never establish our ego securely, our self-identities keep slipping away, and there is nothing to hold on to. Resistance, repression, and defenses are ways that we armor ourselves against this larger openness that threatens our attempt to establish a permanent separate identity. "Normality is neurosis," according to Ernest Becker, because it constitutes a refusal and repression of our essential nature—our complete openness and vulnerability to reality. In this light, it would be important in therapy to help clients make friends with the open nature of their being, rather than colluding with them to avoid it. As therapist Wilson Van Dusen suggests, "The feared empty space is a fertile void. Exploring it is a turning point towards therapeutic change."

Misconceptions of meditation are common in the West. Some view it as a self-improvement technique, others regard it as a passive withdrawal from the world. The approach developed here allows us to avoid both these pitfalls, for it is grounded in an understanding of the total interpenetration of organism and environment, self and world.

In this light, the following description of meditation from a Tibetan text begins to make sense:

> One should realize that one does not meditate in order to go deeply into oneself and withdraw from the world. . . . There should be no feeling of striving to reach some exalted or higher state, since this simply produces something conditioned and artificial that will act as an obstruction to the free flow of the mind. . . . The everyday practice is simply to develop a complete awareness and openness to all situations and emotions, and to all people, experiencing everything totally without mental reservations and blockages, so that one never withdraws or centralizes onto oneself. . . . When performing the meditation practice, one should develop the feeling of opening oneself out completely to the whole universe with absolute simplicity and nakedness of mind.

This understanding allows us to see meditation as a process of self-discovery that is simultaneously a world discovery, in that we are continually co-creating our world, and also, beyond that, we *are* world; we are not other than reality. The way in is the way out.

6

Psychological Space

The essence of mind is like space. Therefore there is nothing that it does not encompass.

—Tilopa

Through every human being, unique space, intimate space, opens up to the world.

—Rainer Maria Rilke

What makes it possible for us to free ourselves from the compulsive habits of the conditioned personality and the conceptual mind? Struggling to change the way we are certainly does not work, for this only produces inner agitation and strain, not genuine freedom or awakening. From the perspective of Buddhist psychology, what allows us to wake up to the very nature of reality and live freshly in the moment is the spacious quality of our being, which is intrinsically free from past conditioning. Our very awareness is, indeed, a kind of open space. Just as the screen on which a film is projected is not touched by the dramas and tragedies playing themselves out upon it (remaining spotless even when a bloody murder takes place in the film), so none of the mind's dramas can stick to spacious awareness. The spacious, transparent, luminous nature of our awareness is much larger and more powerful than any belief, fixation, complex, or compulsion that temporarily arises or resides in it.

Western psychology has mostly failed to recognize any relationship between mind and space.[1] No doubt this is partly due to the lingering influence of Descartes, who divided reality into two separate realms:

mind as thinking substance and matter as spatially extended substance. Yet the notion of psychological space is of central importance for a psychology of awakening. It helps us see more deeply into the nature of consciousness, psychological imprisonment, and spiritual freedom.

Lived Space

Western thought mainly understands space by objectifying it— through measuring its dimensionality, distances, and directionality, or through conceptualizing it as an abstract continuum to account for the relations between objects and forces in the physical world.

But space may also be approached in a different way—in terms of *psychological space*, which is directly experienceable, rather than objectively measurable. The phenomenologist Eugene Minkowski called this *lived space:* "For us, space cannot be reduced to geometric relations, relations which we establish as if, reduced to the simple role of curious spectators or scientists, we were outside space. We *live and act in space*. . . . Life spreads out in space. . . . We have need of expansion, of perspective, in order to live."

Feeling Space

Lived space can be experienced in grosser and more subtle forms. We can distinguish three levels of our experience of space—the space of bodily orientation, the space of feeling, and the open space of being— which roughly correspond to the Tibetan distinction between outer (gross), inner (subtle), and secret (very subtle) space.[2]

At the *outer* level, the body continually orients itself to space "out there," as the medium in which it moves, and to various spatial dimensions—horizontal and vertical planes, location, size, and distance.

On an *inner* level, we continually move through a range of different feeling-states, which also have a certain spatial dimension. Feeling spaces are like changing affective landscapes that we inhabit and move through from moment to moment. If you consider how you feel right now—the affective landscape you are inhabiting—and compare it to the space you were in this morning when you first woke up, or when you were last overcome by some intense emotion, this may help you notice that different inner spaces have entirely different qualities of feeling.

Some feeling spaces seem fluid or watery, others are more sharply defined. Some are diffuse and airy, others are intense and heavy. Some seem flat, others have depth and texture. Each of these affective environments is a kind of space with its own atmospheric quality, texture, density, and flow that seem to surround and envelop us.

Feeling spaces, like weather, are in continual flux. Their qualities shift in accordance with how connected or disconnected we are from our deeper nature. When we are in touch with the ground of our being, we generally feel more expansive. Space feels dynamic, light, or full, and there is more room in which to move and be. The poet Baudelaire used a favorite word, *vast*, to describe these spaces of "vast thoughts," "vast perspectives," "vast silences." But when we are cut off from what is most real and alive in us, the space we inhabit feels heavy, oppressive, and claustrophobic, seeming to press down upon us and impeding our movement. The body feels denser, the pull of gravity seems stronger, and the space around us seems thicker. We feel pushed up against our limitations, with little "wiggle room."

In addition to oscillating between the poles of expansion and contraction, feeling spaces also move between surface and depth. When we are disconnected from the living presence of our source, our affective landscape often feels flat, shallow, and two-dimensional. Life seems like an endless, monotonous parched plain stretching out all around us. When we are inwardly connected, by contrast, feeling space has depth and texture—"filled with countless presences," as Rilke put it.

Open Space

Since feeling space expands, deepens, and flows when we are grounded in our being, and becomes contracted, dry, and flat when we are moving away from it, it is clear that the feeling spaces we inhabit all flow like streams from a central source—our relation to *being space*, the open, omnipotential expanse of pure awareness. Turning away from our being is like shutting ourselves up in a stuffy, cramped cell within the vast mansion of pure awareness, while turning toward our being is like opening the windows and letting in fresh air. Thus, our larger nature exerts a magnetic pull on us, continually calling to us in the claustrophobic mind-states that so often seem to entrap us.

Indeed, even our attraction to wide open spaces in nature—the mysterious pull of unexplored lands, the vast horizon of the restless sea, or the boundless reaches of outer space—is, at bottom, a longing to connect with this expansive dimension of our own nature. As Lama Govinda put it:

> When men look up into the space of heaven and invoke heaven, or a power that is supposed to reside there, they invoke in reality forces within themselves, which, by being projected outward, are visualized or felt as heaven or cosmic space. If we contemplate the mysterious depth and blueness of the firmament, we contemplate the depth of our inner being, of our own mysterious all-comprising consciousness in its primordial, unsullied purity: unsullied by thoughts . . . undivided by discriminations, desires, and aversions.

Yet we tend to feel ambivalent toward the open space at the core of our nature. Although we are drawn to its expansiveness, we also fear its vastness and lack of solidity, which provides no *terra firma* to support our conventional identity. So although we often long for more space, we also quickly flee from it when it is available, or else try to fill it up. Like people fleeing the congestion of cities who bring all the accoutrements of city life with them, thereby turning the open countryside into suburban sprawl, we are initially drawn toward the open space of being but eventually try to fill it with our familiar reference points.

The open space of being continually breaks through into consciousness in unexpected flashes and glimpses; for instance, when we encounter some unfathomable mystery in ourselves or those we love.

This simple awakening also happens in meditation when some burdensome mind-state suddenly falls away. Then we see that even the densest mind-states merely float, like buoys, on the larger open sea of awareness. Meditation opens a gateway into this larger space by relaxing our tendency to identify with the compulsive thinking that usually fills it up. For this reason, the Mahamudra tradition of Tibetan Buddhism describes meditation as "mixing mind and space." Here we come full circle from Descartes's dualistic sundering of these two realms.

One Zen text suggests ten ways in which the nature of awareness is like open space, for it is:

—*unobstructed*, never limited or confined by the thoughts or feelings arising within it

—*omnipresent*, always immediately available, and extending in all directions

—*impartial*, allowing everything to be what it is

—*vast*, extending infinitely beyond all the mind's limitations

—*formless*, unable to be contained within any conceptual box

—*pure*, uncontaminated by anything that arises within it

—*stable*, neither arising nor passing away, but the ever-present ground of all passing experience

—*beyond existence*, for it cannot be located in any definite way

—*beyond nonexistence*, for it is not simply nothing, but rather a clear, bright presence

—*ungraspable*, for it cannot be fixed or held on to in any way

The Tantric tradition also calls the open space of being *secret* because it cannot be located or defined by the mind. Since it is so unfathomable and inscrutable to the conceptual mind, the only way to portray it is symbolically, as Tantric Buddhism does through the mandala. Mandalas are portraits of the creative dance of phenomena at play in the dynamic field of open space. At the center of the mandala is the wisdom of open space, which is centerless and all-pervasive. Unlike the egoic mind, which tries to make itself the central doer or

chief executive of its world, the spacious nature of awareness has neither a fixed center—a definable point of origin—nor a definable outer
circumference or limit. It is not here as opposed to there, mine as
opposed to yours. Nor is it the product of a central thinker, doer, or
controller. As Trungpa describes this:

> In the Tantric version of mandala, everything is centered around cen-
> terless space, in which there is no watcher or perceiver. Because there
> is no watcher or perceiver, the fringe becomes extremely vivid. The
> mandala principle expresses the experience of the relatedness of all
> phenomena. . . . The patterns of phenomena become clear because
> there is no partiality in one's perspective. All corners are visible, aware-
> ness is all-pervading . . . [and] each corner of space is center as well as
> fringe.

Although Jung studied the symbolism of mandalas in Eastern religion and recognized how they represent a profound psychological
shift away from ego fixation, he failed to perceive their larger meaning—as portraits of the vast space of wisdom-mind, the creative openness and potentiality of being in which the play of consciousness
unfolds, without being tied to any central reference point of self.
Jung's understanding of Asian mandalas was more limited, for he saw
them as symbols designed to "aid concentration by narrowing down
the psychic field of vision and restricting it to the center . . . a center
of personality, a kind of central part within the psyche, to which everything is related." Jung's narrow interpretation of mandalas demon-
strates the typical dualistic bias of Western psychology when it tries
to study the larger dimensions of consciousness.

Living in Space

On a personal level, most of us also fail to perceive the sparkling dance
of phenomena that unfolds in the mandala of human consciousness
because of our need to be at the center of things. Because the open
space at the core of our nature provides no support or confirmation
for our identity project, we turn against it, out of fear, and make it

into an enemy. And when we do this, the open space of our being starts to seem like a threatening black hole that could swallow us up.

From this perspective, psychopathology is the result of rejecting our nature as open space. As a consequence, we live in empty, deadened, constricted spaces that feel engulfing or claustrophobic, and that we continually try to ward off. As Wilson Van Dusen describes it, each type of pathology does battle with a different form of black hole:

> More and more it appeared that these holes . . . came to be the key both to pathology and to psychotherapeutic change. . . . In the obsessive compulsive they represent the loss of order and control. In the depressive they are the black hole of time standing still. In the character disorders they are the encroachment of meaninglessness or terror. In every case they represent the unknown, the unnamed threat, the source of anxiety and disintegration. They are nothingness, non-being, threat. . . . Many talk to fill up space. Many must act to fill the empty space with themselves. In all cases it must be filled up or sealed off. I have yet to see a case of psychopathology where the blankness was comfortably tolerated.

For this reason, I have found it essential as a psychotherapist to help people learn to appreciate the open space of their being and regard it as friendly, rather than as threatening. Instead of colluding with the client to fill up space, I continually help clients be aware of the presence of open space, and learn to relax more fully into it.

Psychological problems move in the direction of healing only when we can relate to them in a spacious way, from the space of our being. When we try to fix our problems directly, we usually pit one side of ourselves against another, and this creates inner pressure and stress—which only contract our space. This is what our mind is like most of the time—a crowded, narrow thoroughfare that is choked with traffic trying to move in different directions. One thought moves in one direction, and other thoughts move against it. ("I'm angry"—"I shouldn't be angry"—"Why shouldn't I be angry?"—"But what will people think?") These inner oppositions create a traffic jam and shut down the space. When we can give our experience space in which to be, with awareness, the jam in our mind starts to clear up and the traffic has room to move freely once again. We may not have fixed the problem, but we have found a larger space in which to hold the problems. This is how true healing occurs.

Whenever we allow ourselves to experience some difficult feeling, or whenever an old identity starts to loosen up, the larger space of being that this feeling or identity had been obscuring starts to be revealed. This is a challenging moment, because it can often feel as though we are falling through space. If we resist space at this point, the falling becomes terrifying, and we may try to abort the experience, "pulling ourselves together" by contracting and tensing. This prevents us from freeing ourselves from the old fixation that was starting to dissolve.

Yet if we can learn to relax into the expansiveness that is opening up, then we may begin to discover *space as support:* The ground of our being actually holds us up. We may feel extremely light at the same time, as though we are floating on a bed of clouds. Once we have made this discovery, the shedding of old identities becomes far less frightening.

So when we turn against space, space appears threatening, and then we feel the danger of becoming lost in it—in the black hole of nonbeing. One common way of becoming lost in space is through "spacing out"—when the conceptual mind temporarily loses its bearings and our attention becomes blurred and scattered. When we trust and relax in space as our ground, by contrast, we become *found* in space. Instead of being "spacey," we become spacious. We discover this expansive presence to be who we really are.

This capacity to relax and trust in the open space of being is also essential in creative work. Artists, scientists, inventors, and mathematicians often make their most creative discoveries in moments when they are not directly concentrating on the problem at hand, but relaxing and giving it space to be. The deepest spiritual realizations also arise out of this alert empty-mindedness, which allows the mind to "move upon silence," beyond conventional reference points. In the Buddhist tradition this is called self-arising wisdom.

One striking way that I have experienced the play between opening to space and resisting space is in the presence of a highly awake spiritual teacher, one who abides in the spacious quality of being. When encountering such teachers, I have sometimes been keenly aware of how their vast presence simultaneously triggered in me awe-full attraction as well as tremendous fear and resistance. Depending on which feeling had the upper hand, I might see the teacher as totally appealing or totally threatening. Meanwhile, the teacher's spaciousness seemed to accommodate all my projections, and this would serve as an invitation to open up further. Not only could I find no barriers, limitations, or boundaries in the space the teacher inhabited, but I experienced that his spaciousness did not exclude my space; it was one and the same space.[3] This discovery helped me relax my boundaries and open to the teacher's powerful presence.

Although open space might sound cold or impersonal, it is actually what makes love and intimate human contact possible. It's what allows two lovers to "see each other whole and against a wide sky," as Rilke put it. When we look into the eyes of someone we love, what do we see there after all? Why is eye-to-eye contact such a guarded, revealing, often embarrassing and potentially "cosmic" experience? Just as the eyes looking out relate to physical space, so, looking in, they provide a doorway into the space of being. When we look in the eyes of our beloved, we do not see pupils and irises, but rather a nameless presence that is not separate from our own essential presence, an inner light that calls to our own inner light. Suddenly we cannot objectify or pigeonhole that person, or maintain any artificial separation. Eye-to-eye contact is direct communication through space, taking us beyond the whole subject/object split.

This is why it can be hard to speak intimately with someone on the telephone, and even more so over the Internet, for without the luminous spatial connection through the eyes it is an oblique, incomplete communication. Indeed, perhaps it is the connection with open space that allows us to understand anything at all. Is this why *seeing* is a synonym for understanding? In this sense, the eyes function like the gates of a mandala through which we enter a world of expansive and luminous awareness.

Thus the open space of being—which we *sense* in our receptivity to the world, which we *feel* in our tenderness and sensitivity, which we *share* in loving contact with others, and which we can *know* in the transparency and fullness of human presence—is what allows us to connect with reality in an intimate way and discover the freedom that lies beyond the confines of the conditioned mind.

7

The Unfolding of Experience

Is there even one soul, however materialistic, that does not wish to unfold? There cannot be. It is in the unfoldment of the soul that the purpose of life is fulfilled.

—HAZRAT INAYAT KHAN

I want to unfold. I don't want to stay folded anywhere, because where I am folded, there I am untrue.

—RAINER MARIA RILKE

❀ OUR PATH IN LIFE evolves through a process of *unfolding*, which gives rise to an emerging flow of new discoveries, as what was hidden becomes revealed and what was obscure becomes accessible and clear. At least two different kinds of unfolding operate in human development: a gradual or "horizontal" unfolding, in which new discoveries and developments appear progressively, each one building on those that preceded it; and beyond that, a more sudden and suprising kind of "vertical" emergence, in which a larger, deeper kind of awareness unexpectedly breaks through into consciousness, allowing us to see things in a radically new light. The organic process of unfolding reveals the creative, emergent nature of human experience. It also sheds light on how change happens in psychotherapy and how therapeutic change, creativity, and more radical kinds of spiritual awakening are related to one another.

The Multilevel Texture of Experiencing

Human experiencing is a rich, complex tapestry, consisting of many interwoven strands of feeling, sensing, and knowing. At every moment we are processing much more information, sensing many more levels of meaning and deeper qualities of existence than we are explicitly aware of at the time. William James eloquently describes this holistic tapestry: "In the pulse of inner life immediately present now in each of us is a little past, a little future, a little awareness of our own body, of each other's persons, of these sublimities we are trying to talk about, of the earth's geography and the direction of history, of truth and error, of good and bad, and of who knows how much more?"

Because we thus know, in subtle, nonverbal ways, much more than we can ever articulate at any one time, new meanings—new ways of seeing and new things seen—continually emerge into awareness. Classical depth psychology sees the source of these new meanings as the unconscious. However, this model fosters a deterministic, closed-system view of conscious experience as a derivative of preexisting unconscious contents, such as instincts, drives, archetypes, or object relations. If instead we recognize the emergence of unconscious material as the unfolding of subtle body-mind knowing, which has been enfolded in consciousness in the holistic way described above by William James, this provides a much more dynamic, nondeterministic understanding of how our experience works. As new revelations unfold, they make explicit what was previously implicit—a richly patterned field of body-mind interconnectedness with the world.

For example, a man feels empty after a brief conversation with his father on the telephone, without exactly knowing why. Although his *surface mind*, which operates through linear, focal attention, is still in the dark about what just happened, his *body-mind* senses and seems to know *tacitly* the deeper implications of this exchange. He feels this as a hollowness in his solar plexus. By inquiring into the complex tangle of felt meaning he experiences after getting off the phone, he could begin to unfold various aspects of it—such as guilt, resignation about not being heard, helplessness, and the longing for a more genuine relationship. Some of these are immediate responses to what just transpired, while others go back to a whole relationship of thirty years. Yet all were implicit in his initial empty feeling.

The Holographic Nature of Felt Experience

One analogy that can help us appreciate how implicit experience unfolds is that of the hologram, which Karl Pribram also used to explain certain aspects of memory functioning in the brain. A hologram is a photographic plate that records complex interactions of light waves, from which a realistic three-dimensional picture can be projected. In a hologram, light wave patterns are scattered evenly throughout the whole photographic plate, so that every part of it carries information about the whole. Vast amounts of information are superimposed on each other in a tiny area. As Pribram writes, "Some ten billion bits of information have been usefully stored holographically in a cubic centimeter." The light waves in a hologram overlap in complex ways (called an "interference pattern") to form a blurry whole configuration. The holographic blur neither resembles the object photographed nor has any recognizable form at all. It is the complexity of these wave interactions that gives the holographic image its realistic three-dimensional quality when reproduced from the holographic plate.

The richly patterned texture of our inner experiencing is analogous in certain ways to the structure of a hologram. For instance, if you ask yourself how you feel now, what you get when you first refer inwardly to your bodily felt sensing is a blurry whole. Or try referring to your felt sense of a person in your life. What is your overall feeling about your father, your whole sense of him? Letting go of any specific memory, thought, or image, let yourself feel the whole quality of your relationship with him. Underneath any image you may find a blurry whole felt sense of your father and your relationship with him. This felt sense has a global feeling-texture, feeling-color, or feeling-tone, rather than a definite form you can readily articulate. Nonetheless, it is still quite distinct from your felt sense of other people, as you can see by comparing it to your felt sense of your mother.

A felt sense contains implicit felt meaning. *Felt* refers to the bodily component; *meaning* implies some kind of knowing or patterning, though not of a logical, conceptual kind; *sense* indicates that this meaning is not yet clear. *Implicit* literally means "folded into, enfolded."

Just as a hologram is blurry because it is a compressed record of many overlapping wave patterns, so a felt sense is fuzzy or diffuse because it contains a number of overlapping meanings that a given situation has for you, based on all the different ways you have interacted with it. Notice that your felt sense of your father includes all the ways you have ever experienced him. It is like a holographic record of all your interactions with him (analogous to interference patterns). All your joys, hurts, disappointments, appreciations, angers—all of your whole experience with him is holographically compressed in this one felt sense. The felt sense is blurry in that it includes all of this *implicitly*. This implicitness is not sharply defined, but rather functions as a global background. Much of our everyday experience functions in this holistic background way.

The Unfolding Process

The unfolding that happens in psychological inquiry is a process of making implicit felt meaning explicit. It often begins with a diffuse kind of receptive attention to the whole felt sense of a situation, underneath all one's different thoughts about it. Clients who cannot let go of a strict reliance on focal attention and tolerate ambiguity are much harder to work with, because their words are not coming from a felt sense, but rather from previous ruminations they have thought many times before. Since the way they speak about their problems is not fresh, alive, or connected with present experiencing, no unfolding occurs. Nothing new is happening.

Yet when we can tap into and speak *from* a diffusely felt sense, rather than just pouring out our thoughts *about* it, this allows a fresh articulation of what is true for us, which was not accessible or expressible before. It is only out of the initial blurriness that something fresh can unfold, something we may have vaguely sensed but not yet fully realized. That is why we usually have to let ourselves *not know* before we can discover anything new.

Eugene Gendlin developed the Focusing method in response to research suggesting that psychotherapy clients are more likely to change and move forward if their words tap into and come from presently felt experiencing, which often seems unclear or ambiguous at first. This research also suggested that therapy does not generally teach clients how to tap into this implicit body-mind knowing. Focusing was a major innovation because it showed people exactly how to use diffuse attention to attend to an unclear felt sense.

For example, a client comes in feeling depressed about his marriage. At first he speaks about his unhappiness with his wife, giving voice to complaints, guilt, and frustration. But his words are rather lifeless. He is talking "off the top of his head," without any fresh inward reference going on. As a therapist, I guide him toward his felt sense of this situation underneath all his thoughts and emotional reactions. How does he feel this situation in his body? I might let him feel this out for a while without saying much. Often just connecting with it in this way provides some relief and encouragement to delve further into it.

Describing his felt sense, he says, "It's a heaviness in my stomach." Now that he is in contact with this heavy feeling, he can begin to unfold the implicit meaning contained in it. This involves a certain kind of inquiry and attention that allows the global heaviness to come into sharper focus. This is somewhat analogous to deblurring a hologram by highlighting major contours, so that particular features emerge from the blur. What helps my client bring his attention to the felt implicit is a question from me: "What's so heavy about this for you?" Again he returns to his felt sense and we wait for something to emerge.

"It's anger, just sitting in my gut," he now says, "weighing me down, eating me out from the inside." With this next step of unfolding his words start to gather force. As he feels into the anger he has now articulated, the next direction appears: "But even more than angry, I feel tremendously disappointed in her. She's not there for me the way she used to be." Pause. His words have even more energy now. We seem to be on the verge of something new emerging. "But I'm also disappointed in myself. Things used to be so good between us, and now we don't even listen to each other." He takes a deep sigh now, as he is getting closer to the core of what he is feeling. I can tell by his shaky tone of voice that he is close to opening up something larger and more significant. He is no longer talking *about* his felt sense; he is speaking directly *from* it. His next statement really cracks it open: "And you know, I'm just now realizing that I haven't felt my caring for her in a long time. That's what's so heavy. I've locked away my love and sat on it for months now. I'm having a hard time feeling my love anymore." Something in his body is now releasing—he breathes more deeply, tears start to form, and the blood returns to his face. He is now in a much different place than when he first walked in half an hour ago.

Figure 2 pictures this progressive, zigzag process of unfolding, with the client alternating between a connection to a vague felt sense—represented by the cloudy circles—and articulation of the meaning implicit in that sense. The content of these realizations is not what is significant here. More important than the particular discoveries of anger, disappointment, or blocked love was the dynamic movement of unfolding, which allowed for a spontaneous felt shift as he articulated what his body-mind already sensed and felt implicitly.

FIGURE 2. *Therapeutic Unfolding*

This type of unfolding, which moves back and forth between articulation and the nonarticulated, is at the heart of all creative discovery, whether in therapy, the arts, or the sciences. As therapist Edgar Levinson observes, "The process of therapeutic change has its own phenomenology that is no different from the way an artist arrives at a visual concept or a mathematician at a new formulation." And in words that could apply equally to poetry or psychotherapy, philosopher Max Picard suggests that speech has potency and depth only when it arises out of a larger, undifferentiated space beyond words, moving "from silence into the word and then back again into the silence and so on, so that the word always comes from the center of silence. . . . Mere verbal noise, on the other hand, moves uninterruptedly along the horizontal line of the sentence. . . . Words that merely come from other words are hard . . . and lonely." Physicist David Bohm describes how a creative physicist should proceed in a similar vein, using language also fitting for therapy: "One has to observe the new situation very broadly and tentatively, and to 'feel out' the relevant new features."

In writing this chapter, for instance, I started with a diffuse felt sense of what I wanted to say, which I have to keep referring back to along the way. I can't know exactly what I want to say except by letting it unfold word by word, sentence by sentence. Each sentence leads to the next, which in turn builds on what has previously unfolded. At the end of this chapter I should have discovered the full range of my intent (although of course, there's always more). Similarly, implicit in that whole sense of your father I asked you about earlier there is probably a whole novel about your relationship with him that could unfold from it. Your whole novel (all six hundred pages of it!) is holographically compressed in your very first diffuse felt sense of him.

Once an implicit felt sense has opened up—whether in therapy or in developing a new scientific theory—things are never quite the same again. What is creative or healing about the unfolding process is that it allows us to experience ourselves in a larger way than before. This "larger way" results from the dynamic back-and-forth interaction between two ways of knowing: that of the surface/focal mind and that of the wider body-mind. Each step of the inquiry brings to light a new facet of the felt sense, which starts to move and shift, like a tangled ball of yarn unraveling. As we pull on a given strand, this loosens up the whole tangle, while also revealing the next strand that needs unraveling. Gradually the shape of the bundle changes—the problem no longer feels the same.

While any life problem may have many different angles or many irritating facets, there is usually one central tangle, one central crux (or sometimes two or three). Bringing this central concern—usually some confused or unresolved way of relating to ourselves, to other people, or to life—into awareness helps the tangled situation to unravel and release.

Another client of mine came in feeling a pervasive lack of fulfillment in his life. Over the course of many weeks he had to explore many different facets of this emptiness before the crux of the problem could reveal itself. Finally he realized that it was not that something particular was missing from his life, but that he couldn't let himself consider his heart's desire. "That would make me feel too vulnerable." Many earlier steps of working with the felt sense of emptiness were necessary to lead to this point (just as an artist or scientist has to spend a great deal of time considering the various dimensions of a creative problem before a breakthrough can occur). Now he could see that the real issue was not something missing in his external life, but his own fear of letting himself know what he really wanted. Instead of seeing his life through this distorting lens, he could at last see the lens itself that was causing the distortions. Seeing that he was not just a victim of circumstance brought a huge sense of relief, allowing him to approach his life in a whole new way.

Therapeutic unfolding thus has three main stages: widening attention to feel out a global felt sense of a situation; inquiring directly into this felt sense; and, by successively articulating it from various angles, discovering its crux, which releases its stuckness and allows new directions to reveal themselves. In this way, confusion gradually moves toward clarity, wrongness toward rightness, and disconnection toward connection. As Gendlin suggests, every life problem contains in it a sense of a new direction, if only we can let it unfold: "The sense of what is wrong carries with it . . . inseparably, a sense of the direction toward what is right. . . . Every bad feeling is potential energy toward a more right way of being if you give it space to move toward its rightness."

In psychological work, the dialogue between therapist and client is what facilitates the unfolding process. What makes someone a good listener is the capacity to help another person tune into the silence of pre-articulate experiencing and bring it to fuller and fuller expression, instead of fixating on any particular content that is being articulated. More important than what we say in responding to another is our ability to point to and resonate with the other's (still unclear) felt sense. As Levinson puts it:

It is clear that the therapist would not have to be correct in his formulations as much as he would have to be in harmony or in resonance with what is occurring in the patient. . . . It might sound outrageous to suggest that it would be possible to do good therapy without ever really understanding what is going on, as long as the therapist is involved in an expansion of awareness and is using his own participation to further elaborate and actualize the patient's world. *The therapist does not explain content; he expands awareness of patterning.*

Often it is hard to make sense of therapy sessions when they are transcribed and written out. This is because the words are not the essential thing. The therapeutic process is not just about putting feelings into words. Words, in fact, can never be literal snapshots of felt experience, any more than a three-dimensional holographic image literally reproduces the complex wave patterns stored on a holographic plate. The words spoken by client and therapist have a transforming effect when they resonate with what the client already implicitly feels, thereby helping the feelings to unfold and, in Gendlin's words, "carry forward." In this carrying forward, which happens through unfolding, new understandings, new depths, new ways of being and relating to life reveal themselves.

This understanding of therapeutic working-through as a two-way interactive process—referring inwardly to a felt sense and then carrying it forward through inquiry and unfolding—provides a more dynamic and liberating model of therapy than the one-way street of making the unconscious conscious. The old notion of the unconscious as a separate region of the mind, with its own explicit contents and drives, fosters a deterministic approach to therapy that seeks to uncover, through rational analysis, solid problems stored in the psyche. By failing to recognize or honor the ever-evolving richness and open-endedness of human experiencing—which continually unfolds in surprising and unpredictable ways—deterministic models of therapy reinforce the split between the surface, focal mind and our deeper being, the division that lies at the root of our problems in the first place. As James Hillman has pointed out, this kind of analysis "is really part of the malady itself, and continues to contribute to it."

Spiritual Emergence

Discovering that psychological problems are forever mutable, always capable of unfolding in new ways, rather than being solid, fixed entities lodged inside us, is a liberating realization that leads to a more expansive understanding of human experience. What is it that actually happens when a felt sense unfolds, a frozen feeling thaws, or a tangled life problem unravels? What emerges in this moment of release, when an old fixation suddenly lets go?

Usually when an inner knot releases, we heave a sigh of relief and then go about our business, without noticing how such moments provide a direct experience of our larger being. In the moment when a problem's hold on us dissolves, we gain access to a grounded sense of presence and aliveness. I often call this *finding your seat*, for it is felt as a settling into oneself, into the immediacy of being. This often feels fresh and surprising, like the sudden opening of a flower. It also often allows a new awareness of verticality—or depth of being—to emerge. I call this a *vertical shift*.

Incremental *horizontal shifts* occur throughout the unfolding process, as the ball of yarn unravels and changes shape. In a vertical shift something different happens: we suddenly move from the realm of personality into the realm of pure being. Horizontal unfolding allows us to experience our consciousness growing and expanding as we discover more and more about our situation. Vertical emergence is a breakthrough to our true nature, which lies beyond horizontal evolution and becoming. Here we discover a quality of being that is already complete, intrinsically full, settled in itself. In Tibetan Buddhism, the symbol for the breakthrough of this larger nature, which is complete in itself, is the *garuda*, a mythical bird born fully grown, which begins to soar as soon as it hatches from the egg.

Just as a felt sense is a subtler patterning underneath the grosser forms of thought and concept, so this larger sense of being underlies the whole horizontal realm of personal becoming. This pure beingness is implicit in all our felt experience, just as water is universally present and enfolded in all living things. And just as we do not see water in all the living forms in which it is enfolded (in flesh, grass, or wood), so we usually fail to recognize this ultimate open-heartedness at the core of all our experiences—which in Buddhism is also called *bodhichitta*, the heart/mind of enlightenment. The moment when it fully emerges into awareness is, in Zen terms, like "the bottom of the bucket breaking through."

How then can we let the bottom of our lives break through into this radical openness, without continually having to patch up the bucket because we fear this larger space? While psychological work can provide glimpses of the larger openness at the core of our nature, spiritual practice aims at it more directly. If psychological work helps us *find ourselves*, spiritual work takes a further step, helping us *let go of ourselves*. In this sense, psychological and spiritual work, horizontal unfolding and vertical emergence, finding ourselves and letting go of ourselves, are two sides of one whole dialectic of self-discovery.

Meditation in particular teaches us to let go of the fixations of surface thought and bodily felt meaning—through letting them arise without following or reacting to them. Instead of attempting to unfold felt meaning, meditation allows a continual return to the unknown, so that a larger awareness can start to ventilate and permeate the narrow world of self-preoccupation. With practice, the meditator becomes increasingly able to let the play of the mind happen as it will—habitual thought patterns, subverbal textures of implicit feeling, and the open awareness underlying it all—without becoming carried away by any of it.

Thus meditation practice provides a valuable method for helping us enter the larger sacred ground of being underlying all our thoughts and feelings. Without negating either science, which explains with the surface mind, or psychotherapy, which inquires into the body-mind, it takes us one step further. Through introducing us to the awake, spacious presence of our being, it reveals the essential integrity that lies at the core of human existence. From that vantage point, we can then begin to see and accept all the different levels of human experience as strands of one whole tapestry.

8

Reflection and Presence

The Dialectic of Awakening

✤ WHILE STUDYING CLINICAL PSYCHOLOGY in the 1960s, I was immersed in the cultural changes swirling all around me—the blossoming of political activism, sexual revolution, musical innovation, encounter groups and personal growth work, psychedelic revelation, and not least, the early waves of Eastern spiritual teachings hitting our shores. This cultural flux no doubt stimulated my intense concern in graduate school with the whole question of personality change: What kind of change is really possible for people, what enables it to happen, and how does this come about? When I first heard Eugene Gendlin speaking about the *felt shift*—that transitional moment when an old fixation lets go, bringing fresh insight, release, and new direction—I felt elated and blessed, as though I had just been initiated into a great mystery. And when I finally experienced it for myself, it seemed even more mysterious and profound, almost like a mini–mystical experience.

At the same time I was also delving into Zen, and had become interested in the relationship between the felt shift and *satori*, the sudden awakening that was at the heart of Zen. I was particularly intrigued by the Zen stories where just by hearing the cry of a bird, sweeping the floor, or being slapped by one's teacher, the disciple suddenly woke up and saw reality in an entirely new way. *Satori* seemed like an immense, cosmic felt shift, where one's whole life suddenly changed, and one walked away a new being. I wondered how the felt shift and *satori* were related. Were they relatives of each other, two versions of the same thing or something different altogether?

As a budding student of both Buddhism and psychotherapy, this was not an academic question for me, but one that had important personal and professional implications. If the felt shift was a kind of mini-*satori*, or even a step in that direction, then perhaps Western psychological work could provide a new way to approach the kind of realizations that had previously been the sole province of mystics and monastics.

Psychological Reflection

Later, when I began to practice as a psychotherapist, this question took a new turn. By then I had done a fair degree of both psychological and meditative work, and had experienced powerful results from each. Although both types of work required inner attention and awareness, I was also struck by how different they were in their ways of approaching the flow of experience.

On the one hand, the therapeutic process involved stepping back from one's felt experience in order to inquire into it in a dialogical manner. In the course of the therapeutic dialogue—with the therapist and with one's own feelings—felt experience would open up, hidden felt meanings would unfold, and feelings would shift, leading to important cognitive, affective, and behavioral changes.

At the same time, I was also studying the Mahamudra/Dzogchen meditative tradition of Tibetan Buddhism, which presented a very different approach. The method here involved a more radical opening to whatever experience was at hand, instead of stepping back from it, unfolding felt meanings from it, or engaging in dialogical inquiry. Working with experience in this way could lead to more sudden, on-the-spot kinds of revelation, described variously in terms of *transmutation, self-liberation,* or *spontaneous presence*.

In this approach, one directly recognizes and meets one's experience as it is, without concern for what it means, where it comes from, or where it leads. There is no reinforcement of an observing self trying to grasp, understand, or come to terms with some observed content of consciousness. The early stages of Dzogchen/Mahamudra meditation teach the student to let go of fixation on whatever arises in the mind, and this eventually develops the capacity to relax and abide wakefully in the midst of whatever experience is arising. When there is no identification either with the observer or what is observed, awareness remains undisturbed by any divisions, and a new freedom, freshness, clarity, and compassion become available. This nondual awareness, in the words of the Indian teacher H. L. Poonja, "is your very own awareness, and it is called *freedom from everything*."

While psychotherapy and meditation both led to a freeing of mental and emotional fixations, the meditative approach struck me as the more profound and compelling of the two, because it was more direct, more radical, more faithful to the essential nature of awareness as an open presence intrinsically free of grasping, strategizing, and the subject/object split altogether. At the same time, the reflective dialogical process of psychotherapy provided a more effective and accessible way to work on the issues, concerns, and problems of personal and worldly life—which meditators often tend to avoid dealing with. Yet I had doubts about the ultimate merits of an approach that did not address, and was not designed to overcome, the subject/object struggle that lay at the root of most human alienation and suffering.

Two therapeutic devices I found useful in my early years as a therapist were a particular focus of these doubts. Long before "inner child" work became popularized by John Bradshaw, I discovered that many people who otherwise had trouble relating to their feelings of hurt, fear, helplessness, anger, or sorrow in a helpful, compassionate way could do so when they imagined these feelings as belonging to the child still alive within them. Since I had stumbled on this device on my own, rather than adopting it from a preconceived theoretical framework, it seemed all the more impressive to me. Yet I also remained aware of its shortcoming: it left a person inwardly split between an observing "adult" and an observed "child," with most of the feeling energy seeming to belong to the child.

"Finding the right distance from a feeling" was another useful device, and a central feature of the Focusing method I taught for many years. Many clients who get too close to threatening feelings either become overwhelmed by them or else reject them in order to defend themselves from their intensity. So establishing a certain reflective distance from strong feelings makes it easier to relate to them, just as stepping back from someone who is speaking loudly makes it more possible to hear what they are saying. Finding the right distance involves situating one's attention "next to" the feeling, on the edge of it, close enough to be in contact with it yet far enough away to feel comfortable. This stepped-back position is a useful therapeutic device that allows an interactive dialogue with feelings that might not otherwise be possible. However, if this is the only way one relates to one's experiences, it can also maintain and reinforce an inner separation—between observing ego and the observed flow of experience—that can eventually become a limitation in its own right.

The further I went with meditation, the less satisfied I was only drawing on reflective methods that maintained this inner division. From the perspective of contemplative practice, the root source of human suffering is this very split between "me" and "my experience." Suffering is nothing more than the observer judging, resisting, struggling with, and attempting to control experiences that seem painful, scary, or threatening to it. Without that struggle, difficult feelings can be experienced more simply and directly, instead of as dire threats to the survival and integrity of "me." Conventional psychotherapy teaches clients to understand, manage, and reduce the suffering that arises out of identification with a separate ego-self, but rarely questions the fundamental inner setup that gives rise to it.

Divided and Undivided Consciousness

Although reflective methods are certainly essential for therapeutic work, my experience with Dzogchen/Mahamudra meditation let me see how they were still an expression, in Eastern terms, of divided consciousness. The Sanskrit term for the ordinary, mundane state of consciousness is *vijnana*. *Vi-* could be translated as "divided" and *-jnana* as "knowing." *Divided* here refers to the subject/object split, in which the divide between observer and observed, perceiver and perceived is a primary determinant of how and what we perceive. All conventional knowledge, including what we discover in psychotherapy, happens within the framework of divided consciousness, as phenomenologist Peter Koestenbaum observes: "All knowledge is of this dual sort, and psychotherapeutic intervention is no exception. . . . Psychotherapy, like all other forms of knowledge, is reflection on self; it is self-knowledge and self-consciousness."

When we reflect on self, self becomes divided—into an object of reflection and an observing subject. This is *vijnana* at work. Dividing the field of experience into two poles is a useful device for most purposes and yields relative self-knowledge. We learn about our conditioning, our character structure, our particular ways of thinking, feeling, acting, and perceiving. While these discoveries can be relatively liberating, *who we are* can never be identical with the mind/body patterns we discover through reflective discernment. Nor are we identical with the perceiver that stands back from those patterns and reflects on them. Both these poles are creations of the conceptual mind, which operates by dividing the experiential field in two and interpreting reality through concepts based on this division.

Precise attention to the nature of experiencing reveals that most of our perception and cognition is conditioned by this conceptual divide. For example, we generally do not see a tree in its unique and vivid immediacy—in its suchness. Instead, our experience of the tree is shaped by ideas and beliefs about a category of objects called "tree." Krishnamurti, by contrast, describes what it is like to see a tree in a more direct, unalienated way:

> You look at this magnificent tree and you wonder who is watching whom and presently there is no watcher at all. Everything is so intensely alive and there is only life, and the watcher is as dead as that leaf. . . . Utterly still, . . . listening without a moment of reaction, without recording, without experiencing, only seeing and listening. . . . Really the outside is the inside and the inside is the outside, and it is difficult, almost impossible to separate them.

Just as "the news" pretends to be an accurate and neutral presentation of world events while concealing its hidden biases, so we imagine that conventional divided consciousness gives us an accurate portrayal of what lies before us, while failing to see how our conceptual assumptions usually produce a distorted picture of reality. In this way, we do not experience "things as they are"—in their rich and vivid experiential immediacy. As the great Dzogchen yogi Mipham put it, "Whatever one imagines, it is never exactly like that."

This habitually distorted perception—where we unconsciously mistake our cognitive schema for reality—is, in Buddhist terms, *samsara*, "delusive appearance." The basis of *samsara* is the ongoing habit of dividing the field of experience in two and imagining that the observing self is something set apart from the rest of the field. Meditative experience reveals a different kind of knowing, a direct recognition of *thatness* or *suchness*—the vivid, ineffable nowness of reality, as disclosed in the clarity of pure awareness, free from the constraints of conceptual or dualistic fixation. When this kind of knowing is directed inwardly, it becomes what is called in Zen "directly seeing into one's own nature." In this case, "one's own nature" is not an object of thought, observation, or reflection. Mind in its objectifying mode cannot grasp the immediate beingness of anything, least of all its own nature.

We can only perceive the suchness of things through an awareness that opens to them nonconceptually and unconditionally, allowing them to reveal themselves in their as-it-is-ness. As the poet Basho suggests:

> *From the pine tree*
> *learn of the pine tree.*
> *And from the bamboo*
> *of the bamboo.*

Commenting on these lines, the Japanese philosopher Nishitani Keiji explains that Basho does not mean "that we should observe the pine tree carefully. Still less does he mean for us to study the pine tree scientifically. He means for us to enter the mode of being where the pine tree is the pine tree itself, and the bamboo is the bamboo itself, and from there to look at the pine tree and the bamboo. He calls on us to betake ourselves to the dimension where things become manifest in their suchness." In the same vein, Zen Master Dogen advises: "You should not restrict yourselves to learning to see water from the viewpoints of human beings alone. Know that you must see water in the way water sees water." "Seeing water in the way water sees water" means recognizing water in its suchness, free of all concepts that spring from an observing mind standing back from experience.

Extending these lines from Basho and Dogen into the arena of self-realization, we might say, "If you want to find out who you are, open directly to yourself right now, enter into the mode of being where you are what you are, and settle into your own nature. Just as a snapshot of the bamboo is not the bamboo itself, how can the mental snapshots you have of yourself—the ideas and conclusions about yourself you have come to through reflective observation—be an accurate rendering of who you really are?" Divided consciousness—*vi-jnana*—can never yield *jnana*—direct, unmediated knowing, undivided consciousness, self-illuminating awareness, self-existing wisdom. *Jnana* is a different type of self-knowing, primarily discovered through contemplative discipline, where freedom from the subject/object setup allows direct "seeing into one's own nature."

Stretched between the disciplines of psychotherapy and meditation, I found myself continually revisiting these questions: How might psychological reflection serve as a stepping-stone on the path of awakening? Or since psychological reflection by its very nature was a form of divided consciousness, could it subtly perpetuate a permanent state of inner division in the name of healing? I knew certain spiritual teachers and practitioners who advanced a critique of therapy to this effect. They argued that psychotherapy was just a palliative, a way of making the prison of ego more comfortable, because it did not address, but instead reinforced, the error at the root of all suffering: identification with a separate self that was always trying to control or alter its experience. At the other extreme, many therapists regarded spiritual practice as an avoidance of dealing with the personal and interpersonal knots that interfered with living a full, rich, engaged life.

While psychological and spiritual work can certainly have these pitfalls, I could not side with either of these extreme views. I respected psychotherapy as a domain in its own right, using methods and perspectives that were valid in their own context, without necessarily having to conform to the highest standards of nondual realization. And I also felt that it was possible to build a bridge between psychological reflection, which yields valid relative self-knowledge, even though mediated by divided consciousness, and the deeper, undivided awareness and wordless knowing discovered in meditation. I wanted to see how these two kinds of self-knowing might work together as part of a larger dialectic of awakening that could include and bring together the two poles of human experience—conditioned and unconditioned, relative and absolute, psychological and spiritual, personal and universal.

It was through pursuing these questions that my own therapeutic approach evolved in the direction of what I now call "psychological work in a spiritual context" or "presence-centered psychotherapy." By providing an intermediate step between conventional psychological reflection and the deeper process of meditation, this way of working has proved to be more congruent with my meditative experience than the way I first practiced therapy. In the remainder of this chapter, I situate this intermediate step within a larger dialectic of awakening as it unfolds through psychological reflection and spiritual presence.

The Basic Problem: Prereflective Identification

What makes our ordinary state of consciousness problematic, according to both psychological and spiritual traditions, is unconscious identification. As young children, our awareness is essentially open and receptive, yet the capacity to reflect on our own experience does not fully develop until the early teenage years, during the stage that Piaget termed "formal operations." Until then, our self-structure is under the sway of a more primitive capacity—identification.

Because we lack self-reflective awareness in childhood, we are mostly dependent on others to help us see and know ourselves—to do our reflecting for us. So we inevitably start to internalize their reflections—how they see and respond to us—coming to regard ourselves in terms of how we appear to others. In this way we develop an ego identity, a stable self-image composed of self-representations, which are part of larger object relations—self/other schemas formed in our early transactions with our parents. To form an identity means *taking ourselves to be something*, based on how others relate to us.

Identification is like a glue by which consciousness attaches itself to contents of consciousness—thoughts, feelings, images, beliefs, memories—and assumes with each of them, "That's me," or, "That represents me." Forming an identity is a way in which consciousness objectifies itself, makes itself an object. It is like looking in a mirror and taking ourselves to be the visual image reflected back to us, while ignoring our more immediate, lived experience of embodied being. Identification is a primitive form of self-knowledge—the best we could do as a child, given our limited cognitive capacities.

By the time our capacity for reflective self-knowledge develops, our identities are fully formed. Our knowledge of ourselves is indirect, mediated by memories, self-images, and beliefs about ourselves formed out of these memories and images. Knowing ourselves through self-images, we have become an object in our own eyes, never seeing the way in which we are a larger field of being and presence in which these thought-forms arise. We have become prisoners of our own mind and the ways it has construed reality.

Reflection: Stepping Back from Identification

The first step in freeing ourselves from the prison of unconscious identification is to make it conscious, that is, to reflect on it. We cannot move from prereflective identification directly into nondual awareness. But we *can* use divided consciousness to reflect on divided consciousness. The Buddha likened this to using a thorn to remove a thorn from one's flesh. All reflection involves stepping back from one's experience in order to examine and explore its patterns, its feeling textures, its meanings, its *logos*, including the basic assumptions, beliefs, and ways of conceiving reality that shape our experience. By comparison with identification, this kind of self-reflection represents a giant step forward in the direction of greater self-understanding and freedom. As Gabriel Marcel put it, "reflection . . . is one of life's ways of rising from one level to another."

There are different ways of reflecting on one's experience. Some are cruder, others subtler, depending on the rigidity of the dualism and the size of gap they maintain between observer and observed. I would like to distinguish three levels of reflective method: conceptual reflection, phenomenological reflection, and mindful witnessing.

Conceptual Reflection: Cognitive and Behavioral Analysis

The way most of us begin to reflect on our experience is by thinking about it—using theories and concepts to explain or analyze what is happening. Concepts allow us to step out of prereflective immersion in experience, so that we can see it in a new light or from a new angle. Most psychological and spiritual traditions draw on conceptual reflection at first, introducing certain ideas that help people take a new look at their experience. Buddha's four noble truths, for example, are a way of helping people step back from their unconscious suffering in order to consider its nature and cause, as well as antidotes for it. In Western psychology, developmental theories, maps of consciousness, and character typologies serve a similar purpose, providing frameworks that help people analyze, organize, and understand their experience in more coherent ways.

Some kinds of therapy are based primarily on conceptual reflection. They seek to explain or change the problematic *contents* of a client's experience, rather than working with the client's overall *process* of experiencing. This is a relatively crude approach, in that there is no direct encounter with immediate, lived experiencing. Instead, the relation to experience is always *mediated* by theoretical constructs. The therapist draws on some theory of human development or behavior to interpret the client's experience, while the client's main activity is thinking and talking about his or her experience, at one remove from the experience itself. The therapist might also draw on preformulated techniques to operate on the client's behavior, applying certain cognitive strategies (e.g., reframing, positive affirmations) or behavioral strategies (e.g., desensitization, emotional catharsis) to alter the undesirable contents of experience. This type of approach is often most useful with clients who lack the ego strength or the motivation to encounter their experience in a more direct, immediate way.

Spiritual traditions often formulate the contemplative realizations of great teachers of the past into a "view" that is transmitted to new students in order to help them discover the essence of spiritual realization for themselves. In the Mahamudra tradition, for example, the teacher presents the view, by directly pointing out awareness as intrinsically vast and boundless. Lodro Thaye, a great Mahamudra master of the eighteenth century, uses the image of the *garuda*, a mythical bird that takes to flight as soon as it hatches, to illustrate the effect of this view on consciousness:

> *When one meditates with this view*
> *It is like a garuda soaring through space*
> *Untroubled by fear or doubt.*
> *One who meditates without this view*
> *Is like a blind man wandering the plains.*

Yet such a view cannot have a transformative effect if it remains only conceptual. Therefore, Lodro Thaye adds:

> *One who holds this view but does not meditate*
> *Is like a rich man tethered by stinginess*
> *Who cannot bring fruition to himself or others.*
> *Joining the view and meditation is the holy tradition.*

The danger of any view is that we could start to substitute theory for the reality it points to. That is why, in the Mahamudra/Dzogchen tradition, the master presents the view along with "pointing-out instructions"—which transmit or experientially reveal to the student the actual state that the view describes. Then the view becomes the ground of a contemplative path whose goal is to realize the view in a full experiential way.

Phenomenological Reflection: Meeting Experience Directly

Conceptual reflection that provides a map of where we are or a strategy for how to proceed gives a general orientation but has limited value in helping us relate to where we are right now, more immediately. Conceptual mapping and analysis—thinking and talking about experience—must eventually give way to an approach that helps us work directly with experience.

Phenomenogical reflection is the putting aside of habitual conceptual assumptions in order to explore experience in a fresher, looser way. Because it does not impose preconceived concepts or strategies on experience, it is a more refined approach. The concepts it uses are "experience-near": they grow out of, describe, and point back to what is directly felt and perceived. In this way phenomenology narrows the gap between observer and observed.

Phenomenological approaches to psychotherapy regard experiencing as a complex, living process that cannot be neatly controlled or predicted. Here the observing consciousness stays close to felt experience, inquiring into it gently, and waiting patiently for responses and insights to come directly from there, rather than from some cognitive schema. Experiencing itself is the guide, revealing directions for change that unfold in the course of exploring it.

For example, a tension in the chest might first reveal itself as anxiety, then upon further reflection, as a sense of helplessness, then as an uncertainty that you are worthy of love. Perhaps you started out feeling judgmental toward the anxiety, or threatened by it, but as it reveals itself as an uncertainty about being lovable, a softer tenderness might arise. And this new way of relating to what you are going through allows it to unfold further, as the anxiety relaxes and you feel more compassionate toward yourself. In this kind of reflection, observer and observed become reciprocal poles of a mutual dance. This stepping-back from habitual reactions and assumptions in order to come into a fresher relationship with lived experience is the essence of what is called, in philosophical terms, "the phenomenological reduction."

Reflective Witnessing: Bare, Mindful Attention

An even subtler kind of reflection happens in the early stages of mindfulness meditation, where one is simply attentive to the ongoing flow of the mindstream, without concern about particular contents of experience that arise. In this approach the gap between observer and observed narrows further, in that there is no interest in operating on the mindstream in any way—through understanding, unfolding, articulation, or moving toward any release or resolution. In the context of meditation, any of these aims would indicate the operation of some mental set or attitude, and thus an interference with the process of freeing oneself from identification with all mind-states. While phenomenological reflection is an attempt to find new meaning, new understanding, new directions, meditation is a more radical path of *undoing*, which involves relaxing any tendency to become caught up in feelings, thoughts, and identifications. But mindfulness practice is not yet the totally relaxed nondoing of Dzogchen, for it still requires some effort of stepping back (from identification) and witnessing.

Mindfulness practice provides a transitional step between reflection and nondual presence, incorporating elements of both. Directing mindful attention toward thinking allows us to notice a crucial difference—between thought and awareness, between the contents of consciousness, which are like clouds passing through the sky, and pure consciousness, which is like the wide open sky itself. Letting go of habitual identifications allows us to enter pure awareness, which is intrinsically free of the compulsions of thought and emotion. This is an important step in starting to free ourselves from the prison of dualistic fixation. In the Dzogchen tradition, this is spoken of as distinguishing the mind caught in dualism (Tibetan: *sems*) from pure nondual awareness (*rigpa*). As the Tibetan teacher Chökyi Nyima describes this distinction: "Basically there are two states of mind. *Sems* refers to the state of conceptual thinking, involving fixation on some thing. . . . *Rigpa* means free from fixation. It refers to a state of natural wakefulness that is without dualistic clinging. It is extremely important to be clear about the difference between these two states of mind."

Pure Presence: Awakening within Experience

Before becoming self-reflective, we remain identified with thoughts, beliefs, feelings, and memories arising in consciousness, and this identification keeps us imprisoned in conditioned mind. With reflection, we can start to free ourselves from these unconscious identifications by stepping back and observing them. Yet as long as we are stepping back, we remain in a state of divided consciousness. A further step would be to go beyond reflection and, without falling back into prereflective identification, become at one with our experiencing—through overcoming all struggle with it, through discovering and abiding in the deep, silent source from which all experience arises. This third level of the dialectic, which takes us beyond conventional psychological models and philosophical frameworks, is *post-reflective*, in that it usually follows from a groundwork of reflective work, and *trans-reflective*, in that it discloses a way of being that lies beyond divided consciousness.

Even phenomenology, which, in emphasizing subject/object interrelatedness, is one of the most refined, least dualistic Western ways of exploring human experience, usually fails to go this further step. Peter Koestenbaum, for example, whose work *The New Image of the Person* is a worthy attempt to develop a phenomenological clinical philosophy, and who is generally sympathetic to meditation and transpersonal experience, describes meditation only in terms of stepping back. He considers meditative presence—what he calls the Eternal Now—to be the ultimate phenomenological reduction:

> There is no end to the regressive process of reflection because the field of consciousness is experienced to be infinite. Specifically, *there is infinity in stepping back*. . . . The Eternal Now is an experience in which we are no longer inside space and inside time but *have become an observer* of space and time. . . . In meditation, *the individual takes a spectatorial attitude towards all experiences*. . . . The meditator follows the flow of the body, of a feeling, or of the environment. . . . In this way *individuals can train themselves to become observers rather than participants in life* [my italics].

Koestenbaum's words are accurate up through the early stages of reflective witnessing in mindfulness practice. However, meditation that only goes this far does not lead beyond divided consciousness. The ultimate purpose of meditation goes far beyond training us to be "observers, rather than participants," as Koestenbaum claims. Its aim is full participation in life, but *conscious* participation, rather than the unconscious participation of prereflective identification. What finally replaces divided consciousness is pure presence.

Of all the phenomenologists, Heidegger and Merleau-Ponty have perhaps gone the farthest in acknowledging a mode of awareness beyond subject and object, as well as its sacred import. Borrowing a term from Meister Eckhart, Heidegger speaks of *Gelassenheit*, letting-be, using language reminiscent of Buddhist references to suchness: "To *let be*—that is, to let beings be as the beings which they are—means to engage oneself with the open region and its openness into which every being comes to stand, bringing that openness, as it were, along with itself." Merleau-Ponty suggests the need to develop what he calls *sur-réflection* (which might be translated as "higher reflection") "that would take itself and the changes it introduces into the spectacle into account. . . . It must plunge into the world instead of surveying it, it must descend toward it such as it is . . . so that the seer and the visible reciprocate one another and we no longer know which sees and which is seen." These attempts by two great philosophers to point the way beyond traditional Western dualistic thought are admirable. Yet even at its best, phenomenology can point to but does not provide a true *upaya*, or path, for fully realizing nondual presence.

In the practice of Mahamudra/Dzogchen, meditators discover nondual awareness, at first in glimpses, as the focus on objects of consciousness gradually drops away and they learn to rest in open presence, in what Franklin Merrill-Wolff called "consciousness-without-an-object." This nondual presence could be described in terms of qualities such as depth, luminosity, or spaciousness, yet in its immediacy there is no self-conscious reflection on any such attributes. Instead, one simply rests in the clarity of wide open, wakeful awareness, without any attempt to alter or fabricate one's experience.

Here is direct self-knowing, direct recognition of one's own nature as pure being, without self-reflection. When attention is turned outward, perception is clear and sharp, since it is not clothed in concepts. The world is not seen as something separate from awareness, nor is it any less vivid and immediate than awareness itself. Nor is awareness seen as something subjective, "in here," separate from appearances. Awareness and what appears in awareness mutually coemerge in one unified field of presence.

In this unified field of presence, neither perceptions nor awareness can be objectified as anything for the mind to grasp. This ungraspable quality of experience is the basic meaning of the Buddhist term *emptiness*. The Mahamudra tradition speaks of the inseparability of emptiness and awareness, emptiness and clarity, emptiness and appearance, emptiness and energy. We could also speak of the inseparability of emptiness and being. Pure presence is the realization of being-as-emptiness: being without being some*thing*. Being is empty, not because it lacks anything, but because it cannot be comprehended in terms of any reference point outside itself. Being is precisely that which can never be grasped or contained in any physical boundary or conceptual designation. In Nishitani's words, "being is only being if it is one with emptiness. . . . In that sense, emptiness might be called the field of 'be-ification.' "

Emptiness in this sense is not some "attribute" belonging to awareness, appearance, or being, but their utter transparency when apprehended in pure presence, beyond the subject/object division. This realization is called by many different names, such as self-illuminating awareness, *jnana*, buddha-nature, wisdom mind, great bliss, great perfection. As self-illuminating awareness that simultaneously illumines the whole field of experience, pure presence is intimate engagement, rather than stepped-back detachment. In contrast to reflection, it does not involve any "doing" at all, as the great Dzogchen master Longchenpa indicates when he says, "Instead of seeking mind by mind, let be."

Once awareness extricates itself from the fetters of conceptual mind, through reflection and mindfulness, it can self-realize its intrinsic nature as pure freedom, relaxation, openness, luminosity, and presence. This happens, in Mahamudra terms, through "settling itself in its own nature." Since this resting in presence goes beyond effort, one-pointedness, and witnessing, it is called *nonmeditation*. Although analogies can suggest what this is like, no word or image can describe its radiant immediacy, as Lodro Thaye points out:

It is space, ungraspable as a thing.
It is a flawless precious clear crystal.
It is the lamp-like radiance of your own self-luminous mind.
It is inexpressible, like the experience of a mute.
It is unobscured, transparent wisdom.
The luminous dharmakaya, buddha-nature,
Primordially pure and spontaneous.
It cannot be demonstrated through analogy,
And cannot be expressed in words.
It is the space of Dharma,
Forever overwhelming mind's inspection.

In the state of nonmeditation it is no longer necessary to make a distinction between conceptual mind and pure awareness, in that all mind-states are recognized as forms of awareness and presence. It is more a question of being fully awake within thoughts, feelings, and perceptions when they arise, no longer maintaining a hairbreadth of separation from whatever arises.

This quality of pure presence brings about spontaneous clearings in the mindstream, without any deliberate strategy or intention to create change. There are two closely related ways in which these clearings may come about: through *transmutation*, which involves some effort, and *self-liberation*, which is more effortless and spontaneous.

Transmutation

The Tantric tradition of Vajrayana Buddhism is known as the path of transformation, in which "impure" experience—marked by ignorance, dualism, aggression, grasping—is transmuted into "pure" experience, illumined by awareness, openness, nongrasping, and spontaneous appreciation. The basic Vajrayana methods of visualization, mantra, mudra, and symbolic ritual eventually lead to the more advanced, utterly direct approach of Mahamudra/Dzogchen, where the practitioner finally cuts through the separation between pure and impure by completely meeting and opening to the raw immediacy of experience on the spot.

In this direct encounter, the thick, heavy, fixated quality of experience falls away, revealing a deeper, living intelligence contained within it. Chögyam Trungpa describes this kind of change:

> At this point whatever is experienced in everyday life through sense perception is a naked experience, because it is direct. There is no veil between [you] and "that." . . . Tantra teaches not to suppress or destroy energy but to transmute it; in other words, go with the pattern of energy. . . . When [you] go with the pattern of energy, then experience becomes very creative. . . . You realize that you no longer have to abandon anything. You begin to see the underlying qualities of wisdom in your life-situation. . . . If you are highly involved in one emotion such as anger, then by having a sudden glimpse of openness . . . you begin to see that you do not have to suppress your energy . . . but you can transform your aggression into dynamic energy. . . . If we actually feel the living quality, the texture of the emotions as they are in their naked state, then this experience also contains ultimate truth. . . . We discover that emotion actually does not exist as it appears, but it contains much wisdom and open space. . . . Then the process of . . . transmuting the emotions into wisdom takes place automatically.

Here there is no deliberate effort to transmute the emotions; rather, transmutation happens spontaneously through opening fully to them:

> You experience emotional upheaval as it is but . . . become one with it. . . . Let yourself be in the emotion, go through it, give in to it, experience it. You begin to go toward the emotion rather than just experiencing the emotion coming toward you. . . . Then the most powerful energies become absolutely workable. . . . Whatever occurs in the samsaric mind is regarded as the path; everything is workable. It is a fearless proclamation—the lion's roar.

As a student in this tradition, with a few budding glimpses of what the above words might actually refer to, I began to feel that even

Focusing—which was the simplest, most penetrating, experience-near therapeutic method I knew—still did not go far enough.

Focusing involves attending to an unclear bodily felt sense while remaining extremely respectful, gentle, and attentive toward every nuance of experience that arises from it. Seeing how concrete steps of experiential change can emerge from attending to a felt sense is an important discovery—something that people who use spiritual practice to avoid their feelings and personal experience would do well to learn. Yet as Focusing is commonly practiced, there is often a bias toward unfolding meaning from a felt sense, toward resolution, toward looking for a felt shift. In this way, it can become a form of "doing" that maintains a subtle I/it stance toward one's experience. The bias here can be very subtle. Wanting our experience to change usually contains a subtle resistance to what is, to nowness, to what I call *unconditional presence*—the capacity to meet experience fully and directly, without filtering it through any conceptual or strategic agenda.

The subtle spiritual pitfall of psychological work is that it can reinforce certain tendencies inherent in the conditioned personality: to see ourselves as a doer, to always look for the meaning in experience, or to continually strive for "something better." Although psychological reflection can certainly help people move forward in important ways, at some point even the slightest desire for change or improvement can interfere with the deeper letting go and relaxation that are necessary for moving from the realm of personality into the realm of being, which is only discoverable in and through nowness—in moments when all conceptualizing and striving cease.

When we let experience be as it is, instead of seeking to alter it in any way, the focus of inner work shifts in an important and powerful way. No longer is our experience something apart from us that we need to change or resolve; instead, the focus widens to the larger field: how-we-are-with-our-experience. And when we relate to our experience in a more spacious, allowing way, it becomes less problematic, because we no longer exist in an I/it, subject/object tension with it.

Although the main aim of psychotherapy is to reduce psychological distress and increase self-understanding, rather than to overcome divided consciousness, I nonetheless felt a need to practice therapy in a way that was more congruent with the nondoing quality of meditative presence. I was also inspired in this vision by moments in my own personal work when opening to my experience just as it was brought me into a fuller sense of presence—a kind of "being without agenda" that led to a powerful sense of stillness, acceptance, and aliveness. Such moments afforded a glimpse of what lay on the other side of divided consciousness: being at one with myself in a new and deeper way.

Of course, there is a time for actively trying to penetrate the veils of experience, as well as a time for allowing experience to be as it is. If we are unable or unwilling to actively engage with our personal life issues, then letting-be could become a stance of avoidance, and a dead end. Yet if we are unable to let our experience be, or to open to it just as it is, then our psychological work may reinforce the habitual tendency of the conditioned personality to turn away from nowness. While Focusing showed me a way out of the first pitfall, meditation—which taught me about the wisdom of nondoing—showed me a way beyond the second pitfall.

In training professionals, I also found that the investment in change can introduce a subtle bias into therapists' responses, thereby communicating to their clients: "You're not all right the way you are." And this can reinforce the alienated attitude most people already suffer from: "I should be having a better experience than the one I'm having—what's wrong with me?" When clients pick up this bias from their therapists, it can create a fundamental obstacle in the therapeutic process and relationship. Clients either try to go along with the therapist's agenda, which can disconnect them from their own being, or else they resist the therapist's agenda, which keeps them stuck.

The more I trained therapists, the clearer it became that the most important quality in a therapist was the capacity for unconditional presence—which, oddly enough, is hardly mentioned or taught in most therapy training. When therapists are present with a client's experience in this way, something inside the client can begin to relax and open up more fully. What I have found, again and again, is that unconditional presence is the most powerful transmuting force there is, precisely because it is a willingness to be there with our experience, without dividing ourselves in two by trying to "manage" what we are feeling.

The nondoing of unconditional presence is compatible with a wide range of therapeutic methods, both directive and nondirective. It is not a passive stance, but rather an active willingness to meet and inquire into felt experience in a totally unbiased, nonreactive, noncontrolling way.

In teaching unconditional presence, I have found it helpful to delineate different stages of this coming-into-contact. First of all, there needs to be a *willingness to inquire*, to face directly into our felt experience and see what is there. Then we can begin to *acknowledge* what is happening inside us: "Yes, this is what I'm experiencing right now. I'm feeling threatened . . . hurt . . . angry . . . defensive." Acknowledging involves recognizing and naming what is going on, seeing how it feels in the body, and inviting it more fully into awareness. The power of bare acknowledgment should never be underestimated. To help clients linger here and not rush on toward some hoped-for resolution, I often say something like, "Notice what it's like right now *just to acknowledge* what you're feeling." Attending to the felt quality of this recognition cuts through the impulse to react to the content, allowing the client to be more present with it.

Once we acknowledge what is there, it becomes possible to meet it more fully by *allowing* it to be there as it is. This does not mean wallowing in feelings or acting them out. Instead, allowing means giving our experience space and actively letting it be as it is, putting aside any urge to manage or judge it. Often what interferes with this is either identifying with the feeling ("this anger is me") or resisting it ("this anger is not me"). A certain amount of time and concentration is often necessary before we can let our experience be there in this more allowing way.

Having allowed our experience to be as it is, we can then let ourselves *open to it* more fully, no longer maintaining any distance between it and ourselves as observer, judge, or manager. This is the point where unconditional presence diverges from Focusing and other reflective methods. There is a complete opening to, entering into, and becoming one with the felt experience, without any attempt to find meaning in it, or to do anything with it, to it, or about it. What is most important here is not so much what we are feeling, but the act of opening to it.

For example, a client fears that she is nothing—that if she looks inside, she won't find anything there. Although I first ask her to pay attention to this "fear of being nothing" in her body and we discuss how it relates to situations from her past (this is still reflective inquiry), eventually I invite her to open directly to the sense of being nothing—to enter fully into it and let herself *be* nothing. (Here reflection gives way to presence.) After a while she says, "It feels empty, but there's also a fullness, and a kind of peace." She feels full because she is present now, rather than disconnected. It is her being that feels peaceful and full. And she starts to realize that her sense of nothingness was actually a symptom of being cut off from herself—a disconnection reinforced by stories and beliefs she had about the dreaded void at her core. Of course, feelings don't always transmute this easily. It depends entirely on the client and our relationship. Yet for clients who have experienced this a number of times, it can happen more and more readily.

Feelings in themselves don't necessarily lead to wisdom, but the process of opening fully to them can. When we no longer maintain distance from a feeling, it cannot preserve its apparent solidity, which only crystallizes when we treat it as an object separate from ourselves. In the above example, the client's fear of being nothing persisted only as long as she resisted that experience. But when she opened unconditionally to being nothing, this inner division ceased, at least for a while, as she stepped out of the fixed stance/attitudes/associations she held toward "being nothing," with their long history dating back to childhood. In becoming present in a place where she had been absent, she experienced her being, rather than her nothingness. "Being nothing" transmuted into the empty fullness of being—where the fear of being nothing no longer had a hold on her.

When the focus of awareness shifts from a feeling—as an object of pleasure or pain, like or dislike, acceptance or rejection—to our state of presence with it, this allows us to discover new resources and wisdom hidden within it, as we move from the realm of personality into the larger space of being. Out of presence with anger, strength often emerges; out of presence with sorrow, compassion; out of presence with fear, courage and groundedness; out of presence with emptiness, expansive spaciousness and peace. Strength, compassion, courage, spaciousness, peace are differentiated qualities of being—different ways in which presence manifests.

In this way, being fully present with ourselves overcomes the inner war, at least for a moment, between self and other, between "me" and "my experience." And from there, everything looks and feels different. A felt shift happens, but this is more than the "content mutation" that Gendlin describes as the result of reflective unfolding. An example of content mutation would be anger unfolding to reveal fear, which in turn might unfold further, revealing itself as a desire to be loved, and then a sense of relief at realizing that one's anger was pushing away the love one wanted. I call these "horizontal" felt shifts, because even though deeper feelings and realizations may unfold, the process remains mainly within the realm of personality. But the transmutation that often occurs through unconditional presence is a "vertical" shift, where one moves from personality into a deeper quality of being, as a fixed constellation of observer/observed dissolves, along with all reactivity, contraction, or striving.

Of course, this kind of deepening may not happen quickly or easily, or by itself lead to lasting personal transformation. Often a long sequence of horizontal unfolding must occur before a vertical shift happens, and a long period of integration is necessary before these shifts can lead to real differences in the way one lives. Nor am I suggesting that Focusing and other reflective methods cannot also lead to vertical shifts. But when someone opens completely to what he or she is experiencing, the personality—which is an activity of judgment, control, and resistance—disappears for a moment. Therapists without some background in meditation may have difficulty fully appreciating this or allowing it to unfold.

I make a point of helping clients recognize the nature and significance of this shift into being when it occurs. I encourage them to rest there, appreciate the new quality of presence that has become available, and let it move freely in their body, without having to go on to another problem or anything else. The sense of presence might deepen, and new aspects or implications might reveal themselves. Or perhaps the client starts to feel uneasy, resist, or dissociate. In that case, we might move back into reflective inquiry, to see what is going on—what old beliefs, object relations, or identities may be interfering. We might then explore these obstacles reflectively until at some point I again invite the client to be present with his or her experience in the way described above. In this way, the capacity for presence expands, while obstacles standing in its way are also worked through.

This contemplative approach to psychological work differs from conventional therapy in being more concerned with recovering the presence of being—accessed through opening directly to experience—than with problem resolution. The problem-solving mentality reinforces the inner division between a reformer self and a problematic "me" it wants to change. By contrast, the vertical shift facilitated by unconditional presence is a change of context that alters the whole way a problem is held. People often discover that their alienated, controlling, or rejecting attitude toward the problem at hand is in fact a large part of the problem itself. This allows them to see and consider new ways of relating to the problematic situation.

Unconditional presence is more radical than psychological reflection in that it involves *giving in* to our experience (as in Trungpa's statement, "Let yourself be in the emotion, go through it, give in to it") while learning to ride the energy mindfully, without becoming overwhelmed by it. This approach is clearly not for people lacking in ego strength—those who are unable to step back and reflect on their feelings, or whose primary task is to establish a stable, cohesive self-structure. Focusing, by contrast, helps strengthen the observing ego by helping clients find the right distance from their emotional upheaval. But here one simply dives in, radically erasing any separation from one's experience.

Transmutation through unconditional presence happens somewhat differently in psychological and in meditative practice. In therapy, it is part of a dialogical process, and therefore always develops out of and returns to a reflective interchange. Reflecting on what has happened in a vertical shift also helps integrate the new quality of presence into ongoing daily functioning. In meditative practice, by contrast, mind-states can transmute in a more immediate, spontaneous way, without reference to a prior or subsequent reflective process. By not engaging in reflective articulation, the meditator can often move beyond divided consciousness in a deeper, more sustained way. The challenge here, however, lies in integrating this deeper awareness into daily life and functioning.

Ongoing Self-Liberation

Transmutation, as described above, still involves a slight sense of duality, at least initially, in that one makes some effort to go toward experience, go into it, open oneself to it. Beyond transmutation lie still subtler possibilities of nondual presence, usually realized only through advanced meditative practice. In the Mahamudra/Dzogchen tradition, this is the way of self-liberation. Here one learns to remain continually present within the movement of experience—whether thought, perception, feeling, or sensation. In the words of a great Dzogchen master, Paltrul Rinpoche, "It is sufficient to simply let your mind rest in the state of whatever takes place, in whatever happens." This kind of naked awareness—where there is no mental or emotional reaction to whatever arises—allows each experience to be just what it is, free of dualistic grasping and fixation, and totally transparent. Pure presence makes possible the *self-liberation* of the mindstream. This is Mahamudra—the supreme mudra, the ultimate seeing that "lets beings be as the beings which they are."

What is this supreme mudra? In the words of Tilopa, one of the grandfathers of Mahamudra, "When mind is free of reference points, that is Mahamudra." Not to rely on reference points—attitudes, beliefs, intentions, aversions, self-concepts, object relations—to interpret our experience or evaluate who we are in relation to it is to rest in the "core" of being, "at the still point of the turning world, neither from nor towards." This sense of "resting in the middle of one's experience" is not a "position" in any determinate "place." This use of the term *middle* is taken from Nishitani, who describes it as the "mode of being of things as they are in themselves—namely, the mode of being

wherein things rest in the complete uniqueness of what they themselves are. . . . It is immediately present—and immediately realized as
such—at the point that we ourselves actually are. It is 'at hand' and
'underfoot.' . . . All actions imply an absolute immediacy. And it is
there that what we are calling the 'middle' appears." Resting in the
middle of being means standing in pure presence.

Normal divided consciousness places us on the perimeter of the
field of experience, stepped back from whatever we are observing.
When resting in the middle, by contrast, "the standpoint of the subject that knows things objectively, and likewise knows itself objectively
as a thing called the self, is broken down." The self-knowing that
arises here is immediate and nonobjectifying.

> It is not a "knowing" that consists in the self's turning to itself and
> refracting into itself. It is not a "reflective" knowing. . . . This self-
> awareness . . . is a knowing that comes about not as a *refraction* of the
> self bent into the self but only on a position that is, as it were, abso-
> lutely straightforward. . . . This is because it is a knowing that origi-
> nates in the "middle." It is an absolutely nonobjective knowing of the
> absolutely nonobjective self in itself; it is a completely nonreflective
> knowing. . . . On all other fields the self is at all times reflective, and
> caught in its own grasp in the act of grasping itself, and caught in the
> grasp of things in its attempt to grasp them. . . . It can never be the
> "straight heart" of which the ancients speak.

The ultimate practice here is learning to remain fully present and
awake in the middle of whatever thoughts, feelings, perceptions, or
sensations are occurring and to appreciate them, in Mahamudra/
Dzogchen terms, as *dharmakaya*—as an ornamental display of the
empty, luminous essence of awareness. Like waves on the ocean,
thoughts are not separate from awareness. They are the radiant clarity
of awareness in motion. In remaining awake in the middle of
thoughts—and recognizing them as the luminous energy of awareness—the practitioner maintains presence and can rest within their
movement. As Namkhai Norbu suggests, "The essential principle is
to . . . maintain presence in the state of the moving wave of thought

itself. . . . If one considers the calm state as something positive to be attained, and the wave of thought as something negative to be abandoned, and one remains caught up in the duality of grasping and rejecting, there is no way of overcoming the ordinary state of the mind."

It is dualistic fixation, the tension between "me"—as self—and "my thoughts"—as other—that makes thinking problematic, tormenting, "sticky," like the tar baby to which Brer Rabbit becomes affixed by trying to push it away. Thoughts become thick, solid, and heavy only when we react to them. Each reaction triggers further thought, so that the thoughts become chained together in what appears to be a continuous mind-state. These thought chains are like a relay race, where each new thought picks up the baton from the previous thought and runs with it for a moment, passing it on again to a subsequent thought. But if the meditator can maintain presence in the middle of thinking, free of grasping or rejecting, then the thought has nothing to pass the baton on to and naturally subsides. Although this sounds simple, it is advanced practice, usually requiring much preliminary training and commitment.

When one can rest in presence even in the midst of thoughts, perceptions, or intense emotions, these become an ongoing part of one's contemplative practice, as opportunities to discover a pervasive quality of even awareness in all one's activities. As Tarthang Tulku describes this:

> It's possible to make thought itself meditation. . . . How do we go into that state? The moment you try to separate yourself from thought, you are dealing with a duality, a subject-object relationship. You lose the state of awareness because you reject your experience and become separate from it. . . . But if our awareness is in the center of thought, the thought itself dissolves. . . .
>
> At the very beginning . . . stay in the thoughts. Just be there. . . . You become the center of the thought. But there is not really any center—the center becomes balance. There's no "being," no "subject-object relationships": none of these categories exist. Yet at the same time, there is . . . complete openness. . . . So we kind of crack each

thought, like cracking nuts. If we can do this, any thought becomes meditation. . . .

Any moment, wherever you are, driving a car, sitting around, working, talking, any activities you have—even if you are very disturbed emotionally, very passionate, or even if your mind has become very strong, raging, overcome with the worst possible things and you cannot control yourself, or you feel depressed . . . if you really go into it, there's nothing there. Whatever comes up becomes your meditation. Even if you become extremely tense, if you go into your thought and your awareness comes alive, that moment can be more powerful than working a long time in meditation practice.

Here no antidote need be applied: no conceptual understanding, no reflection, no stepping back, no detachment, no witnessing. When one is totally present in the thought, in the emotion, in the disturbance, it relaxes by itself and becomes transparent to the larger ground of awareness. The wave subsides back into the ocean. The cloud dissolves into the sky. The snake naturally uncoils. These are all metaphors that say: It self-liberates.

Self-liberation is not a dialogical process but a "straight heart" realization of being-emptiness. It makes possible an intimate knowing of reality, as Nishitani suggests when he writes that "things reveal themselves to us only when we leap from the circumference to the center, into their very [suchness]." This "knowing of not-knowing" is a complete openness and attunement to the self-revealing qualities of self, world, and other beings.

For one who can remain fully present even in the middle of deluded thoughts and emotions, the distinction between *samsara* and *nirvana*, conventional and awakened consciousness, duality and nonduality is no longer of great concern. This is known as the awareness of *one taste*. When one is no longer trapped in divided consciousness, the relative duality, or play of self and other, in daily life is not a problem. One can play by the conventional ground rules of duality when appropriate and drop them when they're not useful. The interplay of self and other becomes a humorous dance, an energetic exchange, an ornament rather than a hindrance.

Summary and Conclusion

Most of us live caught up in prereflective identification most of the time, imagining that our thoughts, feelings, attitudes and viewpoints are an accurate portrayal of reality. But when awareness is clouded by prereflective identification, we do not yet fully *have* our experience. Rather, *it has us:* we are swept along by crosscurrents of thought and feeling in which we are unconsciously immersed. Driven by these unconscious identifications—self-images, conflicting emotions, superego commands, object relations, recurring thought patterns—we remain asleep to the deeper import of our experience. We remain angry without even knowing we are angry, anxious without understanding why we are anxious, and hungry without realizing what we are truly hungry for. This is the condition that Gurdjieff called "the machine."

Reflective attention helps us take a major step forward from there. Conceptual reflection allows us to make an initial assessment of what is going on and why. Beyond that, subtler, more direct kinds of phenomenological reflection can help us finally start to *have* our experience. In psychotherapy, it is a major advance when clients can, for example, move from just being angry to *having* their anger. This means that their awareness can hold the anger and reflect on it, instead of being overwhelmed or clouded by it. Beyond that, mindful witnessing allows us to step back from our experience and let it be, without being caught up in reaction or identification.

A further step on the path of awakening involves learning to *be with* our experience in an even more direct and penetrating way, which I call *unconditional presence.* Here the focus is not so much on what we are experiencing as on *how we are with it.* Being fully present with our experience facilitates a vertical shift from personality to being. Being with anger, for instance, involves opening to its energy directly, which often effects a spontaneous transmutation. The anger reveals deeper qualities of being hidden within it, such as strength, confidence, or radiant clarity, and this brings us into deeper connection with being itself. From this greater sense of inner connectedness, the original situation that gave rise to the anger often looks quite different.

Beyond transmutation there lies the still subtler potential to self-liberate experience through naked awareness. Instead of going into the anger, this would mean simply resting in presence as the anger arises and moves, while recognizing it as a transparent, energetic display of being-awareness-emptiness. This possibility is discovered not through a dialogical process like psychotherapy but through contemplative practice.

To summarize the progression described here: it is a movement from unconscious, prereflective immersion in our experience (identification), to thinking and talking about experience (conceptual reflection), to having our experience directly (phenomenological reflection), to nonidentified witnessing (mindfulness), to being-present-with experience (unconditional presence, leading to transmutation), to a transreflective resting in open presence within whatever experience arises, which is no other than pure being/emptiness (self-liberation).

If we use the analogy of awareness as a mirror, prereflective identification is like being captivated by and lost in the reflections appearing in the mirror. Reflection involves stepping back from these appearances, studying them, and developing a more objective relationship with them. And transreflective presence is like being the mirror itself—that vast, illuminating openness and clarity that allows reality to be seen as what it is. In pure presence, awareness is self-illuminating, or aware of itself without objectification. The mirror simply abides in its own nature, without either separating from its reflections or confusing itself with them. Negative reflections do not stain the mirror; positive reflections do not improve on it. They are all the mirror's self-illuminating display.

Psychotherapy as a dialogical process is essentially reflective, although when practiced by a therapist with a contemplative background, it can also include moments of nonreflective presence that facilitate a shift into a deeper dimension of being. In the spiritual traditions, disciplined reflection also serves as a stepping-stone on the way toward greater presence. In Gurdjieff's teaching, for instance, focused self-observation is what allows people to step out of "the machine" and become available to the more pointed presence that he terms "self-remembering." While psychotherapy and spiritual practice may both incorporate reflection and presence, the home base of therapy is reflection and the home base of spirituality is presence.

I would like to close with a few final considerations for Western students of the further reaches of contemplative awareness. From anecdotal evidence, stabilizing the pure presence of *rigpa* in the ongoing realization of self-liberation appears to be quite rare, even among dedicated students of Dzogchen/Mahamudra. This tradition flowered in Tibet, a far simpler and more grounded culture than ours, which also provided a social mandala, or cohesive cultural context, that supported thousands of monasteries and hermitages where meditation practice and realization could flourish. Yet even there, years of preliminary practice and solitary retreat were usually recommended as the groundwork for full nondual realization, which was sometimes described as the golden roof that crowns the entire spiritual enterprise.

The question for modern Westerners, who lack the cultural supports found in traditional Asia and who often find it hard to spend years in retreat or even to complete the traditional Tibetan preliminary practices, is how to build a strong enough base on which this golden roof can rest. What kind of preliminary practices or inner work are most relevant and useful for modern people as a groundwork for nondual realization? What special conditions may be necessary to nurture and sustain nondual presence outside of retreat situations? And how can this spacious, relaxed quality of presence be integrated into everyday functioning in a speedy, complex technological society like ours, which requires such high levels of mental activity and mental abstraction?

Since unresolved psychological issues and developmental deficiencies often present major hurdles to integrating spiritual realizations into daily life, spiritual aspirants in the West may also need to engage in some degree of psychological work, as a useful adjunct to their spiritual work, and perhaps as a preliminary practice in its own right. Perhaps for Westerners genuine nondoing and letting-be can only be fully embodied in a healthy, integrated way once one has learned to attend to bodily feelings and grapple with one's personal experience in a Focusing-style reflective manner. That is why it is important to understand the uses and limitations of psychological reflection, and to study its role as a stepping-stone both toward and "back" from non-dual presence—as a bridge, in other words, that can begin to unlock deeper qualities of being and help to integrate them more fully into everyday life.

PART TWO

✤ Psychotherapy
in a
Spiritual
Context

Introduction

WHILE SEVERAL CHAPTERS in the first section of the book touch on the spiritual dimension of psychological work, the chapters in this section address this issue more directly. My concern here is not so much with conventional psychotherapy, which operates within the medical model of disease and cure and is primarily oriented toward symptom relief and problem solving, as with psychological work in a spiritual context.

Of course there is a place for conventional therapy, and there's certainly nothing wrong with symptom relief, especially when that is all health insurance companies will pay for, or all that a particular person is ready for. But from a larger spiritual perspective, the problem-solving mind-set is extremely limited, in that it diverts us from being fully present with what is actually going on right now. Whenever we work on ourselves with a particular outcome or fix in mind, or strive to get somewhere different from where we are, we cut ourselves off from the immediacy of being—which is the only true agent of healing and transformation that there is. We can access our being only through present experiencing, which is, therefore, the only place where real healing can happen. We can't get there—to healing—from here unless we are fully here, where we are, first of all.

The fix-it mentality only really works on the gross outer level of things. When trying to repair a car or a pipe in the kitchen sink, it is appropriate to take a wrench and exert pressure against the hardened rust to get the nut to turn. But approaching an inner problem in this way usually has the opposite effect, causing the problem to seize up all the more. This is because the part of us we are trying to fix feels unacceptable or rejected, and therefore tightens up. Even more importantly, the source of living change is the self-existing flow of our being. When we exert pressure against some part of our experience, we shut down that flow, and this jams up the works.

Thus if we are working on our fear, for instance, the larger question is not so much, "How can I overcome this fear?," "How can I calm myself down?," or "How can I avoid situations that bring up fear?," but rather, "Can I open to this feeling?," "Can I inquire into where it is coming from?," or "Can I learn to be fully present with this experience, as I feel it in my body, and get to know what is really happening there?" Of course, the intention or desire to overcome our fear is fine, as long as this is not a subtle way of rejecting it. Whenever we turn away from some aspect of our own experience, emotional black holes form in the psyche. Real healing can begin only when we finally learn to be present in the places where we have been absent.

The lifeblood of psychological work in a spiritual context is the healing power of unconditional presence. This involves learning to acknowledge, allow, open to, and inquire into our experience as it is, without trying to have some other experience than the one we're having. Since this involves a practice of presence on the part of both client and therapist, I also call this *presence-centered counseling*.

Unfortunately, there is little in our Western system of education that helps us develop this capacity to be present. In fact, most of our education leads in the opposite direction. Because meditation practice taught me how to stay present with all the ups and downs of the mind, it proved to be an essential foundational training for being a therapist and, beyond that, a good listener, a responsive student, an attuned friend, a sensitive lover, and a kind teacher. Although meditation involves temporarily unplugging from the world and its distractions, it is not about withdrawing from the world. In helping us discover a quality of presence and awareness that is much steadier and more discerning than the habitual whirl of mind and emotion, meditation has tremendous social benefits, helping us to experience others, as well as ourselves, more directly. Then we are able to see people more clearly, understand what they feel more fully, and respond to them more empathically.

The second part of this book opens with an exploration of this core, essential element in psychological healing: the capacity to be fully present with our experience as it is. Chapter 9 shows how unconditional presence is the antidote to the central problem of the conditioned personality—the automatic tendency to turn away from and reject aspects of our experience that are painful, unpleasant, or threatening.

Chapter 10 is a wide-ranging chapter about a central human experience that I call *the moment of world collapse,* and how it can help us appreciate the basic vulnerability of being human, keep growing through identity crisis, and find our genuine power in the process. This chapter also traces some of my own personal development in moving from a heroic, existential approach to dealing with issues of meaninglessness toward a larger understanding of the place of emptiness in human existence.

Chapter 11 explores the place of *heart* in psychological healing, and how the healing relationship calls for a certain kind of unconditional love. This chapter also shows how loving-kindness, or unconditional friendliness, contributes to the discovery of basic goodness at the core of our nature—a discovery that helps us overcome the driving compulsion to prove that we are worthwhile.

Chapter 12 considers depression as a loss of heart, resulting from the loss of familiar reference points that used to provide safety and security. Depression is a negative reaction to the discovery of that open, boundless, ungraspable dimension of reality that Buddhism speaks of as *emptiness.* The depressed person often takes emptiness personally, interpreting it as a sign of failure or deficiency. Seen as a spiritual opportunity, however, depression provides an occasion to look underneath the surface of life and discover the only true support there is—the ground of being.

Chapter 13 looks at the difference between psychological and meditative ways of working with emotion. In psychological work, making the important distinction between mental story lines and felt experiencing is essential for inquiring freshly into emotional upheaval and finding out what is at the bottom of it. A more radical approach is found within Tantric Buddhism, where one learns to overcome all separation from the energy of emotion, thereby transmuting confused, conflicted states of mind into the wisdom of all-pervasive awareness.

This part concludes with the most recent and no doubt the most controversial chapter in the book—on psychological work in the service of spiritual development. My purpose in this chapter is to raise some challenging questions about the integration between psyche and spirit, relative and absolute truth, individuation and liberation—in the service of bringing the teachings and practices of spiritual awakening more fully into everyday life. This chapter takes a different tack from most of the rest of the book, which focuses more on how meditation can inform and illuminate psychological work. Instead of looking at what spirituality has to offer psychotherapy, here I look at what psychological work has to offer spirituality, particularly for modern Westerners on the spiritual path. Although my argument mainly addresses spiritual realization as described in the Eastern nondual contemplative paths, it should apply to other spiritual traditions as well.

Nothing in this chapter should be construed as a criticism or attempt to diminish the teachings or practices of the Eastern traditions. My focus here is not on the these teachings per se but on how Western practitioners tend to understand and apply them. The question of how to incorporate these teachings into life in the West, and the Western psyche, is an extremely challenging one, which raises a host of new issues that the founders of these traditions never had to contemplate. I offer this chapter in a spirit of inquiry, rather than as a final, definitive statement. Originally delivered as a talk to a conference in England, this was the most difficult chapter to bring into shape, as I sought to craft a finely balanced understanding of how psychological and spiritual work might support and complement each other at this time in the West.

9

The Healing Power of
Unconditional Presence

*If your everyday practice is to open to all your emotions, to all the
people you meet, to all the situations you encounter, without closing
down, trusting that you can do that—then that will take you as far
as you can go. And then you'll understand all the teachings that
anyone has ever taught.*

—Pema Chödrön

✤ What is the essence of psychological healing—the
core, indispensable element that allows us to leave old, self-destructive
patterns behind and turn in a new direction? To answer this question,
we first need to understand the basic dis-ease or distress at the root of
all psychological problems: we are engaged in a continual struggle
with our experience; we have a hard time letting it be as it is.

Why is it so hard to just let our experience be what it is? Why are
we so uncomfortable with it? What is this uneasiness we feel in relation to our own feelings and states of mind?

The Basic Dis-ease

The nature of our dis-ease is this: we continually judge, reject, and
turn away from certain areas of our experience that cause us discom-
fort, pain, or anxiety. This inner struggle keeps us inwardly divided,
creating pressure and stress and cutting us off from the totality of who
we are. We first learned to reject our experience when we were grow-

ing up. As children, our feelings were often too overwhelming for our fledgling nervous systems to handle, much less understand. So when an experience was too much, and the adults in our environment could not help us relate to it, we learned to contract our mind and body, shutting ourselves down, like a circuit breaker, so that our fuses would not blow. This was our way of preserving and protecting ourselves. In this way, we began to cut off our anger, our need for love, our tenderness, our will, or our sexuality. And we formed negative, even harsh, judgments about these parts of ourselves that caused us pain, and withdrew our awareness from them.

For instance, if our need for love was continually frustrated, it became too painful to feel this need. So when the need came up, we learned to contract against it and its associated pain, shutting them out of awareness. In later life, our need for love will still feel overwhelming whenever it arises, and so we will continue to contract against it. In this way we become disabled, unable to function in areas of our lives that evoke feelings we've never learned to tolerate. Turning away from this primary pain creates a second, ongoing level of suffering: living in a state of contraction and constricted awareness.

Creating an Identity Based on Contraction

In time these contractions form the nucleus of an overall style of avoidance and denial. We develop a whole identity, or view of ourselves, based on rejecting painful aspects of our experience. If we can't handle anger, for instance, we might try to be "a nice person" instead. Such an identity is always partial or lopsided and never reflects the totality of our experience, the whole of who we are. It is based on grasping and identifying with aspects of our experience that we like and rejecting those we dislike.

Because such identities are not really who we are, they require ongoing maintenance. We continually have to prop them up and defend them against the onslaughts of reality that threaten to undermine them. It is as though we are trying to maintain a fragile dike against a restless ocean constantly smashing into it. Life is like the ocean, forever trying to wear away our narrow self-concepts, which compromise its freedom of movement. The continual need to monitor our experience, in order to ward off something that might threaten our identity, creates a third level of suffering: an ongoing state of tension, anxiety, and stress.

Thus our psychological distress is composed of at least three elements: the basic pain of feelings that seem overwhelming; the contracting of mind and body to avoid feeling this pain; and the stress of continually having to prop up and defend an identity based on this avoidance and denial.

One of the main ways we try to hold our identity together is by developing an elaborate web of rationalizations—*stories* about the way we are or the way reality is—to justify our denial and avoidance. A story in this sense is a mental interpretation of our experience, a way of organizing our beliefs into an overall view of reality. Such stories may not be entirely conscious. Often they are more like dreams, consisting of subconscious imaginings and expectations.

For example, a woman whose father had been remote in childhood had difficulty acknowledging her need for emotional contact. She justified her rejection of this need through a story she told herself: "Men are not emotionally available. Since you can never trust them, it would be foolish to ever let myself need a man." When this woman was in a relationship, she would contract against her own need and hold herself back because she never wanted to be in such a vulnerable position again. As a result, men would always leave her because they couldn't feel a real connection with her. And this reinforced her story, "You can never count on men to be there."

That is how stories work—they become self-fulfilling prophecies. A story creates a reality that in turn reinforces the story. In this way, we become more and more locked into a false self and a distorted view of reality.

Why do we spend so much energy maintaining a false self that cuts us off from our larger being? Our self-concept endures, despite all the pain it causes, because it provides a sense that "this is who I am." Even though this false self creates inner division and distress, at least it provides some illusion of stability and permanence amid the uncertainty and flux of existence. Even if your story is, "I am nothing, nobody," at least *that is something*. You know who you are, and this provides a sense of comfort and security.

Unconditional Presence and Healing

If we could *completely* identify with the false self, it wouldn't cause us distress—it would just be who we are. The pain it causes arises from something deeper within us that feels constricted by this identity and suffers when we are not living fully. This deeper intelligence within us feels the pain of being caught in a web of stories and beliefs, scripts and behaviors that cut us off from our true nature and potential. If we do not realize the expansive possibilities that are our birthright, we suffer.

The first and most difficult step in healing is to expose this wound—our disconnectedness from our larger being, and the suffering it creates. *In this pain is our healing.* If we turn away from it, we only add another link in the chain of contraction and denial that constitutes our dis-ease. If we open to it, however, it will put us in direct contact with those aspects of our experience we have cut off or denied. The first step in healing is to acknowledge our dis-ease.

Of course, it is often hard to let ourselves feel our pain and disconnection. As soon as we start to look at it, a story comes up, a distracting belief, thought, or fantasy. As soon as we ask ourselves, "What is this? Why am I feeling so bad?" our mind steps in and says, "Oh, I know what it is. It's *x* or *y*. It's my hang-up with my mother. It's my inferiority complex. It's nothing serious, nothing worth giving any energy to. Everyone has problems like these, don't indulge them." Such stories are a major obstacle to healing because they keep us separate from our experience, stuck in contraction and rejection.

This is why it is important for psychotherapists to help people make an essential discrimination—between their stories and their living experience. For example, if I ask a client how he feels and he says, "I feel stupid," I would say, "That's not a feeling. You don't *feel* stupid—that's a story you have about yourself. What's the actual feeling?" Then he might say, "Well, I feel shaky and scared when I try to speak my mind." *That's* a feeling.

To be effective, therapists or healers continually need to sift through their own stories as well as their clients' stories about what is happening. This can be tricky. Therapists like to think that they know what's going on with people. They are professionals, they've been trained for many years, they have all this knowledge about psychological dynamics. Yet when they're actually working with someone, this knowledge in itself is not an agent of healing. It can be useful; it can be an aid. But a therapist's knowledge and expertise can easily be experienced by clients as another form of rejection. The only way to promote healing is by reversing the condition of rejection that creates dis-ease in the first place.

Since the condition that has created our dis-ease is a fixed, partial view of our experience, we can't promote healing just by adopting a different view. It might be a better view, it might be a wonderful view, it might be the greatest view of reality in the world, but it will not be healing if it's just another set of beliefs and attitudes. It will be another frame that screens out some aspect of experience, another box we will eventually have to outgrow.

Instead of building bigger or fancier boxes, we need to develop the antidote to all our partial views of reality: *being present with our experience as it is.* This is *unconditional presence.* We could also call it *beginner's mind.* As Suzuki Roshi put it, "In the beginner's mind there are many possibilities, in the expert's there are few." We have all become experts at being ourselves, and in so doing we have lost our ability to be present with our experience in a fresh, open-minded way.

Although therapists often think of themselves as experts at knowing people, the truth is that there are no experts in the realm of human experience. That is because the nature of human experience is unbounded and open-ended—it doesn't come boxed to begin with. If you're an expert, your expertise is based on what you know; and what you know is a set of boxes, a collection of concepts, memories, beliefs, ideas about reality—not reality itself.

Beginner's mind, by contrast, is a willingness to meet whatever arises freshly, without holding to any fixed idea about what it means or how it should unfold. As a powerful state of openness that cuts through old prejudices and beliefs, it lets us see things freshly and find new directions. What could be simpler than this? And yet what could be more difficult?

If I ask you, "How do you feel right now? What's going on for you?" and you look inside yourself, the most honest first answer would probably be, "I don't know." If you know right away what's going on inside you, that's probably just a thought—your mind hopping onto a familiar island in the larger sea of the unknown. Let that go and just stay with the question.

Looking within, you may find no single thing to grasp onto, nothing that easily fits into a conceptual box. Indeed, the totality of our present experiencing is much larger and richer than anything we can know or say about it at any moment. To tap the healing power within us, we first have to let ourselves *not know*, so that we can make contact with the fresh, living texture of our experience, beyond all our familiar thoughts. Then when we express what we are feeling, our words will have real power.

The therapeutic dialogue, like any intimate encounter between two human beings, is full of mystery, surprise, and unpredictable turns. Therefore, great therapists are likely to be more interested in what they don't know about their clients than what they do know. When therapists operate primarily from knowledge, they are more likely to be manipulative; when they operate from not-knowing, they are more likely to embody authentic presence. Letting themselves not know what to do next invites a deeper quality of stillness and attentiveness into the work.

In supervising therapists, I have found that they often have an inordinate fear of these moments of uncertainty. Therapeutic training rarely teaches people to remain open and alert in the face of the unknown. So when therapists don't know what to do or say next, they usually feel deficient. And they search around in their bag of tricks, or else quickly shift the client's attention to safer and more familiar ground—thereby leaving the creative edge of the present moment far behind.

How then can we go about being present with our experience?

Actually, the deeper, background presence of our being is happening all the time, although we usually don't recognize it. What we notice instead are the islands in the stream of consciousness—the islands in this case being our thoughts, the places where our busy mind lands from moment to moment. We only notice where our mind lands, not the spaces through which the mind moves like a bird in flight. We don't notice the gaps between our thoughts, even though they are happening all the time. If I talk very slowly, you . . . will . . . begin . . . to . . . notice . . . the . . . spaces . . . between . . . the . . . words.

What is happening in these gaps? Usually we don't notice them because we're too busy weaving together the strands of our thought into the familiar fabric of our ego identity. From ego's point of view, these gaps are scary; they represent absence of control. Yet these gaps are entry points into a still, nonconceptual awareness that is always there, self-existing. When we settle into this awareness, it becomes unconditional presence—just being with what is, open and interested, without agenda. So when we relate to our experience in a friendly, nonreactive, and allowing way, we open ourselves to the embrace of our larger, unconditioned nature. And it is here—as the spark of our basic sanity reveals itself, like a lotus rising out of the muck of neurosis and confusion—that the healing of our conditioned self takes place.

So we don't have to manufacture unconditional presence; in fact, we can't, because it is already there, like the sun, behind the clouds of our busy mind. This is the great discovery of the meditative traditions, going back thousands of years. Pure awareness is direct, unfabricated knowing, clear and fluid like water. Although we swim in this sea of pure awareness, our busy mind is constantly hopping from island to island, from thought to thought, jumping over and through this awareness, which is its ground, without ever coming to rest there. Meanwhile, our unconditioned awareness operates silently in the background, no matter what our busy mind is doing. Everyone has access to this. It is our most intimate reality, so close that it is often hard to see.

Of course, whenever we open into a larger presence, our conditioned personality often tries to flee from that experience, or else grasp it and put it in a familiar box. For example, though we may open in a wonderful new way with someone we love, this may also be scary, so we quickly do something to shut the energy down. One moment we may be there freshly with a piece of music and the next moment we're distracted. Or we try to recapture that moment—which is another way of shutting presence down. Instead of trying not to shut down, all we can do is to see how we do this, again and again, and notice how it affects us. The key to waking up from our distraction is to bring awareness to our lack of awareness, and be present with our lack of presence.

Therapists often inadvertently close down their clients' experience by putting it in familiar interpretive boxes as well. When a client starts to open into the larger space of being, if the therapist cannot allow this opening to take its own course, or interprets it in some conventional way, the client may quickly fall right back into his or her old, familiar identity. At other times a client may open up a feeling that the therapist has some resistance to experiencing. Here is where therapists must also be willing to hang out with their own raw edges, or else when their clients activate these touchy areas, they will pull back, offer a quick fix, or try to steer the client in some other direction.

The most powerful healers or teachers are those who can model authentic presence and bring it into their work. Inviting and allowing another person to have his or her experience just as it is—this is perhaps the greatest gift anyone can offer. Yet though open presence is natural and spontaneous, the capacity to recognize and sustain it in the midst of the mind's distractions requires training and practice. Unfortunately, professional psychology training consists mostly of transmitting knowledge and information. The most important thing—the ability to bring a quality of unbiased presence to experience just as it is—is hardly even mentioned.

That is why meditation is such a useful training for therapists and healers. It teaches us to be there with our experience as it is and become more comfortable with the gaps where our identity doesn't exist. We discover that letting go of our familiar identity will not kill us. We find that pain and fear become solid and overwhelming only when we contract against them. We see that no states of mind have any finality; they become fixed only when we make up stories about what they mean. We learn to trust in the unknown as a guide to what is most fresh and alive in the moment. With this trust, therapists can begin to let go of their knowledge and let what is needed to help others emerge spontaneously from the fresh edge of the moment.

Unconditional presence promotes healing by allowing us to *see* the ways in which we are contracted and *feel* their impact on our body and on our relations with the world. It is not enough just to see, not enough just to feel. We must both see *and* feel. Of course, it may take months or years to clearly see, feel, and penetrate with awareness a pattern in which we are stuck. As the pattern becomes less solid and more transparent, gaps open up in it, and these gaps become doorways that let us tap deeper resources that pattern has been blocking.

For example, when we have shut fear out of awareness, it remains frozen deep within the body, manifesting as background anxiety, tension, worry, insecurity. When we finally bring full attention to the fear, feeling and opening to it, our larger being makes contact with the fear, perhaps for the first time. As this happens the fear starts to loosen; it cannot remain so tightly contracted in the embrace of our full, caring presence. As the fear loosens, we may also gain access to our compassion, the antidote that could allow our fear to relax even further. Of course, for deeper, older patterns that have been with us since childhood, we may have to meet them like this many times before they fully relax or transform.

When children are in pain, what they most want is this kind of presence, rather than band-aids or consolations. They want to know we are really there with them in what they are going through. That's what our wounded places most need from us as well—just to be there with them. They don't need us to say, "Things are getting better every day." The full presence of our being is healing in and of itself.

Trying to fix a problem without being fully present with it would be like trying to use drugs to create a state of health. Although drugs may relieve symptoms, relieving symptoms does not produce health. What keeps the organism healthy are the immune system and the vital resources of the body. If these are not activated, no amount of symptom relief will ever keep us healthy. Thus, certain therapeutic technologies may relieve symptoms without ever promoting real healing.

Seeking a "fix" cannot lead to genuine healing because it keeps us in the same mind-set—wanting our experience to be other than it is—that created our dis-ease in the first place. Our natural healing resources become mobilized only when we see and feel the truth—the untold suffering we cause ourselves and others by rejecting our experience, thus shutting down our capacity to be fully present. When we recognize this, our dis-ease starts to become conscious suffering. As our suffering becomes more conscious, it starts to awaken our desire and will to live in a new way.

Genuine Compassion

In opening to our experience of life as it is, we often find that it does not meet our expectations of what it should be. Perhaps we don't fit the picture in our mind of who we should be. Perhaps those we love don't measure up to our ideals. Or we find the state of the world disheartening, even shocking. Reality is continually breaking open our heart by not living up to how we would like it to be.

If we can also open to our "broken-open heart," it has a bittersweet quality. Reality never quite fits our fond hopes—that is the bitter taste. The sweetness is that when reality breaks our heart open, we discover a sweet, raw tenderness toward ourselves and the fragile beauty of life as a whole.

This is the beginning of feeling real compassion toward ourselves and others—for the difficulties we are facing in our lives. A friend who was dying of cancer tried every possible treatment she could find. Nothing worked. At first she blamed herself, but she finally realized that the greatest healing was not in curing the cancer but in coming to terms with it. We all need to heal our separation from reality and our struggle with it. The whole world is in need of that.

So the greatest difficulties we face also offer the greatest opportunities to practice unconditional presence. What is especially helpful in this practice is recognizing again and again that our experience is not as solid as we think. Indeed, nothing is what we think it to be. Meditation helps us recognize this by letting us notice and relate to the gaps or open spaces in our experience, from which genuine clarity and wisdom arise.

If we take this approach, our old wounds from the past can reveal hidden treasure. In the places where we have contracted and turned away from our experience we can begin to uncover genuine qualities of our being that have long been veiled. In the most painful corners of our experience something alive is always waiting to emerge. So whatever pain or problem we have, if it helps us find a quality of presence—where we can open to it, see it, feel it, include it, and find the truth concealed in it—*that* is our healing.

10
Vulnerability, Power, and the Healing Relationship

❖ THERE IS A CENTRAL HUMAN EXPERIENCE that will shake us to the roots and that each of us must eventually face. Nobody likes to acknowledge or talk much about it. So we usually try to ignore it, wrapping ourselves in habitual routines to avoid having to face it. Since there is no ready-made term for this experience, I will call it *the moment of world collapse*. This experience of the ground falling out from under us is at the core of both the existential and the Buddhist traditions. For existentialism, it is a source of existential anxiety, while for Buddhism, it is the beginning of a path that leads toward enlightenment, awakening, or liberation.

World collapse occurs when the props that have supported our life give way unexpectedly. Suddenly the meaning our life previously had seems to lack weight and substance and no longer nourishes us as it once did. Before, we may have been motivated by dreams of success, achievement, wealth, or simply by a desire to be loved or to provide for our family. Now, suddenly, we wonder why we're doing all of this and what it's all about. We may cast about in vain for some absolute, unwavering reason for it all, some unshakable ground, yet all we are left with is the arbitrariness of it all and our hopeless attempts to grasp onto something solid and secure.

At the same time we feel raw and shaky when our old structures fall away and we don't have anything to replace them with. Yet the tenderness and nakedness we discover here are essential qualities of being human—which we usually try to cover up and hide. When the props of our identity start to crumble, what we encounter is our *basic vulnerability.* The kind of vulnerability that accompanies moments of world collapse is one I have also come to know quite intimately through extended meditation practice. It is clear to me, as an existentially trained psychotherapist who has also practiced meditation for many years, that we cannot fully appreciate either therapy or meditation, or how they help us access deeper qualities of our nature, without taking account of the central importance of world collapse and basic vulnerability.

Existential Heroism

In the existential tradition, the feeling that accompanies moments of world collapse is called *existential anxiety* or, in Kierkegaard's words, *dread (angst)*. Existentialists regard this kind of anxiety as ontological, that is, as a response to potential *loss of being.* When we perceive the basic groundlessness of all our finite projects, our whole sense of who we are is put in question. This kind of anxiety emerges from, and is intimately connected with, the very nature of human existence. Meaning, purpose, support, direction, stability, coherence—none of these are givens on which we can securely rely. Since our mind creates them, we can just as easily see through them, or suddenly find ourselves unable to depend on them. The dread of facing death is perhaps the most dramatic instance of this loss of familiar supports and reference points.

Existential psychology makes a distinction between this kind of ontological anxiety and ordinary neurotic anxiety—about threats to our self-esteem, pleasure, or security. Ordinary anxiety is often a smoke screen that allows us to distract ourselves from the scary groundlessness that underlies our life. Worrying about what people think of us or about whether we are getting ahead, for instance, keeps us from having to face the deeper existential dread of our whole ground falling out from under us. We often seem to be in love with our neurosis because at least it occupies us and gives us something to hold on to. It gives us a sense of self—unlike those moments of world collapse, when there seems to be nothing there at all.

In the existential tradition, Sartre's notion of nausea, Camus's investigation of suicide, Kierkegaard's alienation from conventional rational, philosophical, and religious structures, and Nietzsche's attempt to create new values based on life rather than fear all grew out of a keen perception that the old structures of meaning that formerly guided and supported people's lives no longer held up. There was no longer a clear, absolute ground for human life; in Nietzsche's words, "God is dead." Existentialism developed out of this loss of an absolute, unshakable ground that justified people's lives. It sought a way to *create* meaning out of a person's own individual existence. The only authentic source of meaning was your own individual conviction, action, and choice.

Human life thus took on a heroic dimension for the existentialists, who tried to find and create their own meaning in a meaningless world. One archetype of this heroic effort was the myth of Sisyphus, as Camus wrote about it. Although the rock keeps rolling back down the hill, Sisyphus keeps rolling it up again, finding heroic meaning in his own will and determination.

From this perspective, existential anxiety is a given; there is no way to finally overcome the sense of groundlessness and dread. For there can never be a guarantee that the personal meanings you create for yourself are going to hold up for very long, especially in the ever-impending face of death. What's meaningful today is not necessarily meaningful tomorrow, and what has been meaningful throughout your whole life may not do much for you at the moment when you're dying. You may cast a look backward at the moment of death and wonder, "What have I done with my life that really matters?" Since self-created meaning cannot provide any absolute ground, *angst* is inescapable.

Before exploring the role that world collapse and basic vulnerability play in psychological healing, I would like to describe the transition I went through in shifting from the existential perspective—the heroic attempt to create my own meaning—to a more Buddhist-inspired contemplative outlook. During the early 1960s I went to live and study in Paris—when I was in my early twenties, at a time when I was extremely influenced by the existentialists. That was the place to soak up the existential flavor of the time. The existentialists were my personal heroes because the world I had grown up in didn't make much sense to me, and these were people who were at least trying to establish a new sense of meaning for themselves and the world. So I'd sit in the cafés that Sartre frequented, and I'd walk along the streets that Rilke wrote about. Even the stones, the streets, and the walls in Paris exuded a certain existential aura. I would walk along the bridges over the Seine that I imagined Camus had thought about throwing himself off. It was wonderfully romantic and painful at the same time. Yet I was in despair because I didn't find it really satisfying just to acknowledge the absurdity of the world and heroically struggle on from there.

Fortunately, just when I was starting to feel that I had rolled the rock up the hill a few too many times, I came across the teachings of Zen, which showed me a way out of the existential impasse. The real problem wasn't that human existence was absurd or that there wasn't any absolute basis for a meaningful life. The basic problem lay instead in the nature of the self we create, who we think we are. I realized, in other words, that life was not the problem, but rather that "I" was the problem. This realization made sense of things in a whole new way for me. Anxiety, meaninglessness, and despair did not have to be denied but could become stepping-stones to something deeper.

Emptiness and the Fabricated Self

Existentialism tries to fill the void that opens up in moments of world collapse through the heroic attempt to forge one's own authentic response to reality. By contrast, Buddhism does not try to fill this emptiness at all, but rather provides a way to enter into it more deeply. When I read the playful stories about the Zen masters, it seemed that they had found a way to actually enjoy and even celebrate this emptiness. This led to a radical shift in my perspective. I could see the despair of world collapse, in the Buddhist context, as one moment in a larger journey of transformation, rather than as a final or ultimate condition.

Like existentialism, Buddhism developed as a response to the experience of world collapse. The Buddha himself, as an Indian prince, was born into a world of coherent social traditions and meanings. His life had been preprogrammed for him by his father and his social caste. Although he was supposed to inherit his father's kingdom, he found his life permanently altered by four moments of world collapse—when he saw an old person, a sick person, a dying person, and a wandering holy man. The shock of these encounters, which undermined the meaning that had supported his life until then, started him on his own personal quest to find out what really mattered. After trying the various ascetic practices of his day, he finally decided to sit still in meditation until he got to the bottom of things. One of his major discoveries was the central fact I'd like to emphasize here: the illusory nature of the conventional self. He saw that all his ideas about himself had no ground, no substance, no solidity, no continuity. In fact, they only prevented him from having a direct, immediate experience of himself and life.

As Western psychology also shows, the conventional self is not something given in the nature of things, but is, rather, a construct. We fabricate our notion of who we are out of "self-representations"— images of ourselves internalized from our early interactions with our parents and social environment. Our consciousness comes to identify itself with various objects of consciousness—ideas about ourselves and the world, the work we do, the things we own, our personal history, dramas, and achievements, the intimate relationships we hold most dear. We hold on to all these things because they are supports for our identity, because they make us feel that we exist, that we are real.

The word *identity* comes from a Latin word that means "the same." Maintaining an identity literally means that we are trying to establish some kind of sameness from day to day. Our identity is what holds us together, and we use it to avoid the frightening experience of our world collapsing. Yet identification is a form of false consciousness. Our fabricated identity can never be real, because it is based on identifying with things that are extrinsic to us. Therefore, it can never provide true satisfaction or security.

Why do we need to identify so tightly with things that are not who we are—beliefs, images, possessions, behaviors, social status? Here is where the Buddha inquired more deeply than the existentialists. Through his meditation experience, he discovered the nature of consciousness to be a radical openness, wide open to the whole of reality.

Of course, Sartre also described consciousness as a no-thingness. Yet in his view the human being is destined to feel this as a lack, in comparison with the apparently solid rockness of a rock or treeness of a tree (what he called the *en-soi*, the in-itselfness of things). The tree is clearly just what it is. But what is a human being? My father is who he is, a tree is what it is, yet who am I by comparison? We would like to possess the same kind of solidity that we tend to perceive in the Other. "They seem to have no trouble being what they are, so why is it so hard for me to be what I am?"

Yet in envying the apparently solid realness of Other, we fail to appreciate how our awareness is a kind of illuminating presence that allows things to stand out and be revealed as what they are—in their suchness. We regard our spaciousness and nonsolidity as a deficiency, something that should be filled up or nailed down. Yet the very fact that we can take things into us and let them affect us, or see Other as solid at all, means that we ourselves are not solid, but rather empty like a mirror, open like space.

Here is where meditation practice can be extremely helpful—in helping us appreciate our nonsolidity as a powerful clarity and presence, rather than a terrifying deficiency. Meditation allows you to observe the mind in its attempts to grasp onto the stream of passing thoughts, feelings, and perceptions, or identify with them, yet never getting anywhere with this. You keep trying to come to some conclusion about things, but every position the mind takes is succeeded by a different one a few moments later. You find that you can't hold on to anything. This provides a direct experience of the lack of solidity of the self.

Yet this need not lead to existential dread. When you first learn to meditate, you find yourself constantly trying to do something with your thoughts—identify with them or disidentify with them, fight them or make love to them, own them or disown them. But as you continue to meditate, you find it's impossible to maintain this grasping and rejecting one hundred percent of the time. You discover moments of space between each mental fixation, where something different, something unknown is happening, which is not grasping. Gradually you find you can relax a little into these gaps. As you keep sitting, relaxing into these open spaces, you discover the larger ground of awareness and peace in which grasping takes place—what we could call the *open ground* of our being. This discovery points toward a liberation that lies far beyond the existential freedom to make meaningful choices. It is the beginning of a path beyond existential despair.

Many of us recognize that life is a continual process of moving forward, and that it's impossible to move gracefully through life unless we can let go of where we have already been. Though we may know this rationally, it is still hard it to let go, and still painful when old structures collapse on their own, without consulting us first. The crumbling of our own identity right before our eyes is especially painful. Yet since life is continual flux, this means that we must be prepared to go through a series of identity crises. Especially in this era of advanced future shock, when the meanings holding people's lives together erode ever more rapidly, identity crises inevitably escalate at an ever-increasing rate.

Meditation is a way of learning to accept and welcome this, by letting go and falling apart gracefully. As we sit, we can see that most of our thoughts are about ourselves; in fact, they are our way of trying to keep ourselves together from moment to moment. When we no longer reinforce these thoughts, the self we've been trying to hold together in a nice, neat package begins unraveling right before our eyes. As soon as we stop trying to glue it together, it quickly comes unglued. This allows us to see how we are constructing and maintaining it, and how that causes endless tension and stress.

The nonexistence of a solid, continuous self-identity is not an idea unique to Buddhism. We find it in the Western tradition as well, though it develops out of philosophical analysis rather than meditative practice. David Hume, for instance, observed that we can only observe various objects of consciousness, never a separate subject: "For my part, when I enter most intimately into what I call myself, I always stumble on some particular perception or other. I never catch *myself*." William James found that the continuous self was a belief constructed out of the endless sequence of thoughts overlapping each other and, in the process, passing along an illusion of ownership (see the James quotation on p. 39). This trick that each thought plays—immediately taking up the baton passed on by the preceding expiring thought and handing it on to the subsequent arising thought—creates the illusion of a central thinker lying above or behind the mindstream. Sartre also wrote about the illusoriness of the managerial ego: "Everything happens as if consciousness were hypnotized by this ego which it has established, which it has constructed, becoming absorbed in it as if to make the ego its guardian and law."

Meditation and the Path beyond Dread

Yet we might well wonder, "So what if our identity is an arbitrary construction—how does that help relieve anxiety and suffering?" Having discovered the insubstantiality of the ego identity, we still need a path that can help us discover what is on the other side of our conventional, limited notions of self. Otherwise, we could easily fall into nihilistic despair.

Similarly, in psychotherapy it is not enough just to help people deconstruct their old false self. It is also crucial to help them see what lies beyond it. As a meditator, I'm keenly aware of the beauty of the first moment when a client comes to realize, "I don't know who I am." I consider these moments sacred, because they potentially mark the birth of a whole new way of being. The realization "I don't know who I am" emerges at a point in therapy when the old structures have started to collapse and fall away under the weight of greater consciousness, yet before some new direction has emerged. This leaves the client in an in-between zone, which is the threshold of new birth.

If we can stay present and not recoil from the emptiness we encounter when our familiar sense of self breaks down, we eventually discover not just a meaningless void but a fresher quality of presence that feels awake, alive, and liberating. But because conventional therapists are often unfamiliar with the path that leads through emptiness, they often try to steer their clients away from such moments, or else smooth them over. There is little in Western culture or Western psychology to prepare people for dealing with moments of identity loss. Because most Western therapies are based on theories of *personality*, they are geared toward knowing, rather than not-knowing. An unspoken assumption in the therapeutic world is that we should always know who we are, and if we don't, that's a real problem.

So when an old maladaptive identity starts to break down and the client finds nothing to hold on to, this may be frightening for client and therapist alike. What do I as a therapist do at that point? Should I try to shore up the old structure or patch together a new one? Or is it all right to let the client dangle in space on the edge of the abyss? At times like this I rely on my own realization that none of us really knows who we are, that this is the nature of our being, that if we have a true self at all, it somehow lies in the heart of the unknowingness that opens up when we inquire deeply into our experience, and that if we can hang out on the edge of this unknown, we may discover how to let ourselves be, without having to be some*thing*.

In providing me with that realization, meditation has also furnished a context for working with these moments in therapy. I once had a powerful experience of world collapse during a three-month meditation retreat with my teacher. About six weeks into it, I found the patterns and meanings holding me together radically falling away, at a level of intensity that reminded me of my old existential days, magnified a few extra degrees. I realized that I didn't really believe in the self I was holding on to for dear life, even though it was a better self than I'd ever had before. And yet, if I let go of myself, what then? I knew I would fall, and I didn't know where I would land.

It was extremely helpful to work with that fear in an environment of meditation. I found that I *could* let my self fall apart. The atmosphere of the practice environment encouraged that in a friendly sort of way—other people were also practicing, and the whole purpose of being there was to let your world collapse, to keep going, and to let something new and unexpected happen. I don't want to say it was "meaningful" because I didn't necessarily find some new meaning there, something that I could hold on to and use as the basis for constructing a new and improved self-structure. And yet neither did I fall back into a sense of utter meaninglessness or existential despair.

Letting go of the need to be some*thing*, giving up the struggle to hold on to the old meanings that support our identity, if only briefly, allows a clearing to open in the mind. And this in turn reveals a basic intelligence and well-being, known as *buddha-nature* in the Buddhist tradition—an essential clarity, transparency, and warmth intrinsic to human consciousness. This is not the neutral or scary emptiness that existentialism addresses, but a fullness of presence whose brightness and sharpness cuts through confusion, rationalization, projection, self-deception, and all the other tricks we play on ourselves.

Therapists often try to help their clients move away from the utter vulnerability of not having anything to identify with and not knowing who they are. But this vulnerability is an important stepping-stone that can lead to a deeper recognition of what it means to be human.

As humans, we are the animals that stand erect with a soft front, fully exposing our heart and belly to the world. We take the world into us through this soft front. To have sensitive skin means that it can be easily pierced. This literal vulnerability is reflected in our psychological makeup as a basic tenderness and receptivity that often feels raw and shaky when we first encounter it. In touching this vulnerability, clients start to connect with their own living heart, which can shift the whole way they relate to their problems. In my work, I usually don't have to try to make someone feel their vulnerability; it usually comes up on its own.

It's interesting that the word *vulnerability* usually has a pejorative meaning in our culture. That's because we associate it with loss of power and strength. If we say that someone is vulnerable, this usually means he is weak, overly sensitive, and easily hurt. But it's important to distinguish our basic human vulnerability from the fragility of the ego identity, that brittle shell we construct around our soft receptive core where the world flows into us. Feeling essentially tender at heart, we usually hide our vulnerability behind a facade or mask that puts distance between us and the world. But the shell we construct is fragile and always susceptible to being punctured, if not demolished (in moments of world collapse). Other people can usually see through our facades, and death or some other vicissitude will eventually break through this shell. Continually having to maintain and patch up our shell leaves us fragile and defensive—and *this* is the vulnerability that we usually associate in our culture with weakness. In fact, that kind of brittleness *is* weak; continually having to be on guard is a position of weakness.

Power and Vulnerability

Learning to accept and relate to our vulnerability, by contrast, is a source of real inner power and strength. Fake power of the macho kind—which is really a form of control, tightness, and tension—has no real strength in it. As an attempt to have power *over*, it is top-heavy and thus forever in danger of being toppled. Trying to maintain control in this way keeps us highly vulnerable in the fragile ego sense. Since life constantly challenges our attempts to control it, the amount of energy we put into guarding and defending only drains our strength away.

The power that comes from relaxing into the open ground of being and making friends with the rawness and vulnerability we find there is more grounded and real. This kind of strength is powerful in the way that water is. Water is the softest element, in that anything can penetrate it; it shapes itself to any mold and follows any contour. And yet, as the *Tao Teh Ching* points out, nothing surpasses it for wearing down what is hard and tough. The way that leads from basic vulnerability to genuine power lies through gentleness and loving-kindness, which help soothe the panic that surrounds our vulnerability. Indeed, kindness and gentleness are our most natural response to vulnerability—as when we see a young child, an animal, or a close friend in pain. Not so, usually, with ourselves, strangely enough. Somehow we have to *learn* to be kind to ourselves.

I would like to illustrate this through a case example. A client in his mid-thirties, call him Ray, came to see me with the presenting problems of exhibitionism and alcoholism, as well as a fear that he was homosexual because of problems relating to women. His mother had abandoned him at age six, and he'd been adopted by an uncle. The uncle was a macho type who was not able to be kind or tender with him. Nonetheless, he came to identify strongly with the uncle.

I've chosen this client to discuss because all his symptoms kept pointing back to the issue of vulnerability in one way or another. His exhibitionism was one of those strangely appropriate symptoms that are perfectly symbolic. It was his way of exposing his vulnerability while not having to give up control. His fear of being homosexual was connected with fear of his tenderness. His alcoholism—getting drunk and busting loose—was a way in which his aliveness was trying to break free from his overcontrolling ego. And his coldness toward women grew out of a fear of being at their mercy, being in a vulnerable position again.

Ray's way of feeling strong and manly was to be on edge all the time. Those were his words—"I'm always on edge." One way he conveyed this was through an image of driving a car on the freeway stuck behind people who were driving too slowly. This portrayed his frustration with how he was driving himself. Yet keeping himself on edge was also a way of trying to keep himself together, stay in control, and feel like a man.

What I did with Ray was to hang out with him in the raw places that came up for him as we worked together. I never introduced the word *vulnerability*—that came from him. But this side of him clearly wanted to be recognized and included in his life. It was important for him to discover that vulnerable didn't have to mean victimized. One day he said, "It's okay to be hurt. That doesn't mean that I'm bad or unlovable." And he began to see how he created anger and struggle with women in order to feel strong rather than tender.

Another image that Ray had of being on edge was hanging on to the side of a cliff. We often came back to that sense of holding on to a cliff's edge, and what that was like for him. A third image was of being out on a limb—how he felt when he was in love. If his love wasn't fully reciprocated, or if his lover left him, he was afraid he would fall into an abyss and be swallowed up by dreaded feelings of terror and emptiness. Once when he felt out on a limb, I asked him to shift his attention to the feeling of "nothing there if she leaves me." Staying present with the emptiness, without judging it, reacting against it, or drawing conclusions about himself from it, he experienced an inner warmth, which was all red and yellow, arising in that void. This experience helped undermine the equation in his mind between vulnerability and being a victim.

Ray was in a classic macho bind—he could feel strong only by maintaining tight control, which kept him forever on edge. Yet an occasional helpless look in his eyes, his longing to be spontaneous (which he acted out through getting drunk and busting loose), as well as his willingness to keep coming and working on his problems, revealed a deep tenderness that was trying to find expression. What he needed, without realizing it, was to have his vulnerability held—something that had never happened before in his life. I don't mean that he needed to be literally held, but rather that he needed to have his vulnerability seen, recognized, and accepted, that is, *held in awareness*. After all, our larger awareness is the ultimate holding environment that can allow us to embrace all our different feelings and experiences, so that they no longer have to terrorize or overwhelm us.

What I most remember from the time Ray and I spent together is that sense of being there together, hanging out on the edge of that cliff—exploring what it was like to hold on for dear life, what it was like to let go and fall into the void, and what it was like to have his feelings held in a friendly, open space of awareness and compassion. Through this work, Ray came to realize that vulnerability did not have to mean annihilation, disgrace, humiliation, dishonor, or abandonment. He discovered to his great surprise that it was possible to be gentle and strong at the same time. Eventually he was able to overcome his alcoholic binges and enter a marriage partnership, although his marriage also opened up further levels of vulnerability for him to face.

Of course someone could object: "Maybe it's all right for people with intact egos to open up their vulnerability, but what about people who can't hold themselves together in the first place because their world is always collapsing?" I would work with clients with a weak ego structure differently from those who have an intact set of defenses. If they are continually falling apart, then my first concern is to help them develop firmer inner support, self-confidence, and self-respect. If the conventional ego is ultimately a fiction in *absolute* terms, it still has *relative* usefulness, especially for those whose sense of self is weak or damaged. Once there is some sense of support and confidence, then it becomes more possible to open to the feelings of vulnerability that go along with being open. Establishing this kind of inner trust and friendliness is especially important with highly disturbed clients, so that their vulnerability is not a constant source of panic.

The more therapists distrust their own vulnerability, the more likely they are to worry, "What will happen if I let clients face their existential void? They might go over the edge!" In fact, Ray had "gone over the edge" earlier in his life. Once when he had been high on drugs, he felt his whole world fall apart and checked into a mental hospital for several weeks. That reinforced his feeling of "I can't go near that scary place again. It's off limits." But directly experiencing our fear or vulnerability is not what causes this kind of "freak-out." The real problem is how we react to those feelings and freeze into panic about them. This is like hitting an icy patch on the road and then slamming on the brakes, causing the car to go out of control. What is important is how people relate to their vulnerability and fear. And this is where meditation can be of particular value, especially for therapists. If therapists can learn to work directly with their own vulnerability and loss of identity, they are less likely to steer their clients away from their raw edges, out of their own anxiety.

Meditation teaches us to be spacious, kind, and gentle through letting our world collapse and discovering that this does not kill us but makes us stronger. Through facing our raw edges, we can become more compassionate with others and can better help them to accept their vulnerability as well. In the Buddhist perspective, our basic vulnerability is the seed of enlightenment already present within us. It is said that when we let this tender heart fully ripen and develop, it becomes a powerful force that can cut through all the inner barriers we have constructed. In its fully developed form tender heart becomes transformed into awakened heart, *bodhichitta*.

The mutual vulnerability between two people who meet each other transparently—client and therapist, lover and beloved, guru and disciple—is what allows them to affect each other deeply. If we look at the god and goddess of love in Greek mythology, we see Aphrodite associated with instruments of war and Eros armed with arrows. This suggests that we can only truly love if we are willing to let ourselves be wounded. In this sense, vulnerability means "able to connect." As we will explore further in part 3, this capacity to be vulnerable—to the raw edges in our own experience—is what allows us to truly connect with ourselves, with others, and with life itself.

11

Psychotherapy as a Practice of Love

Genuine psychotherapeutic eros must be a selflessness and reverence
before the patient's existence and uniqueness.

—MEDARD BOSS

✦ FREUD ONCE ADMITTED in a letter to Jung that "psychoanalysis is essentially a cure through love." Yet while many psychotherapists might privately agree that love has some kind of role in the healing process, the word *love* is curiously absent from most of the therapeutic literature. The same is true for the word *heart*. Not only is this term missing from the psychological literature, but the tone of the literature itself also lacks heart.

My interest in the place of heart in psychotherapy developed out of my experience with meditation. Although Western thought often defines mind in terms of reason and heart in terms of feeling, in Buddhism *heart* and *mind* can both be referred to by the same term (*chitta* in Sanskrit). Indeed, when Tibetan Buddhists refer to mind, they often point to their chest. Mind in this sense is not thinking mind but rather big mind—a direct knowing of reality that is basically open and friendly toward what is. Centuries of meditators have found this openness to be the central feature of human consciousness.

Heart and Basic Goodness

Heart, then, is a direct presence that allows a complete attunement with reality. In this sense, it has nothing to do with sentimentality.

Heart is the capacity to touch and be touched, to reach out and let in. Our language expresses this twofold activity of the heart, which is like a swinging door that opens in both directions. We say, "My heart went out to him," or "I took her into my heart." Like the physical organ with its systole and diastole, the heart-mind involves both receptive letting in, or letting be, and active going out to meet, or being-with. In their different ways, both psychological and spiritual work remove the barriers to these two movements of the heart, like oiling the door so that it can open freely in both directions.

What shuts down the heart more than anything is not letting ourselves have our own experience, but instead judging it, criticizing it, or trying to make it different from what it is. We often imagine there is something wrong with us if we feel angry, needy, dependent, lonely, confused, sad, or scared. We place conditions on ourselves and our experience: "If I feel like this, there must be something wrong with me. . . . I can only accept myself if my experience conforms to my standard of how I should be."

Psychological work, when practiced in a larger spiritual context, can help people discover that it is possible to be unconditional with themselves—to welcome their experience and hold it with understanding and compassion, whether or not they like it at any given moment. What initially makes this possible is the therapist's capacity to show unconditional warmth, concern, and friendliness toward the client's experience, no matter what the client is going through. Most people in our culture did not receive this kind of unconditional acceptance in their childhood. So they internalized the conditions their parents or society placed on them: "You are an acceptable human being only if you measure up to our standards." And because they continue to place these same conditions on themselves, they remain alienated from themselves.

The Dalai Lama and many other Tibetan teachers have spoken of their great surprise and shock at discovering just how much self-hatred Westerners carry around inside them. Such an intense degree of self-blame is not found in traditional Buddhist cultures, where there is an understanding that the heart-mind, also known as buddha-nature, is unconditionally open, compassionate, and wholesome. Since we are all embryonic buddhas, why would anyone want to hate themselves?

Chögyam Trungpa described the essence of our nature in terms of *basic goodness*. In using this term, he did not mean that people are only morally good—which would be naive, considering all the evil that humans perpetrate in this world. Rather, basic goodness refers to our primordial nature, which is unconditionally wholesome because it is intrinsically attuned to reality. This primordial kind of goodness goes beyond conventional notions of good and bad. It lies much deeper than conditioned personality and behavior, which are always a mix of positive and negative tendencies. From this perspective, all the evil and destructive behavior that goes on in our world is the result of people failing to recognize the fundamental wholesomeness of their essential nature.

Meditation, Psychotherapy, and Unconditional Friendliness

While studying Rogerian therapy in graduate school, I used to be intrigued, intimidated, and puzzled by Carl Rogers's term "unconditional positive regard." Although it sounded appealing as an ideal therapeutic stance, I found it hard to put into practice. First of all, there was no specific training for it. And since Western psychology had not provided me any understanding of heart, or the intrinsic goodness underlying psychopathology, I was unclear just where unconditional positive regard should be directed. It was only in turning to the meditative traditions that I came to appreciate the unconditional goodness at the core of being human, and this in turn helped me understand the possibility of unconditional love and its role in the healing process.

The Buddhist counterpart of unconditional positive regard is loving-kindness (*maitri* in Sanskrit, *metta* in Pali). Loving-kindness is unconditional friendliness—a quality of allowing and welcoming human beings and their experience. Yet before I could genuinely express this kind of acceptance toward others, I first had to discover what it meant for myself. Meditation is what allowed me to do this.

Meditation cultivates unconditional friendliness through teaching you how to *just be*, without doing anything, without holding on to anything, without trying to think good thoughts, get rid of bad thoughts, or achieve a pure state of mind. This is a radical practice. There is nothing else like it. Normally we do everything we can to avoid just being. When left alone with ourselves, without a project to occupy us, we become nervous. We start judging ourselves or thinking about what we *should* be doing or feeling. We start putting conditions on ourselves, trying to arrange our experience so that it measures up to our inner standards. Since this inner struggle is so painful, we are always looking for something to distract us from being with ourselves.

In meditation practice, you work directly with your confused mind-states, without waging crusades against any aspect of your experience. You let all your tendencies arise, without trying to screen anything out, manipulate experience in any way, or measure up to any ideal standard. Allowing yourself the space to be as you are—letting whatever arises arise, without fixation on it, and coming back to simple presence—this is perhaps the most loving and compassionate way you can treat yourself. It helps you make friends with the whole range of your experience.

As you simplify in this way, you start to feel your very presence as wholesome in and of itself. You don't have to prove that you are good. You discover a self-existing sanity that lies deeper than all thought or feeling. You appreciate the beauty of just being awake, responsive, and open to life. Appreciating this basic, underlying sense of goodness is the birth of *maitri*—unconditional friendliness toward yourself.

The discovery of basic goodness can be likened to clarifying muddy water—an ancient metaphor from the Taoist and Buddhist traditions. Water is naturally pure and clear, though its turbulence may stir up mud from below. Our awareness is like that, essentially clear and open, but muddied with the turbulence of conflicting thoughts and emotions. If we want to clarify the water, what else is there to do but let the water sit? Usually we want to put our hands in the water and do something with the dirt—struggle with it, try to change it, fix it, sanitize it—but this only stirs up more mud. "Maybe I can get rid of my sadness by thinking positive thoughts." But then the sadness sinks deeper and hardens into depression. "Maybe I'll get my anger out, show people how I feel." But this only spreads the dirt around. The water of awareness regains its clarity through seeing the muddiness for what it is—recognizing the turbulence of thought and feeling as noise or static, rather than as who we really are. When we stop reacting to it, which only stirs it up all the more, the mud can settle.

This core discovery enabled me to extend this same kind of unconditional friendliness toward my clients. When I first started practicing therapy and found myself disliking certain clients or certain things about them, I felt guilty or hypocritical. But eventually I came to understand this differently. Unconditional love or loving-kindness did not mean that I always had to like my clients, any more than I liked all the twists and turns of my own scheming mind. Rather, it meant providing an accommodating space in which their knots could begin to unwind.

Part of what had been confusing for me was that I identified unconditional positive regard with Carl Rogers's personality and nondirective way of responding to people. I finally realized that unconditional friendliness did not mean always having to be nurturing, nondirective, or nice. In truth, I often don't like to be nice. Sometimes I want to confront clients in a more challenging way. When I got out from under my client-centered superego, which whispered in my ear that I should be like Carl Rogers and always have positive feelings toward my clients, I was actually able to be more fully present with them. The more I could let myself *be*, the more I could be with others and let *them* be *themselves*.

It was a great relief to realize that I did not have to love or accept unconditionally that which is conditioned—another's personality. Rather, unconditional friendliness is a natural response to that which is itself unconditional—the basic goodness and open heart in others, beneath all their defenses, rationalizations, and pretenses. Unconditional love is not a sentiment but a willingness to be open. It is not a love of personality but the love of being, grounded in the recognition of the unconditional goodness of the human heart.

Fortunately, unconditional friendliness does not mean having to like what is going on. Instead, it means allowing whatever is there to be there, and inviting it to reveal itself more fully. In trying to help clients develop unconditional friendliness toward a difficult feeling, I often say, "You don't have to like it. You can just let it be there, and make a place for your dislike of it as well."

The metaphor of letting the dirt settle out of the water also applies to therapeutic work. At its best, therapy does not involve analyzing problems or coming up with solutions. When a therapist can extend unconditional friendliness toward whatever is arising in his or her clients—letting it be and being with it—this helps them settle down with themselves and their experience. Then they can take the next step—meeting their experience fully, which invites what is going on under the surface to be revealed and met.

The health of living organisms is maintained through the free-flowing circulation of energy. We see this in the endless cycles and flow of water, the cradle of life, which purifies itself through circulating, rising from the oceans, falling on the mountains, and rushing in clear streams back to the sea. Similarly, the circulation of blood in the body brings new life in the form of oxygen to the cells, while allowing the removal of toxins from the body. Any interference with circulation is the beginning of disease.

Similarly, when we do not recognize our basic goodness, self-doubt blooms like algae in water, clogging up the natural flow of self-love that keeps us healthy. When loving-kindness does not circulate throughout our system, blockages and armoring build up and we get sick, psychologically or physically. When a therapist extends *maitri*, unconditional friendliness, toward a client's whole range of experience and very being, this begins to penetrate the clouds of self-judgment, so that person's life energy can circulate freely again.

This understanding allowed me to approach psychotherapy in a new way. I found that if I could connect with the basic goodness in those I worked with—the underlying, often hidden longing and will to be who they are and meet life fully—not just as an ideal or as positive thinking but as a living reality, then I could start to forge an alliance with the essential core of health within them. I could help them meet and go through whatever they were experiencing, as frightening or horrifying as it might seem, just as I myself had done on the meditative cushion. Orienting myself toward the basic goodness hidden beneath their conflicts and struggles, I could contact the deeper aliveness circulating within them and between the two of us in the present moment. This made possible a heart connection that promoted real change.

I was inspired in this approach by the example of the bodhisattvas in Buddhism, who, in their commitment to help all sentient beings, join compassion with the discriminating wisdom that sees through people's suffering to the embryonic buddha within. For me, seeing the buddha in others is not a way of denying or minimizing their suffering or conflicts. Rather, in the words of Robert Thurman, "A bodhisattva sees simultaneously how a being is free from suffering as well as seeing it with its suffering, and that gives the bodhisattva great compassion that is truly effective." When bodhisattvas engender this kind of all-seeing compassion, according to the *Vimalakirti Sutra*, they "generate the love that is truly a refuge for all living beings; the love that is peaceful because free of grasping; the love that is not feverish, because free of passions; the love that accords with reality because it contains equanimity; the love that has no presumption because it has eliminated attachment and aversion; the love that is nondual because it is involved neither with the external nor the internal; the love that is imperturbable because totally ultimate."

The Aikido of Therapy

The poignant truth about human suffering is that all our neurotic, self-destructive patterns are twisted forms of basic goodness, which lies hidden within them. For example, a little girl with an alcoholic father sees his unhappiness and wants to make him happy so that she can experience unconditional love—the love of being—flowing between them. Unfortunately, out of her desire to please him, she also winds up bending herself out of shape, disregarding her own needs and blaming herself for failing to make him happy. As a result, she ends up with a harsh inner critic and repeatedly reenacts a neurotic victim role with the men in her life. Although her fixation on trying to please is misguided, it originally arose out of a spark of generosity and caring for her father.

Just as muddy water contains clear water within it when the dirt settles out, all our negative tendencies reveal a spark of basic goodness and intelligence at their core, which is usually obscured by our habitual tendencies. Within our anger, for instance, there may be an arrow-like straightforwardness that can be a real gift when communicated without attack or blame. Our passivity may contain a capacity for acceptance and letting things be. And our self-hatred often contains a desire to destroy those elements of our personality that oppress us and prevent us from being fully ourselves. Since every negative or self-defeating behavior is but a distorted form of our larger intelligence, we don't have to struggle against this dirt that muddies the water of our being.

With this understanding, psychological work becomes like aikido, the martial art that involves flowing with the attack, rather than against it. By recognizing the deeper, positive urge hidden within our ego strategies, we no longer have to treat them as an enemy. After all, the strategies of the ego are all ways of *trying to be.* They were the best we could do as a child. And they're not all that bad, considering that they were dreamed up by the mind of a child. Realizing that we did the best we could under the circumstances, and seeing ego as an imitation of the real thing—an attempt to be ourselves in a world that did not recognize, welcome, or support our being—helps us have more understanding and compassion for ourselves.

Our ego itself is testimony to the force of love. It developed as a way to keep going in the face of perceived threats to our existence, primarily lack of love. In the places where love was missing, we built ego defenses. So every time we enact one of our defensive behaviors, we are also implicitly paying homage to love as the most important thing.

As a therapist, meditation was my aikido teacher. As I sat on the meditation cushion with a whole range of "pathological" mind-states passing through my awareness, I began to see depression, paranoia, obsession, and addiction as nothing more than the changing weather of the mind. These mind-states did not belong to me in particular or mean anything about who I was. Recognizing this helped me relax with the whole spectrum of my experience and meet it more inquisitively.

This helped me relax with my clients' mind-states as well. In working with someone's terror, I could honor it as the intense experience it was, without letting it unsettle me. I also took it as an opportunity to meet and work with my own fear once again. Or if I was helping someone explore an empty, lonely place inside, this gave me a chance to check in with that part of myself as well. It became clear that there was only one mind, though it may appear in many guises. While this might sound strange and mystical, I mean it in a very practical sense: the client's awareness and mine are two ends of one continuum when we are working together. Fear is essentially fear, self-doubt is self-doubt, blocked desire is blocked desire—though these may take on a variety of forms and meanings for different individuals. Realizing that I shared one awareness with the people I worked with allowed me to keep my heart open instead of retreating into a position of clinical distance.

When two people meet and connect, they share the same presence of awareness, and there is no way to divide it neatly into "your awareness" and "my awareness." I am not speaking here about losing my conventional boundaries or identifying with clients' problems, but rather about letting the other person's experience resonate in and through me. I find that I most enjoy my work and am most helpful when I can respond to the other person's work as part of our journey in common—toward discovering an authentic ground of human presence amidst the turbulent crosscurrents of the mind.

12

Depression as a Loss of Heart

❖ DEPRESSION IS PERHAPS the most widespread psychological problem of modern times, afflicting people in both chronic low-grade forms and more acute attacks that are completely debilitating. By framing depression as a "mental illness" to dispose of as quickly as possible, the psychiatric profession and the culture at large make it difficult to approach this experience with curiosity and interest, or to find any meaning in it. While there is certainly a somatic component of depression that can be usefully addressed through drugs, exercise, lifestyle changes, diet, herbs, or biofeedback, the focus on simply getting rid of depression prevents us from recognizing it as a potential teacher that can convey an important message about our relationship with ourselves, the world, or life as a whole. If we want to *heal* depression, instead of just suppressing it, we need to approach it not just as an affliction but as an opportunity to free ourselves from certain obstacles that prevent us from living more fully.

In the simplest human terms, depression can be understood as a loss of heart—our basic openness and responsiveness to reality. Since this openness to reality, which, in Buddhist terms, is "unborn and unceasing," allows us to be intelligently attuned to life and grateful for the wonder of existence, it is the basis of sanity and well-being. If we construct elaborate systems of defenses to buffer us from reality, this is but further testimony to the raw, responsive quality of the open mind and heart that lies behind these defenses. The basic goodness of the human heart—in its intrinsic responsiveness to life—is unconditional. It is not something we have to achieve or prove.

The Genesis of Depressions: Bitterness toward What Is

Depression is a symptom that arises when we cannot feel the goodness and aliveness of our heart. It is a feeling of weight and oppression that often contains suppressed anger and resentment. Instead of taking a defiant or fluid expression, this anger is muted and frozen into bitterness. Reality takes on a bitter taste. Depressed people hold this bitterness inside, chew it over, and make themselves sick with it. Having lost touch with their own basic goodness, they become convinced that they or the world are basically bad.

This loss of heart usually follows from a deep sense of sorrow or defeat, which may stem from specific losses: loss of a loved one, a career, cherished illusions, material possessions, or self-esteem. Or there may be a more global sense of defeat that has persisted since childhood. These losses tend to undermine the stable reference points that people count on to provide security, meaning, or support for their lives. Depressed people take this loss personally. They blame themselves for the lack of love in their family of origin, for failing to save their mother or please their father, for their difficulty finding satisfaction in work or intimate relationships, for the way their life has not turned out as planned. They feel a sense of powerlessness, loss of control, and pervasive distrust.

Two elements are at work here: a sorrow that stems from something missing in their lives, and a belief that this is their fault, that there is something basically wrong with them, and that there is nothing they can do about it. When people imagine that their sorrow and helplessness are signs of something wrong with them, it becomes too painful to open and relate to these feelings. So they turn away from their pain. The pain begins to congeal, and this is when depression starts to set in.

The Flight from Emptiness

While depression is an extreme reaction to loss, meditation practice reveals that the stable reference points we rely on for security are actually slipping away all the time. Buddhist psychology describes this situation in terms of the "three marks of existence"—three unavoidable facts of life that shape the basic context in which human existence unfolds.

The first mark of existence is *impermanence*—the fact that nothing ever stays the same. On the outer plane, our bodies and the physical world are continually changing, while on the inner plane our mental and emotional states are ceaselessly shifting and passing away. Every mind-state brings with it a new take on reality, only to be replaced minutes later by a somewhat different take. No state of mind is ever complete or final.

The second mark of existence, often termed *egolessness*, follows from this all-pervasive impermanence. Like everything else, the self we consider ourselves to be is in constant flux. While it may be useful to speak of a functional ego structure as an explanatory concept, it is impossible to pin down, locate, or establish a substantial, continuous self-entity in any concrete, definitive way. If we see this as a threat, we may panic, but if we can understand it as a gateway into a larger truth, it can give rise to profound relief.

The third mark of existence is that human life always entails some kind of unsatisfactoriness or *pain*—the pain of birth, old age, sickness, and death; the pain of trying to hold on to things that change; the pain of not getting what you want; the pain of getting what you don't want; and the pain of being conditioned by circumstances beyond your control. Because nothing in life is ever final or complete, everything is in flux, and we cannot even control what happens to us, dependable satisfaction remains as elusive as a rainbow in the sky.

These three marks all point to a more fundamental condition of existence, known as *emptiness* in the Buddhist tradition. *Emptiness* is a term that points to the ungraspable, unfathomable nature of everything. Nothing can be grasped as a solid object that will provide enduring, unshakable meaning, satisfaction, or security. Nothing is ever what we expect, hope, or believe it to be. We marry the person of our dreams and find out that marriage does not yield the predictable happiness we had imagined. We spend a fortune on a new car, and three weeks later no longer find it all that exciting. We achieve a major career success and discover that it does not deliver the fulfillment we had hoped for. Moreover, we can never get a firm grip on what we are doing here, what we ultimately want, what life is all about, or where it is going. All of these experiences point to the truth of emptiness—the fact that there is no way to carve anything solid out of the flow of reality or pin down any part of it as "just *this*, only *this*, forever *this*."

From the perspective of trying to get somewhere or establish security, emptiness seems frightening and disheartening. So we can understand various forms of psychopathology as reactions against emptiness and the three marks of existence. The paranoid resents his vulnerability and tries to blame others for it: "Who's doing this to me? Is everyone out to get me?" The sociopath tries to gain the upper hand over the slipperiness of existence. The schizoid and catatonic simply shut down, as an outright refusal to be susceptible to life's vicissitudes. Narcissism is a dogged attempt to solidify a self at any cost. And depression results from blaming ourselves for the way things are, for the sorrow we feel when we discover life slipping through our fingers.

Depression starts creeping up on us the moment we imagine there is something wrong with us because we cannot keep pain at bay, because we feel vulnerable or sad, because we cannot rest on our laurels, because we do not achieve total fulfillment through work, relationships, or any other finite worldly arrangement, or because we sense the hollowness of our self-created identity. If we were to look more deeply into any of these experiences, it could help us awaken to the essential openness of our nature, which is the only real source of happiness and joy. But depression takes a different route—blaming and recriminating when we cannot control reality. And this inevitably shuts down our capacity to respond and feel grateful for the beauty of life just as it is.

Emptiness—the ungraspable, open-ended nature of reality—need not be depressing. For it is what allows life to keep creating and recreating itself anew in each moment. And this makes creativity, expansiveness, growth, and real wisdom possible. If we regard our intrinsic lack of solidity as a problem or deficiency to overcome, this only turns against ourselves. We fall prey to our "inner critic"—that voice that continually reminds us we are not good enough. We come to regard the three marks of existence as evidence for the prosecution in an ongoing inner trial, where our inner critic presides as prosecutor and judge. And, imagining that the critic's punitive views are equivalent to reality, we come to believe that our self and world are basically bad.

Modern consumer culture fosters depression. All our materialistic addictions are desperate attempts to run away from the truth of emptiness by desperately trying to hold on to form for dear life. Then when marriage, wealth, or success fail to bring true satisfaction, depression is inevitable.

One young man who came to me for treatment of a clinical depression had suddenly found that he no longer enjoyed the things he used to: surfing, going out with the guys, chasing women. He was undergoing a major identity crisis, but because he believed in the ideology of materialism so thoroughly, he was ill-prepared for the life passage facing him. Rather than considering that his depression might hold an important message for him—that it was time to move beyond the carefree life of a perpetual adolescent—he only wanted to get rid of the depression so he could go back to his old lifestyle. He regarded his depression as an arbitrary quirk of fate that had singled him out for mysterious reasons. Although he was getting his first real glimpse of the three marks of existence, the only framework he had for interpreting them made them seem like signs of ultimate failure. No wonder he felt so depressed.

Stories and Feelings

Since depression is maintained through stories we tell ourselves about how we or the world are fundamentally flawed, it is essential in working with depression to distinguish between our actual feelings and the stories we tell ourselves about these feelings. By *story* I mean a mental fabrication, judgment, or interpretation of an experience. We usually do not recognize our stories as inventions; we think that they portray reality.

Meditation is a highly effective method for seeing through our stories. Through sharpening our mindfulness, we start to catch ourselves in the act of constructing stories and can see them as the fabrications they are. We start to see how we are continually trying to draw conclusions about who we are, what we are doing, and what will happen next. With continued practice, meditators can learn to develop a healthy skepticism toward this storytelling aspect of mind. In Buddhist terms, they are cultivating *prajna*—the discriminating intelligence that lets them distinguish between what is real and what is a fabricated belief about reality, between immediate experience and mental interpretations of that experience.

Underneath the stories that keep depression frozen lie more vulnerable feelings such as uncertainty, sorrow, anger, helplessness, or fear. The stories the inner critic fabricates about these feelings—"I'm no good," "I'll never get it together," "The world is a cold, hard place"—are negative, rejecting judgments that freeze our feelings into a hardened state. And this frozenness is what makes depression a problem, not the vulnerable feelings underlying it.

Any feeling in its fluid state is workable, but when we interpret it with negative stories, it freezes and becomes a roadblock. Frozen fear contributes to the constriction, dullness, and lethargy commonly associated with depression. Yet where there is fluid fear, there is also openness and responsiveness to life. Frozen anger turns in on itself and becomes a weapon of self-punishment wielded by the critic. Yet fluid anger can unlock passion and power we can draw on to effect change. Frozen uncertainty results in confusion and apathy; fluid uncertainty allows for alertness to new possibilities.

In addition to fear and anger, the main feeling underlying depression is sorrow or sadness. What is sadness? The word *sad* is related etymologically to *satisfied* or *sated*, meaning *full*. So in sadness there is a fullness of heart, a fullness of feeling in response to being touched by the sweet, transitory, ungraspable quality of human existence. This empty fullness is one of the most significant of human experiences. The poignancy of not knowing who we are and not being able to hold on to or control our quickly passing life connects us with the vastness and depth of the living heart. It invites us to let go of the fixed reference points we use to prop ourselves up. If we judge or reject this sadness, then its vital intelligence congeals into the heaviness of depression. In overlooking the opportunity that sadness provides for touching and awakening the heart, we quite literally lose heart.

Thus it is important to help people suffering from depression to relate more directly to their actual moment-to-moment experience, so that they can see through the negative stories told by their critic and contact their genuine heart. When they directly experience what they are going through, it is rarely as bad as they imagined it to be. In fact, it is actually impossible to *experience* their nature as basically bad. The idea of basic badness turns out to be nothing more then a story told by the inner critic; it is a figment of our imagination, never an immediate felt experience. People can discover basic goodness only through opening to their experience. Unlike their fictional basic badness, basic goodness *can* be concretely felt—in their unconditional openness and attunement to life.

A Case Example

One of the clients who most challenged my own faith in basic goodness was a successful lawyer in his mid-fifties whom I saw for more than two years. When he first came to see me, Ted had hardened into one of the most unyielding states of depression I had encountered. Growing up during the Great Depression as the son of immigrant parents who taught him to hate and fear the white Anglo-Saxon world, he had fought to get ahead at any cost and had driven himself hard to achieve material and professional success. He had reached the top of his profession yet was completely miserable and desperate. His body gave the impression of an armored tank, and his health was suffering from the amount of tension he carried around. He spoke at a raised pitch, as though he were delivering proclamations.

Ted had a sharp lawyer's mind that literally attacked whatever he turned his attention to. His mind continually constructed arguments to buttress his dark views of reality. His themes were always the same: his weariness with life, his fear of death and letting go, the meaninglessness of everything, the demands people were always making on him, his enslavement to *should*s and *ought*s, and the distrust he felt toward everything. His rule of life was "attack or be attacked."

His life had been a series of unsuccessful attempts to overcome the three marks of existence. The more he struggled to gain the upper hand over them, the more he fell victim to the very circumstances he was trying to avoid. He had tried to escape his fear of his own insubstantiality by climbing the professional ladder, but in the stress of doing so, he was literally killing himself. He desperately wanted to be *somebody*. Yet in continually trying to win recognition from others, he had become so overbearing that people rejected him—which left him feeling even more like a nobody. In trying to escape the pain of his life, Ted had numbed himself into an profound state of depression. The three marks of existence persistently haunted him in the form of a continual sense of despair, loneliness, and death-in-life.

Initially I felt assaulted by Ted's manner and presence. To be able to stay present in the room with him, I found that I had to engage in swordplay with his sharp mind during our first few months together. Through these encounters, which involved some intense confrontations, I was eventually able to penetrate his stories and contact him in a more human way. As Ted began recognizing the difference between his real feelings and the rejecting attitude he held toward them, he could see how his negative stories only dug him deeper into his rut. Through developing some skepticism toward these stories, he no longer felt the need to broadcast them so loudly. This helped him slow down, so that he could start to pay attention to what he was feeling in the moment.

The next step in my work with Ted involved helping him recognize and step back from the inner voice that kept telling him what he "should, must, ought" to do. We came to call this voice by various names: "the critic," "the driver," "the tyrant," "the judge." As we proceeded, Ted discovered that his main aim in life had been to win approval and recognition from others, as well as from his own inner critic. He had pursued the more tangible comforts of recognition and approval as a way of not feeling the vulnerability of his own need for love. Feeling that need terrified him because it put him back in touch with the helplessness and despair he had known as a child. Ted had come to hate his vulnerability so much that he had abandoned his own heart. As he realized this, he began to feel his anger, sadness, and fear more directly, instead of just blaming the world for his condition.

Eventually Ted reached an important turning point that enabled him to start choosing life over death-in-life: Underneath all his compulsive striving and attempts to win recognition, he felt the tremendous sorrow of having lost touch with his heart. It took a long time for him to let this pain really touch him. Yet as he did so, Ted began to acknowledge his desire *just to be*, without having to be an important *somebody*. He started to feel his humanness.

Invitation to the Dance

All our reference points are continually slipping away. We can never create an unassailable position or identity that will guarantee happiness or security. Shall we let this depress us, or can we dance with it? The grand cosmic dance of Shiva in the Hindu tradition or Vajrayogini in the Tibetan Buddhist tradition takes place on the groundless ground where everything is continually giving birth and dying, slipping away. These ancient images of the cosmic dance portray egolessness and impermanence as a source of exhilaration, rather than depression.

Depression is the loss of heart that results from turning against the unfathomable flux of life. Yet at the root of this condition—in the rawness, vulnerability, and poignancy underlying it—our basic sanity is still operating. That is why depression, like all psychopathology, is not merely a disease to be simply eradicated. Instead, it is an opportunity to awaken our heart and deepen our connection to life.

13

Making Friends with Emotion

✤ EMOTIONS ARE OFTEN PROBLEMATIC because they are our most common experience of being taken over by forces seemingly beyond our control. Usually we regard them as a threat, imagining that if we really let ourselves feel our anger or depression, they would totally overwhelm us. Maybe we would be unable to function or go berserk! So we engage in a struggle with our emotions—which is like trying to stand up against a powerful wave that is heading into shore. If we resist the wave, it is indeed overwhelming. And our resistance prevents us from learning to work with emotions more skillfully—perhaps by learning to ride the waves—and thereby discovering the spiritual challenge and opportunity they represent.

Is it possible then to make friends with our emotions? How could we learn to accept them fully, go *toward* them willingly, and face them directly and fearlessly, so that their energy could become a force of awakening in our lives?

If we could learn to enter more deeply into emotion and let ourselves feel what we feel instead of reacting against it, condemning it, or trying to suppress it, we would be able to face more confidently whatever life hands us. After all, life's challenges are painful and difficult only to the degree that we are uncomfortable with the feelings they stir up within us.

Emotion in Western Psychology

The subject of emotion is one of the most confusing chapters of modern psychology. Anyone wishing to learn about emotion from the literature of Western psychology finds a bewildering array of conflicting theories about what it is, how it arises, and what it signifies. James Hillman, at the end of an exhaustive study of these theories, could only conclude that "the problem of emotion remains perennial and its solution ineffable."

In Western culture we have a history of treating emotions with suspicion and contempt, as something alien, *other*, separate from us. From Plato on, the "passions" have been viewed as our "lower nature." Regarding the source of the passions, as Freud did, as an *it* ("id"), "a primitive chaos, a cauldron of seething excitement," makes it hard to develop a friendly relationship with emotions or accept them as part of ourselves. This view of emotion as primitive and alien is a classic form of dualistic Western thinking.

As a result of regarding emotions as *other*, we feel the need to rid ourselves of these alien forces invading our system, either by acting them out or suppressing them. Yet this fear of our emotions indicates how alienated we are from ourselves. First we are alienated from our own energy, making it *other* and judging it negatively. Then we start to imagine that emotions are demonic, that we have monsters inside us. The irony is that in judging and controlling our emotions, we become further overwhelmed by them, which leads to explosive eruptions that leave us all the more alienated from ourselves. In treating emotions as other, we grant them dominion over us. Suppressing emotions and acting them out are both alienated, afflicted strategies that prevent us from experiencing emotions as they are, face to face.

The Spectrum of Felt Experience

Before we can see how to work with emotion in a more wholesome way, we must understand how emotion arises and gathers force. Our feeling life takes a whole range of forms, from global and diffuse to sharp and intense. This spectrum of felt experience can be pictured, as in figure 3, in a cone shape, with a wide base that becomes more narrow and intense at its peak:

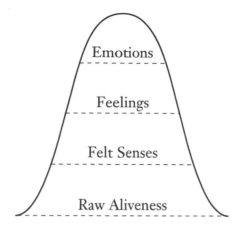

FIGURE 3. *The Spectrum of Felt Experience*

The Ground of Feeling: Raw Aliveness

All feelings and emotions arise as expressions of a more basic life energy coursing through us. The biologist René Dubos describes this basic aliveness as an unconditional sense of wholesome vitality underlying all the ups and downs of circumstance:

> About the experience of life, most people are under the illusion that they can be happy only if something especially good happens. Oddly enough, there is only one phrase I know to express that life is good *per se*, that just being alive is good . . . the French expression, *joie de vivre*. *Joie de vivre* simply means that just being alive is an extraordinary experience. The quality of that experience anyone can see by watching a young child or a young animal playing in the spring. It is totally immaterial what goes on, except for the fact that you are alive. It does not mean that you are very happy with the way you live. You can even be suffering; but just being alive is a quality *per se*.

What Dubos is describing here is the simple joy of just being—*basic goodness*, in fact, that primordial responsiveness to reality that lies at our core, and that is not dependent on whether current circumstances are good or bad.

Our raw aliveness is both the source of particular feelings and the energy circulating fluidly within them, just as water is the cradle of life as well as a universal element in all living tissues. Like earth, our aliveness is the ground that encompasses and nurtures us, with specific feelings arising from this ground. Like air, which quickens the whole body with vital energy, our aliveness is a mutable openness at the core of all feelings, which keeps them from ever becoming something totally solid or fixed. And like fire, our raw aliveness is a warmth that radiates freely in all directions.

This primordial vitality is the source of our sensitivity as well as our sanity. Our soft skin, the intricate workings of our senses, brain, and nervous system are all geared toward *letting the world in* and responding in appropriate ways. Feelings and emotions are our responses to the world as we let it touch us.

Felt Sense

Between this wide-open aliveness and our more familiar feelings and emotions, lies a subtle zone of sensibility, which Gendlin calls the *felt sense*. Your anger with a friend, for instance, is but the tip of an iceberg—which is a more global sense of frustration in your relationship with him. This larger "iceberg" is wider and deeper than your anger and can be experienced as a felt sense in the body, perhaps as burning heat or prickly tension. In this prickly felt sense there is a lot more going on than just anger. There may also be disappointment, hopelessness, sorrow, or pressure.

We can often tap into the larger felt sense underlying an emotion by asking ourselves, "What kind of an impact is this whole situation having on me?" Although a felt sense is often unclear at first, because it contains many facets of our response to a situation, once we tap into it and start to articulate what is there, we discover much more new information and possibilities than our more familiar emotional reactions allowed for.

Feeling and Emotion

Feelings, such as sadness, gladness, or anger, are more clearly recognizable than a felt sense, which is often unclear at first. And emotions are a more intense form of feeling. The feeling of sadness may build into grief, a feeling of irritation may erupt into rage, a feeling of fear may turn into panic. The distinguishing characteristic of emotion is that it totally dominates our attention and cannot be ignored, and it usually takes a repetitive, predictable form. Feelings are more subtle and fluid than emotions.

The Birth of Emotional Entanglement

How do emotions start to build steam and take over, becoming claustrophobic or explosive? And what is the difference between wallowing in emotions and working with them more constructively? Suppose you wake up feeling sad. Instead of letting the sadness touch you and alert you to something that may need attention in your life, you focus instead on how it threatens your ego identity: "If I wake up feeling sad, there must be something wrong with me. Only losers wake up feeling sad." When a feeling threatens your self-image, you will want to push it away. So as you judge your sadness negatively and reject it, it freezes up, losing its connection with your raw aliveness. You become caught up in dark, depressive story lines—melancholy thoughts and imaginings you project into the past and the future ("What is the matter with me? Why do I always feel this way? I'll never get it together.").

The more you mull over these stories, the sadder you become, and the sadder you feel, the darker your stories become—a vicious circle that starts generating more intense emotion, such as depression and despair, which in turn lead to more depressing thoughts. As depression starts to congeal out of the simple sadness you turned away from, you may start to see the entire world, your whole life history and future prospects in this dreary light. Your depressed thoughts extend in all directions and keep you stuck in the mire. In this way, what started out as a fluid feeling becomes thick, solid, heavy, and entrapping.

Thus reacting against feelings—fearing fear, being outraged about anger, becoming depressed about sadness—is much worse than the primary feelings themselves, for it turns us against ourselves and causes us to go around in emotional circles. As we spin around in the cycle of feelings-giving-rise-to-highly-charged-thoughts, our perception becomes cloudy, and we often say or do things we later regret.

Cutting through this tendency to get lost in emotionally driven thoughts and stories requires a certain discipline, which psychotherapy and meditation each provide in their different ways.

The Therapeutic Approach to Emotion

Through unpacking the wider felt sense underlying an emotion, psychotherapeutic inquiry can help us free ourselves from the spin of this kind of emotional vortex. In a felt sense we discover a much wider range of meanings and responses than in the emotion itself. For example, underneath the heavy depression you have worked up, you may find that you are sad about not knowing what to do with your life. Discovering this helps you look more deeply into the issue of life direction, instead of remaining stuck in depression. Or underneath your anger with your friend you may discover a need to communicate something essential that you only just now recognize, which releases you from being stuck in the anger.

Although emotional release may be important and helpful in this process, what finally dissolves emotional entanglement is not catharsis per se, but the unpacking of a wider felt sense, which illuminates our larger relationship to the situation in question. And this can lead to a bodily felt shift that breaks through the logic of our story lines and reveals a new way of relating to the problematic situation. Felt shifts break up logjams in the mindstream, allowing our raw aliveness to flow freely once more.

Therapeutic work also brings to light conditioned identity structures that contribute to our emotional entanglement. For instance, working with your sadness and depression may reveal psychological fixations that usually remain hidden—your view of yourself as inadequate to meet life's challenges or your view of the world as overwhelming—so that these can be addressed more directly. In this way, working psychologically with emotional reactions provides an important stepping-stone toward freeing up deep-set conditioned patterns.

One limitation of a purely psychological approach to emotion is the tendency to make the exploration of feelings an endless project, or an end in itself. A psychotherapy that focuses solely on emotional and psychological patterns often fails to help a person recognize and access the larger ground of primordial aliveness that reveals itself in moments of felt shift and release.

The Meditative Approach to Emotion

By teaching us to relate to emotions in a more nonconceptual, naked way, the practice of meditation provides direct access to our raw aliveness. The meditative approach to emotion, unlike the psychological approach, is not oriented toward the content of feelings, their meaning, or the psychological structures underlying them. Instead, meditation involves opening to feelings directly, without trying to discover their meaning. When surges of emotional turbulence arise, we practice keeping our seat and opening to their energy.

While psychotherapy unpacks the meanings in our feelings, meditation relates to feelings purely as energetic phenomena, as expressions of our basic aliveness. Uncovering the raw energy of emotions is like moving into the depths of the ocean, underneath the whitecaps of emotional frenzy and the broader swells of feeling, where all remains calm, where our personal struggles empty into the larger currents of life.

Thus meditation allows us to discover a freer, more open awareness that is always available, even when we are caught up in emotional reactions. By helping us recognize the gaps and discontinuities that spontaneously appear in the thick logic of our story lines, meditation can also help us wake up in the midst of intense emotional states when they arise. A meditator might be able to wonder, in the midst of an eruption of anger, "Am I really this angry? Do I really need to make such a big deal out of this? Is this really as important as I am making it? Are these people as wrong as I am making them?"

Transmutation

Drawing on emotion as a vehicle for self-illumination is known as *transmutation* in Tantric Buddhism. As an alchemical term, *transmutation* implies converting something apparently worthless into something extremely valuable, like lead into gold.

The first step in taming the lion of emotion, in transmuting its fierce energy into illumination, is to feel it and let it be, without judging it as good or bad. Running away from a fierce animal or trying to thwart its energy only provokes further attack. We must learn to open directly to the energy of emotions and become one with it, as Chögyam Trungpa points out, "When we are able to become completely one with irritations or feel the abstract quality of the irritation as it is, then irritation has no one to irritate. It becomes a sort of judo practice." Although emotions seem to have us in their grip, as soon as we turn to face them directly, we find nothing as solid or fixed as our judgments or stories about them. In their raw state, emotions are simply expressions of our own energy. It is only our reactions against them and the story lines we weave out of them ("My anger is right because . . . ," "My sadness is bad because . . .") that make their energetic presence thick and heavy.

Instead of trying to control emotions, judge ourselves for them, or react against them, we can learn to experience them in their immediacy, as a living presence. Trungpa describes several aspects of this process:

> There are several stages in relating with the emotions: seeing, hearing, smelling, touching, and transmuting. In the case of seeing the emotions, we have a general awareness that the emotions have their own space, their own development. We accept them as part of the pattern of mind, without question. And then hearing involves experiencing the pulsation of such energy, the energy upsurge as it comes toward you. Smelling is appreciating that the energy is somewhat workable. Touching is feeling the nitty-gritty of the whole thing, that you can touch and relate with it, that your emotions are not particularly destructive or crazy, but just an upsurge of energy, whatever form they take.

If ego is the tendency to hold on to ourselves and control our experience, then feeling our emotions directly and letting their energy flow
freely threatens ego's whole control structure. When we open to the
actual texture and quality of a feeling, instead of trying to control or
judge it, "I"—the activity of trying to hold ourselves together—starts
to dissolve into "it"—the larger aliveness present in the feeling. If I
fully open to my sorrow, it may intensify for a while, and I may feel
all the grief of it. Yet opening to this pain, without stories, also makes
me feel more alive. As I turn to face my demons, they reveal themselves as my very own life energy.

Emotions, we could say, are the blood shed by ego—they start to
flow whenever we are touched, whenever the defensive shell around
the heart is pierced. Trying to control them is an attempt to keep this
shell from cracking. Letting ego bleed, on the other hand, opens the
heart. Then we rediscover ourselves as living beings who are exposed
to the world, interconnected with all other beings. Letting go of judgments and story lines and feeling this naked quality of being alive
wakes us up and nurtures compassion for ourselves and others.

Facing into the turbulence of emotions is like entering the eye of a
hurricane. The surrounding winds may be turbulent, but eventually
we arrive at a clear opening in the midst of the storm, as Tarthang
Tulku suggests:

> When you are emotionally upset, stay within the emotion . . . without
> grasping or holding on to it. . . . Likewise, when anxiety or any other
> disturbing feeling arises, concentrate on the feeling, not on thoughts
> about it. Concentrate on the center of the feeling: penetrate into that
> space. . . . If we go directly into the center of the emotion, there's
> nothing there! . . . There is a density of energy in that center that is
> clear and distinct. This energy has great power, and can transmit great
> clarity. . . . We can transmute this samsaric mind because the mind
> itself is emptiness—total openness, total honesty with each situation
> . . . direct seeing, total freedom from obscurations, complete recep-
> tivity.

Entering emotions in this way may be a delicate maneuver at first.
We may have a brief glimpse of the space within them, but then

quickly fall back into fearful stories. Meditation practice helps develop
the sustained attention necessary here, through which we learn to stop
being "hijacked" by our thoughts. When we enter an emotion in this
naked way, it cannot persist for long because it does not actually have
any independent, solid existence of its own, apart from our concepts
or reactions.

This kind of understanding can also help clients in psychotherapy
face their emotions more directly. For example, one man I worked
with felt terribly burdened by his hunger for love. The first task was
to cut through his critical stories about his need. ("I shouldn't need
. . . It's not manly . . . I should be self-reliant.") When he could let
himself feel the need fully and directly, he discovered his aliveness in
it, as the following condensed transcript illustrates:

THERAPIST: What happens when you let that need be there?

CLIENT: It says: "I'm unhappy. I'm all alone. I'm scared. It's hard to
make it on my own. I need someone to love and care for me."

THERAPIST: Can you let yourself just have that need for love right
now? What would it be like to let yourself have your need one hundred percent?

CLIENT: (*long pause*) It really shifts things around inside me to do that.
. . . When I really go into it, it gives me a feeling of power. . . . It really
feels different. . . . I feel more balanced . . . grounded. . . . There's
much more space. . . . There's no desperation or fear. . . . Letting
myself have this need is very nurturing, even though no one else is
there. . . . I feel full.

Various metaphors have been used to describe the transmutation
of emotional energy. The French psychoanalyst Hubert Benoit com-
pares it to the metamorphosis of coal into diamonds, where "the aim
is not the destruction of the ego, but its transformation. The conscious
acceptance results in the coal which has become denser, and so blacker
and more opaque, being instantaneously transformed into a diamond
that is perfectly transparent."

This image of transparency and lucency, where emotion becomes a clear window opening onto a deeper aliveness, is particularly prominent in Vajrayana or Tantric Buddhism. *Vajra* is the diamondlike, indestructible clarity of the awake state of mind, which manifests as mirrorlike wisdom. Because it signifies absolute clarity, the Vajrayana (the "diamond path") sees the world in terms of luminosity, lit up with brilliance. The struggle to shore up a self-image only generates a film of confusion that dulls the natural brilliance of our diamondlike awareness. Transmuting emotion turns the dark, murky world of the confused mind into the radiance of clear seeing.

Transmutation can be a sudden change or happen more gradually, through increasing friendliness with our experience. Other metaphors emphasize the gradual, organic nature of this process. In Trungpa's words: "Unskilled farmers throw away their rubbish and buy manure from other farmers, but those who are skilled go on collecting their own rubbish, in spite of the bad smell and the unclean work, and when it is ready to be used they spread it on their land, and out of this they grow their crops. . . . So out of these unclean things comes the birth of the seed which is Realization." Suzuki Roshi speaks in a similar vein of how the weeds of the mind can be used to feed the awakening of awareness: "We pull the weeds and bury them near the plant to give it nourishment. . . . You should be grateful for the weeds, because eventually they will enrich your practice. If you have some experience of how the weeds in your mind change into mental nourishment, your practice will make remarkable progress."

Transmutation comes about through discovering the open space of being at the core of all experience. This spaciousness cuts our emotional turmoil down to size, so that it appears as a small drama in the middle of a vast expanse of awareness. When we no longer fear our emotions, this promotes greater fearlessness toward life as a whole, known in Buddhism as the "lion's roar":

> The lion's roar is the fearless proclamation that any state of mind, including the emotions, is a workable situation. Then the most powerful energies become absolutely workable rather than taking you over, because there is nothing to take over if you are not putting up any resistance. Indian Ashokan art depicts the lion's roar with four lions

looking in four directions, which symbolizes the idea of having no back. Every direction is a front, symbolizing all-pervading awareness. The fearlessness covers all directions.

In sum, the meditative approach to emotion, as cultivated particularly in Tantric Buddhism, involves keeping our seat and staying present in the middle of emotional turbulence, cutting through judgments and story lines in order to enter the emotions more directly, and opening to their energy in all its rawness and power. In so doing, we discover the intense tenderness of our aliveness.

Befriending emotions in this way also allows us to discover the larger intelligence contained within them. Liberated from reactivity, anger can become a means of direct communication, rather than a weapon. Fear can be an alert that perks up our attention, rather than a trigger to run and hide. And when we appreciate loneliness as a longing to connect and sadness as a fullness of heart, these feelings regain their essential dignity, instead of being a burden.

In the Vajrayana tradition, the complete path of transmutation depends on careful understanding and qualified guidance. It is considered essential to have a firm foundation in meditation practice, which helps free one from the grip of thought and fantasy. It is also important to work with a living, realized teacher who is deeply grounded in the energies of life, and who can guide the student through the many twists and turns along the way. Then, through discipline and practice, the confusion of the emotions may become transformed into the wisdom of seeing things as they are.

14

Embodying Your Realization

Psychological Work in the Service of
Spiritual Development

> *The technique of a world-changing yoga has to be as multiform,*
> *sinuous, patient, all-including as the world itself. If it does not deal*
> *with all the difficulties or possibilities and carefully deal with each*
> *necessary element, does it have any chance of success?*
>
> —SRI AUROBINDO

> *The impersonal is a truth, the personal too is a truth; they are the*
> *same truth seen from two sides of our psychological activity; neither*
> *by itself gives the total account of Reality, and yet by either we can*
> *approach it.*
>
> —SRI AUROBINDO

❖ WHEN I FIRST ENCOUNTERED ZEN in the 1960s, I
found myself especially drawn to the mysterious *satori*—that moment
of seeing into one's own nature, when all the old blinders were said to
fall away, so that one became an entirely new person, never to be the
same again. In D. T. Suzuki's words, "The opening of satori is the
remaking of life itself . . . a complete revolution . . . cataclysmic" in its
consequences. A revelation that led to a whole new way of being—I
found this prospect compelling enough to make it a central focus of
my life.

Many of us who have been involved in meditative practices during
the past few decades have had a direct taste of this realization, which

inspires great joy and gratitude while bringing fresh insight and clarity. Yet at the same time I have also developed a profound respect for how difficult it is to embody such realizations in everyday life—especially for modern Westerners who live in the world, rather than in monastic settings. Monastic or retreat situations are designed to help people devote themselves one-pointedly to seeing through the veils of the conditioned mind and realizing Being, spirit, or naked awareness as their own true nature. Yet the full embodiment of such realizations—manifesting as a wise and balanced way of engaging in livelihood, intimate relationships, and the complex challenges of modern society—presents another type of hurdle altogether. We who live as householders, husbands, wives, parents, or working people may also need other methods to help us integrate spiritual realization into our busy, complex lives.

Realization and Transformation

The hard truth is that spiritual realization is relatively easy compared with the much greater difficulty of actualizing it, integrating it fully into the fabric of one's embodiment and one's daily life. By *realization* I mean the direct recognition of one's ultimate nature, while *actualization* refers to how we live that realization in all the situations of our life. When people have major spiritual openings, often during periods of intensive practice or retreat, they may imagine that everything has changed and that they will never be the same again. Indeed, spiritual work can open people up profoundly and help them live free of the compulsions of their conditioning for long stretches of time. But at some point after the retreat ends, when they encounter circumstances that trigger their emotional reactivity, their unresolved psychological issues, their habitual tensions and defenses, or their subconscious identifications, they may find that their spiritual practice has barely penetrated their conditioned personality, which remains mostly intact, generating the same tendencies it always has.[1]

Of course, there are many levels of realization, ranging from temporary experiences to more stable attainment that alters one's whole way of being. Yet even among advanced spiritual practitioners who have developed a high degree of insight, power, even brilliance, certain islands—unexamined complexes of personal and cultural conditioning, blind spots, or areas of self-deception—often seem to remain intact within the pure stream of their realization. They may even unconsciously use their spiritual powers to reinforce old defenses and manipulative ways of relating to others. For others, spiritual practice may reinforce a tendency toward coldness, disengagement, or interpersonal distance. How is it possible for spiritual realization to remain compartmentalized, leaving whole areas of the psyche apparently untouched? Why is it so hard to bring the awareness developed in meditation into all the areas of one's life?

Some would say that these problems are signs of deficiency or incompleteness in one's spiritual practice or realization, and this is undoubtedly true. Yet since they are almost universal, they also point to the general difficulty of integrating spiritual awakenings into the entire fabric of our human embodiment. It is said in the Dzogchen teachings that only the rare highly endowed person attains full liberation upon realizing the essential nature of mind. For the rest of us, liberation does not follow quickly from realization. As Sri Aurobindo put it, "Realization by itself does not necessarily transform the being as a whole. . . . One may have some light of realization at the spiritual summit of consciousness but the parts below remain what they were. I have seen any number of instances of that." Because problems with integration are so widespread, we need to consider more fully the relationship between these two different movements in spiritual development: realization and transformation, liberation and complete integration of that liberation in all the different dimensions of one's life.

Realization is the movement from personality to being—leading toward liberation from the prison of the conditioned self. *Transformation* involves drawing on this realization to penetrate the dense conditioned patterns of body and mind, so that the spiritual can be fully integrated into the personal and the interpersonal, so that the personal life can become a transparent vessel for ultimate truth or divine revelation.

In the traditional cultures of Asia, it was a viable option for a yogi to live purely as the impersonal universal, to pursue spiritual development without having much of a personal life or transforming the structures of that life. These older cultures provided a religious context that honored and supported spiritual retreat and placed little or no emphasis on the development of the individual.[2] As a result, spiritual attainment could often remain divorced from worldly life and personal development. In Asia, yogis and *sadhus* could live an otherworldly life, have little personal contact with people, or engage in highly eccentric behavior and still be supported and venerated by the community at large.

Many Westerners have tried to take up this model, pursuing impersonal realization while neglecting their personal life, but have found in the end that this was like wearing a suit of clothes that didn't quite fit. Such attempts at premature transcendence—taking refuge in the impersonal absolute as a way to avoid dealing with one's personal psychology, one's personal issues, feelings, or calling—leads to inner denial. And this can create monstrous shadow elements that have devastating consequences, as we have seen in many American spiritual communities in recent years. For whatever reasons, for better or for worse, it has become problematic in our culture to pursue spiritual development that is not fully integrated into the fabric of one's personal experience and interpersonal relationships.

Here is where psychological work might serve as an ally to spiritual practice—by helping to shine the light of awareness into all the hidden nooks and crannies of our conditioned personality, so that it becomes more porous, more permeable to the larger being that is its ground. Of course, what I am describing here is a special kind of psychological self-inquiry, which requires a larger framework, understanding, and aim than conventional psychotherapy. I am hesitant to call this psychotherapy at all, for the word *therapy* has connotations of pathology and cure that place it in a medical, rather than a transformative, context. Moreover, conventional therapy often involves only talk, failing to recognize ways in which the body holds defensive patterns and also manifests the energies of awakening. Truly transformative psychological work must also help us unlock the body's contractions and gain access to its larger energies.

Of course, spiritual work has a much larger aim than psychological work: liberation from narrow identification with the self-structure altogether and awakening into the expansive reality of primordial being. And it does seem possible to glimpse and perhaps even fully realize this kind of awakening, whether or not one is happy, healthy, psychologically integrated, individuated, or interpersonally sensitive and attuned. Yet after centuries of divorce between the spiritual and the worldly life, the increasingly desperate situation of a planet that human beings are rapidly destroying cries out for a new kind of psychospiritual integration, which has only rarely existed before: namely, an integration between liberation—the capacity to step beyond the individual psyche into the larger, nonpersonal space of pure awareness—and personal transformation—the capacity to bring that larger awareness to bear on all one's conditioned psychological structures, so that they become fully metabolized, freeing the energy and intelligence frozen inside them, thereby fueling the development of a fuller, richer human presence that could fulfill the still unrealized potential of life on this earth.

For most of my career I have explored what the Eastern contemplative traditions have to offer Western psychology—an inquiry that has been extremely fruitful. I have only the greatest respect and gratitude for the spiritual teachings I have received and for the Asian teachers who have so generously shared them with me. Yet in recent years I have become equally interested in a different set of questions. How might Western psychological understandings and methods serve a sacred purpose, by furthering our capacity to embody our larger awakenings in a more personally integrated way? Is our individuality a hindrance on the path of awakening, as some spiritual teachings would claim, or can true individuation (as opposed to compulsive individualism) serve as a bridge between the spiritual path and ordinary life?

The Challenge of Psychospiritual Integration

The question of how psychological self-inquiry could serve spiritual development forces us to consider the complex issue of the relationship between the psychological and the spiritual altogether. Confusions about this are rampant. Conventional therapists often look askance at spiritual practice, just as many spiritual teachers often disapprove of psychotherapy. At the extremes, each camp tends to see the other as avoiding and denying the real issues.

For the most part, psychological and spiritual work address different levels of human existence. Psychological inquiry addresses relative truth, personal meaning—the human realm, which is characterized by interpersonal relations and the issues arising out of them. At its best, it also reveals and helps deconstruct the conditioned structures, forms, and identifications in which our consciousness becomes trapped. Spiritual practice, especially of the mystical bent, looks beyond our conditioned structures, identifications, and ordinary human concerns toward the transhuman—the direct realization of the ultimate. It sees what is timeless, unconditioned, and absolutely true, beyond all form, revealing the vast open-endedness, or emptiness, at the root and core of human existence. Yet must these two approaches to human suffering work in different directions? Or could they be compatible, even powerful allies?

If the domain of psychological work is *form*, the domain of spiritual work is *emptiness*—that unspeakable reality which lies beyond all contingent forms. Yet just as form and emptiness cannot be truly separated, so these two types of inner work cannot be kept entirely separate, but have important areas of overlap. Psychological work can lead to spiritual insight and depth, while spiritual work, in its movement toward embodiment, transformation, and service, calls on us to come to grips with the conditioned personality patterns that block integration.

The question of whether and how psychological work might further spiritual development calls for a new type of inquiry that leads back and forth across the boundary of absolute and relative truth, taking us beyond orthodoxy and tradition into uncharted territory. If, instead of leaping to facile or definitive conclusions, we start by honoring the question itself in a spirit of open inquiry, it takes us right to the heart of the issue of how spirituality in general, and Eastern transplants such as Western Buddhism in particular, need to develop if they are truly to take hold in, and transform, the modern world.

As a psychotherapist and student of Buddhism, I have been forced to consider this question deeply. My initial interest in psychotherapy developed in the 1960s, at the same time as my interest in the Eastern spiritual traditions. I was inspired to become a psychotherapist largely because I imagined that psychotherapy could be our Western version of a path of liberation. But I quickly found Western psychology too narrow and limited in its view of human nature. And I wondered how I could help anybody else if I didn't know the way out of the maze of human suffering myself. Although I had one great teacher in graduate school—Eugene Gendlin, a pioneer in existential therapy, who taught me much of what has proved useful to me as a therapist—I became quite disillusioned with Western psychology as a whole.

In looking for a way to work on myself and understand my life more fully, I became increasingly drawn toward Buddhism. After finding a genuine master and beginning to practice meditation, I went through a period of aversion to Western psychology and therapy. Now that I had "found the way," I became arrogant toward other paths, as new converts often do. I was also wary of getting trapped in my own personal process, addicted to endlessly examining and processing feelings and emotional issues. In my newfound spiritual fervor, however, I was falling into the opposite trap—of refusing to face the personal "stuff" at all. In truth, I was much more comfortable with the impersonal, timeless reality I discovered through Buddhism than I was with my own personal feelings or interpersonal relationships, both of which seemed messy and entangling, compared with the peace and clarity of meditative equipoise—sitting still, following the breath, letting go of thoughts, and resting in the open space of awareness.

Yet as I continued studying Tantric Buddhism, with its emphasis on respecting relative truth, I began to appreciate many aspects of Western psychology more fully, perhaps for the first time. Once I accepted that psychology could not describe my ultimate nature, and I no longer required it to provide answers about the nature of human existence, I began to see that it had an important place in the scheme of things. Facing some extremely painful relationship struggles, I began to do my own intensive psychological work. Despite my clinical training, I was surprised at the power of psychological inquiry to help me uncover blind spots, address leftover issues from the past, move through old fears, and open up in a more grounded, personal way, both with myself and with others. This work also helped me approach spiritual practice in a clearer way, not so encumbered by unconscious psychological motivations and agendas.

Cultural Factors East and West

Learning to appreciate the respective value of psychological and spiritual work brought up another set of questions for me: Why was it so easy to see the value of psychological work for Western people, yet so hard to imagine traditional Asian people utilizing the services of a psychotherapist? And why did most of the Eastern spiritual teachers I knew have so much difficulty understanding psychological work and its potential value for a spiritual practitioner? What accounts for this disparity?[3]

In presenting my hypotheses about this, I am not trying to advance a full-blown anthropological theory. Nor do I wish to idealize the societies of ancient India or Tibet, which certainly had many serious problems of their own. Rather, my intention is to point out some (admittedly generalized) social and cultural differences that may help us consider how we in the West may have a somewhat different course of psychospiritual development to follow than people in the traditional cultures where the great meditative practices first arose and flourished.

Some would argue that psychotherapy is a sign of how spoiled or narcissistic Westerners are—that we can afford the luxury of delving into our psyches and fiddling with our personal problems while Rome burns all around. Yet though industrial society has alleviated many of the grosser forms of physical pain, it has also created difficult kinds of personal and social fragmentation that were unknown in premodern societies, generating a new kind of psychological suffering that led to the development of modern psychotherapy.

Traditional Asian culture did not engender the pronounced split between mind and body that we in the West know so well. In giving priority to the welfare of the collective, Asian societies also did not foster the division between self and other, individual and society, that is endemic to the Western mind. There was neither a generation gap nor the pervasive social alienation that has become a hallmark of modern life. In this sense, the villages and extended families of traditional India or Tibet actually seem to have built sturdier ego structures, not so debilitated by the inner divisions—between mind and body, individual and society, parent and child, or weak ego and harsh, punishing superego—characteristic of the modern self. The "upper stories" of spiritual development in Asian culture could be built on a more stable and cohesive "ground floor" human foundation.

Early child-rearing practices in some traditional Asian cultures, while often far from ideal, were in some ways more wholesome than in the modern West. Asian mothers often had a strong dedication to providing their children with strong, sustained early bonding. Young Indian and Tibetan children, for instance, are continually held, often sharing their parents' bed for their first two or three years. As Alan Roland, a psychoanalyst who spent many years studying cross-cultural differences in Asian and Western self-development, describes Indian child rearing:

> Intense, prolonged maternal involvement in the first four or five years with the young child, with adoration of the young child to the extent of treating him or her as godlike, develops a central core of heightened well-being in the child. Mothers, grandmothers, aunts, servants, older sisters and cousin-sisters are all involved in the pervasive mirroring that is incorporated into an inner core of extremely high feelings of esteem. . . . Indian child rearing and the inner structuralization of heightened esteem are profoundly psychologically congruent with the basic Hindu concept that the individual soul is essentially the godhead (*atman-brahman*). A heightened sense of inner regard and the premise that a person can strive to become godlike are strongly connected. . . . This is in contrast to the Western Christian premise of original sin.

According to Roland, this nurturing quality of the Indian extended family helps the child develop an ego structure whose boundaries are "on the whole more flexible and permeable than in most Westerners," and "less rigorously drawn."[4]

Growing up in extended families, Asian children are also exposed to a wide variety of role models and sources of nurturance, even if the primary parents are not very available. Tibetan tribal villages, for instance, usually regarded the children as belonging to everyone, and everyone's responsibility. Extended families mitigate the parents' tendency to possess their children psychologically. By contrast, parents in nuclear families often have more investment in "This is *my* child; my child is an extension of me"—which contributes to narcissistic injury and intense fixations on parents that persist for many Westerners throughout their lives.

Certain developmental psychologists have argued that children with deficient parenting hold on to the internalized traces of their parents more rigidly inside themselves. This might explain why the Tibetans I know do not seem to suffer from the heavy parental fixations that many Westerners have. Their self/other (object relational) complexes would not be as tight or conflicted as for Westerners who lack good early bonding, and who spend their first eighteen years in an isolated nuclear family with one or two adults, who themselves are alienated from both folk wisdom and spiritual understanding. Asian children would be less burdened by what the psychologist Guntrip considers the emotional plague of modern civilization: ego weakness, the lack of a grounded, confident sense of oneself and one's capacities.

In addition to fostering strong mother-infant bonding, intact extended families, and a life attuned to the rhythms of the natural world, traditional Asian societies maintained the sacred at the center of social life. A culture that provides individuals with shared myths, meanings, religious values, and rituals provides a source of support and guidance that helps people make sense of their lives. In all these ways, a traditional Asian child would likely grow up more nurtured by what pediatrician and psychoanalyst D. W. Winnicott called the "holding environment"—a context of love, support, belonging, and meaning that contributes to a basic sense of confidence and to healthy psychological development in general. By contrast, children today who grow up in fragmented families, glued to television sets that continually transmit images of a spiritually lost, fragmented, and narcissistic world, lack a meaningful context in which to situate their lives.

One way these differences manifest is in how people inhabit their bodies. In observing Tibetans, I am often struck by how centered they are in the lower half of the body and how powerfully they are connected to the ground beneath their feet. Tibetans naturally seem to possess a great deal of *hara*—grounded presence in the belly—which is no doubt a result of the factors mentioned above. Westerners, by contrast, are generally more centered in the upper half of their body and weak in their connection to the lower half.

Hara, which Karlfried Graf Dürckheim calls the *vital center* or *earth center*, is connected with issues of confidence, power, will, groundedness, trust, support, and equanimity. The child-rearing deficiencies, disconnection from the earth, and overemphasis on rational intellect in Western culture all contribute to loss of *hara*. To compensate for the lack of a sense of support and trust in the belly, Westerners often try to achieve security and control by going "upstairs"—trying to control life with their mind. But behind the ego's attempts to control reality with the mind lies a pervasive sense of fear, anxiety, and insecurity.

Another difference that has important consequences for psychospiritual development is the greater value traditional Asian cultures place on being, in contrast to Western cultures, which put more emphasis on doing. Winnicott in particular stressed the importance of allowing a young child to remain in unstructured states of being: "The mother's nondemanding presence makes the experience of formlessness and comfortable solitude possible, and this capacity becomes a central feature in the development of a stable and personal self. . . . This makes it possible for the infant to experience . . . a state of 'going-on-being' out of which . . . spontaneous gestures emerge." Winnicott used the term *impingement* to describe a parent's tendency to interrupt these formless moments, forcing children to separate abruptly from the continuity of their "going-on-being." The child is "wrenched from his quiescent state and forced to respond . . . and to mold himself to what is provided for him. The major consequence of prolonged impingement is fragmentation of the infant's experience. Out of necessity he becomes prematurely and compulsively attuned to the claims of others. . . . He loses touch with his own spontaneous needs and gestures . . . [and develops] a false self on a compliant basis."

Traditional Asian families often give the young child plenty of room and permission just to be, in an unstructured way, free from the pressures to respond and perform that Western parents often place on their children at an early age. Allowed to be in that way, these children would be more comfortable with emptiness, which we could define here as *unstructured being*. But in our culture, which emphasizes doing, having, and achieving at the expense of simply being, emptiness can seem quite alien, threatening, and terrifying. In a family or society that does not recognize or value being, children are more likely to interpret their own unstructured being as some kind of deficiency, as a failure to measure up, as an inadequacy or lack. Thus the Western ego structure seems to form in a more rigid and defended way, in part to ward off a terrifying sense of deficiency born out of fear of the open, unstructured nature of one's very being.

As a result of this brittle ego having to work overtime to compensate for a lack of inner trust and confidence, many Western seekers find that they are not ready, willing, or able to let go of their ego defenses, despite all their spiritual practice and realization. On a deep, subconscious level, it is too threatening to let go of the little security that their shaky ego structure provides. That is why it can also be helpful for Westerners to work on dismantling their defensive personality structure in a more gradual and deliberate way, through psychological inquiry—examining, understanding, and dissolving all their false self-images, their self-deceptions, their distorted projections, and their habitual emotional reactions, one by one—and developing a fuller, richer connection with themselves in the process.

In sum, to the extent that traditional Asian children grew up supported by a nurturing holding environment, they would be more likely to receive more of what Winnicott defined as the two essential elements of parenting in early childhood: sustained emotional bonding and space to be, to rest in unstructured being. As a result, these children would tend to grow up with a more stable, grounded sense of confidence and well-being—what we call in the West "ego strength"—in contrast to the self-hatred, insecurity, and shaky sense of self that modern Western people often suffer from.

In discussing Asian child development here, I am speaking of influences in the first few years of childhood, when the ego structure first starts to coalesce. In later childhood, many Asian parents become much more controlling, exerting strong pressure on children to conform and to subordinate their individuality to collective rules and roles. Thus Roland notes that most neurotic conflicts among modern Asians are found in the area of family enmeshment and difficulties with self-differentiation. Indeed, while Eastern culture more generally values and understands being and emptiness, as well as interconnectedness, the West values and has a deeper appreciation of individuation.

Cultivating one's own individual vision, qualities, and potentials is of much greater significance in the West than in traditional Asia, where spiritual development could more easily coexist alongside a low level of individuation. Here is where psychological work may serve another important function for Westerners, by helping them to individuate—to listen to and trust their own experience, to develop an authentic personal vision and sense of direction, and to clear up the psychological conflicts that prevent them from authentically being themselves.[5]

Buddhist scholar Robert Thurman has argued that since Buddhism is a path of individuation, it is inaccurate to characterize this tradition as not promoting individual development. Certainly the Buddha gave birth to a new vision that encouraged individuals to pursue their own spiritual development, instead of depending on conventional religious rituals. In that broad sense, Buddhism can be regarded as a path of individuation. But this is a different model of individuation from the one that has developed in the West. As Roland notes, individuation in Asian cultures was usually limited to the arena of spiritual practice, rather than supported as a general norm.

The Western notion of individuation involves finding one's own unique calling, vision, and path, and embodying these in the way one lives. To *become oneself* in this sense often involves innovation, experimentation, and the questioning of received knowledge. As Buddhist scholar Anne Klein notes: "Tibetans, like many Asians who have grown up outside Western influence, do not cultivate this sense of individuality."

In traditional Asia, the teachings of liberation were geared toward people who were, if anything, *too* earthbound, too involved in family roles and social obligations. The highest, nondual teachings of Buddhism and Hinduism—which show that who you really are *is* absolute reality, beyond *you*—provided a way out of the social maze, helping people discover the transhuman absolute that lies beyond all worldly concerns and entanglements. Yet these teachings rest on and presume a rich underpinning of human community, religious customs, and moral values, like a mountain arising out of a network of foothills and valleys below. The soulful social and religious customs of traditional India and Tibet provided a firm human base out of which spiritual aspirations for a transhuman absolute, beyond human relationships and human society, could arise.

Because the traditional Asian's sense of self is embedded in a soulful culture rich in tradition, ritual, close-knit family and community life, people in these cultures did not lose themselves or become alienated from their own humanness in the way that Westerners have. And since soul—the deep, rich, colorful qualities of our humanness—permeated the whole culture, the need to develop individuated soul qualities never assumed the importance that it has in the West. Never having lost their soul, traditional Asians never had to develop any consciousness about how to find it—that is, how to individuate in a distinctly personal way.

In the modern West, it is quite common to feel alienated from the larger social whole—whose public spaces and architecture, celebrations, institutions, family life, and even food are lacking in nourishing soul qualities that allow people to feel deeply connected to these aspects of life, as well as to one another. The good news, however, is that the soullessness of our culture is forcing us to develop a new consciousness about forging an individuated soul—an authentic inner source of personal vision, meaning, and purpose. One important outgrowth of this is a refined and sophisticated capacity for nuanced personal awareness, personal sensitivity, and personal presence.

This is not something the Asian traditions can teach us much about. If the great gift of the East is its focus on *absolute* true nature—impersonal and shared by all alike—the gift of the West is the impetus it provides to develop an *individuated expression* of true nature—which we could also call *soul* or *personal presence*.[6] Individuated true nature is the unique way that each of us can serve as a vehicle for embodying the suprapersonal wisdom, compassion, and truth of absolute true nature.

We in the West clearly have much to learn from the Eastern contemplative teachings. But if we only try to adhere to the Eastern focus on the transhuman, or suprapersonal, while failing to develop a grounded, personal way of relating to life, we may have a hard time integrating our larger nature into the way we actually live.

Spiritual Bypassing

While many Eastern teachers are extremely warm, loving, and personal in their own way, they often do not have much to say about the specifically personal side of human life.[7] Coming out of traditional Asian societies, they may have a hard time recognizing or assessing the personal, developmental challenges facing their Western students. They often do not understand the pervasive self-hatred, shame, and guilt, as well as the alienation and lack of confidence in these students. Still less do they detect the tendency toward spiritual bypassing—using spiritual ideas and practices to sidestep personal, emotional "unfinished business," to shore up a shaky sense of self, or to belittle basic needs, feelings, and developmental tasks, all in the name of enlightenment. And so they often teach self-transcendence to students who first of all need to find some ground to stand on.[8]

Spiritual practice involves freeing consciousness from its entanglement in form, matter, emotions, personality, and social conditioning. In a society like ours, where the whole earthly foundation is weak to begin with, it is tempting to use spirituality as a way of trying to rise above this shaky ground. In this way, spirituality becomes just another way of rejecting one's experience. When people use spiritual practice to try to compensate for low self-esteem, social alienation, or emotional problems, they corrupt the true nature of spiritual practice. Instead of loosening the manipulative ego that tries to control its experience, they are further strengthening it.

Spiritual bypassing is a strong temptation in times like ours when achieving what were once ordinary developmental landmarks— earning a livelihood through dignified, meaningful work; raising a family; sustaining a long-term intimate relationship; belonging to a larger social community—has become increasingly difficult and elusive. Yet when people use spirituality to cover up their difficulties with functioning in the modern world, their spiritual practice remains in a separate compartment, unintegrated with the rest of their life.

For example, one woman I know went to India at age seventeen to get away from a wealthy family that had provided her with little love or understanding and no model of a meaningful life. She spent seven years studying and practicing with Tibetan teachers in India and Nepal, participated in many retreats, and had many powerful realizations. She experienced states of bliss and inner freedom lasting for long periods of time. Upon returning to Europe, however, she could barely function in the modern world. Nothing made any sense to her, and she did not know what to do with herself. She became involved with a charismatic man and wound up having two children by him before she knew what had happened to her. In looking back at that time she said, "This man was my shadow. He represented all the parts of myself I had run away from. I found him totally fascinating and became swept up in a course of events over which I had no control. Clearly, all my spiritual practice had not touched the rest of me—all the old fears, confusions, and unconscious patterns that hit me in the face when I returned to the West."

Using spirituality to make up for failures of individuation— psychologically separating from parents, cultivating self-respect, or trusting one's own intelligence as a source of guidance—also leads to many of the so-called perils of the path: spiritual materialism (using spirituality to shore up a shaky ego), grandiosity and self-inflation, "us versus them" mentality, groupthink, blind faith in charismatic teachers, and loss of discrimination. Spiritual communities can become a kind of substitute family, where the teacher is regarded as the good parent, while the students are striving to be good boys or good girls by toeing the party line, trying to please the teacher-as-parent, or driving themselves to climb the ladder of spiritual success. And spiritual practice becomes co-opted by unconscious identities and used to reinforce unconscious defenses.

For example, people who hide behind a schizoid defense (resorting to isolation and withdrawal because the interpersonal realm feels threatening) often use teachings about detachment and renunciation to rationalize their aloofness, impersonality, and disengagement, when what they really need is to become more fully embodied, more engaged with themselves, with others, and with life. Unfortunately, the Asian emphasis on impersonal realization makes it easy for alienated Western students to imagine that the personal is of little significance compared with the vastness of the great beyond. Such students are often attracted to teachings about selflessness and ultimate states, which seem to provide a rationale for not dealing with their own psychological wounding. In this way, they use Eastern teachings to cover up their incapacity in the personal and interpersonal realm.

People with a dependent personality structure, who try to please others in order to gain approval and security, often perform unstinting service for the teacher or community in order to feel worthwhile and needed. They confuse a codependent version of self-negation with true selflessness. Spiritual involvement is particularly tricky for people who hide behind a narcissistic defense, because they use spirituality to make themselves feel special and important, while supposedly working on liberation from self.

Spiritual bypassing often adopts a rationale based on using absolute truth to deny or disparage relative truth. Absolute truth is what is eternally true, now and forever, beyond any particular viewpoint. When we tap into absolute truth, we can recognize the divine beauty or larger perfection operating in the whole of reality. From this larger perspective, the murders going on in Brooklyn at this moment, for instance, do not diminish this divine perfection, for the absolute encompasses the whole panorama of life and death, in which suns, galaxies, and planets are continually being born and dying. However, from a *relative* point of view—if you are the wife of a man murdered in

Brooklyn tonight—you will probably not be moved by the truth of ultimate perfection. Instead you will be feeling human grief.

There are two ways of confusing absolute and relative truth. If you use the murder or your grief to deny or insult the higher law of the universe, you would be committing the relativist error. You would be trying to apply what is true on the horizontal plane of *becoming* to the vertical dimension of pure *being*. The spiritual bypasser makes the reverse category error, the absolutist error: he draws on absolute truth to disparage relative truth. His logic might lead to a conclusion like this: Since everything is ultimately perfect in the larger cosmic play, grieving the loss of someone you love is a sign of spiritual weakness.

Psychological realities represent relative truth. They are relative to particular individuals in particular circumstances. Even though one may know that no individual death is ultimately important on the absolute, transhuman level, one may still feel profound grief and regret about a friend's death—on the relative, human level. Because we live on both these levels, the opposite of whatever we assert is also true in some way. Jesus' advice, "Love thine enemies" and "Turn the other cheek," did not prevent him from expressing his anger toward the money changers in the temple or the hypocritical Pharisees. Likewise, our everyday experiences may often appear to be at odds with the highest truth. This creates uncertainty and ambiguity. For many people, the disparity between these two levels of truth is confusing or disturbing. They think reality has to be all one way or the other. In trying to make everything conform to a single order, they become New-Age Pollyannas or else bitter cynics.

Because we live on two levels as human beings, we can never reduce reality to a single dimension. We are not just this relative body-mind organism; we are also absolute being/awareness/presence, which is much larger than our bodily form or personal history. But we are also not *just* this larger, formless absolute; we are also incarnate as this particular individual. If we identify totally with form—our body, mind, or personality—our life will remain confined to known, familiar structures. But if we try to live only as pure emptiness, or absolute being, we may have a hard time fully engaging with our humanity. At the level of absolute truth, the personal self is not ultimately real; at the relative level, it must be respected. If we use the truth of no-self to avoid ever having to make personal statements such as "I want to know you better" to someone we love, this would be a perversion.

A client of mine who was desperate about her marriage had gone to a spiritual teacher for advice. He advised her not to be so angry with her husband, but to be a compassionate friend instead. This was certainly sound spiritual advice. Compassion is a higher truth than anger; when we rest in the absolute nature of mind—pure open aware-ness—we discover compassion as the very core of our nature. From that perspective, feeling angry about being hurt only separates us from our true nature.

Yet the teacher who gave this woman this advice did not consider her *relative* situation—that she was someone who had swallowed her anger all her life. Her father had been abusive and would slap her and send her to her room whenever she showed any anger about the way he treated her. So she learned to suppress her anger and always tried to please others and "be a good girl" instead.

When the teacher advised her to feel compassion rather than anger, she felt relieved because this fit right in with her defenses. Since anger was terrifying and threatening to her, she used the teaching on com-passion for spiritual bypassing—for refusing to deal with her anger or the message it contained. Yet this only increased her sense of frustra-tion and powerlessness in her marriage.

As her therapist, taking account of her relative psychology, my aim was to help her acknowledge her anger and relate to it more fully. As a spiritual practitioner, I was also mindful that anger is ultimately empty—a wave arising in the ocean of consciousness, without any so-lidity or inherent meaning. Yet while that understanding may be true in the absolute sense and be valuable for helping dissolve attachment to anger, it was not useful for this woman at this time. Instead, she needed to learn to pay more attention to her anger in order to move beyond a habitual pattern of self-suppression, to discover her inner strength and power, and to relate to her husband in a more active, assertive way.

Given that compassion is a finer and nobler feeling than anger, how do we arrive at genuine compassion? Spiritual bypassing involves imposing on oneself higher truths that lie far beyond one's immediate existential condition. My client's attempts at compassion were not entirely genuine because they were based on rejecting her own anger. Spiritual teachers often exhort us to be loving and compassionate, or to give up selfishness and aggression, but how can we do this if our habitual tendencies arise out of a whole system of psychological dynamics that we have never clearly seen or faced, much less worked with? People often have to feel, acknowledge, and come to terms with their anger before they can arrive at genuine forgiveness or compassion. That is relative truth.

Psychological inquiry starts there, with relative truth—with whatever we are experiencing right now. It involves opening to that experience and exploring the meaning of that experience, letting it unfold, step by step, without judging it according to preconceived ideas. As a therapist, I find that allowing whatever arises to be there as it is and gently inquiring into it leads naturally in the direction of deeper truth. This is what I call psychological work in the service of spiritual development.

Many people who seek out my services have done spiritual practice for many years. They do not suffer from traditional clinical syndromes, but from some impasse in their lives that their spiritual practice has failed to penetrate: they cannot maintain a long-term relationship, feel real joy, work productively or creatively, treat themselves with compassion, or understand why they continue to indulge in certain destructive behaviors.

I have often been struck by the huge gap between the sophistication of their spiritual practice and the level of their personal development. Some of them have spent years doing what were once considered the most advanced, esoteric practices, reserved only for the select few in traditional Asia, without developing the most rudimentary forms of self-love or interpersonal sensitivity. One woman who had undergone the rigors of a Tibetan-style three-year retreat had little ability to love herself. The rigorous training she had been through only seemed to reinforce an inner discontent that drove her to pursue high spiritual ideals, without showing any kindness toward herself or her own limitations.

Another woman had let an older teacher cruelly manipulate her. She had a habitual tendency from childhood to disregard her own needs and feelings, which, using "dharma logic," she lumped in the category of samsaric hindrances. I have also worked with seasoned spiritual teachers who felt conflicted, guilty, and hypocritical because they were not embodying the teachings they were imparting to others. Often in the course of our work, they would discover narcissistic motives underlying their spiritual ambitions: Holding a position of power and knowledge was a way to be seen as special and important, and to avoid facing their own psychological wounding.

Spiritual Superego

In addition to spiritual bypassing, another major problem for Western seekers is their susceptibility to the "spiritual superego," a harsh inner voice that acts as relentless critic and judge telling them that nothing they do is ever quite good enough: "You should meditate more and practice harder. You're too self-centered. You don't have enough devotion." This critical voice keeps track of every failure to practice or live up to the teachings, so that practice becomes more oriented toward propitiating this judgmental part of themselves than opening unconditionally to life. They may subtly regard the saints and enlightened ones as father figures who are keeping a watchful eye on all the ways they are failing to live up to their commitments. So they strive to be "dharmically correct," attempting to be more detached, compassionate, or devoted than they really are. In trying to live up to high spiritual ideals, they deny their real feelings, becoming cut off from their bodily vitality, the truth of their own experience, and their ability to find their own authentic direction.

Spiritual seekers who try to be more unemotional, unselfish, or compassionate than they really are often secretly hate themselves for the ways they fail to live up to their high ideals. This makes their spirituality cold and solemn. Their self-hatred was not created by the spiritual teaching; it already existed. But by pursuing spirituality in a way that widens the gap between how they are and how they think they should be, they wind up turning exquisite spiritual teachings on compassion and awakening into further fuel for self-hatred and inner bondage.

This raises the question of how much we can benefit from a spiritual teaching as a set of ideals, no matter how noble those ideals are. Often the striving after a spiritual ideal only serves to reinforce the critical superego—that inner voice that tells us we are never good enough, never honest enough, never loving enough. In a culture permeated by guilt and ambition, where people are desperately trying to rise above their shaky earthly foundation, the spiritual superego exerts a pervasive unconscious influence that calls for special attention and work. This requires an understanding of psychological dynamics that traditional spiritual teachings and teachers often lack.

Overcoming Praise and Blame: A Case Study

The following case study illustrates both how spiritual teaching and practice can be used to reinforce psychological defenses, and how psychological work can be a useful aid to embodying spirituality in a more integrated way.

Paul had been a dedicated Buddhist practitioner for more than two decades. He was a husband, father, and successful businessman who had recently been promoted to a position that involved public speaking. At first, he took this as an interesting challenge, but after a few experiences in front of large audiences, he started feeling overwhelmed by anxiety, worry, tension, sleeplessness, and other physical symptoms. At first, he tried to deal with his distress by meditating more. While these periods of practice would help him regain some equilibrium, the same symptoms would start to recur when he was about to face an audience again. After a few months of this, he gave me a call.

From the Buddhist teachings, Paul knew the importance of not being attached to praise and blame, two of the eight worldly concerns—along with loss and gain, pleasure and pain, success and failure—that keep us chained to the wheel of suffering. Yet it was not until his fear of public speaking brought up intense anxiety about praise and blame that he realized just how concerned he was about how people saw him. Recognizing this was extremely upsetting for him.

At first Paul waxed nostalgic about his periods of retreat, when he felt detached from such concerns, and we discussed how living in the world often brings up unresolved psychological issues that spiritual practice is not designed to address. As our work progressed, he realized that he used detachment as a defense to deny a deeper, underlying fear about how other people saw him.

He had developed this defense in childhood as a way to cope with not feeling seen by his parents. His mother had lived in a state of permanent tension and anxiety and regarded him as her potential savior, rather than as a separate being with his own feelings and life apart from her. To shield himself from her pain and intrusiveness, Paul had developed a defensive stance of not feeling his need for her and, by extension, for other people in his life.

Having tried all his life not to care about how people regarded him, he was particularly attracted to the Buddhist teachings of no-self when he first encountered them. After all, in the light of absolute truth there is nobody to be seen, nobody to be praised, nobody to be blamed—and Paul found great comfort in this. Yet on the relative level he carried within himself a denied and frustrated need to be seen and loved. In denying this need, Paul was practicing defensiveness, not true nonattachment. He was using spiritual teachings as a rationale for remaining stuck in an old defensive posture.

How could Paul be truly detached from praise and blame as long as he had a buried wish to be loved and appreciated, which he couldn't admit because it felt too threatening? Before he could truly overcome his anxieties about praise and blame, he would first have to acknowledge this wish—a prospect that was frightening and risky.

Along with his conflicted feelings about being seen, Paul also had a fair share of buried self-hatred. As his mother's appointed savior, he had desperately wanted her to be happy, and felt guilty about failing to save her. In fact, he was stuck in many of the ways his mother was stuck. His guilt and self-blame about this made him hypersensitive to blame from others.

So Paul was doubly trapped. As long as he could not acknowledge the part of him that felt, "Yes, I want to be seen and appreciated," his frustrated need for love kept him tied in knots, secretly on the lookout for others' praise and confirmation. And his inability to say, "No, I don't exist for your benefit," kept him susceptible to potential blame whenever he failed to please others.

Yes and *no* are expressions of desire and aggression—two life energies that philosophers, saints, and psychologists, from Plato and Buddha to Freud, have considered particularly problematic. Unfortunately, many spiritual teachers simply criticize passion and aggression instead of teaching people to unlock the potential intelligence hidden within them.

The intelligent impulse contained in the yes of desire is the longing to expand, to meet and connect more fully with life. The intelligence contained in no is the capacity to discriminate, differentiate, and protect oneself and others from harmful forces. The energy of the genuine, powerful no can be a doorway to strength and power, allowing us to separate from aspects of our conditioning we need to outgrow. Our capacity to express the basic power of yes and no often becomes damaged in childhood. And this incapacity becomes installed in our psychological makeup as a tendency to oscillate between compliance and defiance, as Paul exemplified in his attitude toward others—secretly feeling compelled to please them, yet secretly hating them for this at the same time.

As long as Paul failed to address his unconscious dynamic of compliance and defiance, his spiritual practice could not help him stabilize true equanimity, free from anxiety about praise and blame. Although he could experience freedom from praise and blame during periods of solitary spiritual practice, these realizations remained compartmentalized and failed to carry over into his everyday functioning.

There were two defining moments in our work together, in which Paul connected with his genuine yes and no. These two moments are also of interest in highlighting the difference between psychological and spiritual work.

Before Paul could find and express his genuine yes—to himself, to others, to life—he had to say no to the internalized mother whose influence remained alive within him: "No, I don't exist to make you happy, to be your savior, to give your life meaning." But it was not easy for him to acknowledge his anger and hatred toward his mother for the ways he had become an object of her own narcissistic needs. Quoting spiritual doctrine, Paul believed it was wrong to hate. Yet in never letting himself feel the hatred he carried unconsciously in his body, he wound up expressing it in covert, self-sabotaging ways. I did not try to push past his inner taboo against this feeling, but only invited him to acknowledge his hatred when it was apparent in his speech or demeanor. When Paul could finally let himself feel his hatred directly, instead of judging or denying it, he came alive in a whole new way. He sat up straight and broke into laughter, the laughter of an awakening vitality and power.

Articulating his genuine no, the no of protection—"I won't let you take advantage of me"—also freed him to acknowledge his hidden desire, his dormant yes—"Yes, I want to be seen for who I am, the being I am in my own right, apart from what I do for you." The second defining moment happened as Paul acknowledged this need to be seen and loved for who he was—which triggered a surge of energy coursing through him, filling his whole body. Yet this was also scary for him, for it felt as though he were becoming inflated. And for Paul, with his refined Buddhist sensibilities, self-inflation was the greatest sin of all—a symptom of a bloated ego, the way of the narcissist who is full of himself.

Seeing his resistance, I encouraged him to explore, if only for a few moments, what it would be like to let himself become inflated, to feel full of himself, and to stay present with that experience. As he let himself fill up and inflate, he experienced himself as large, rich, and radiant. He felt like a sun king, receiving energy from the gods above and below, radiating light in all directions. He realized that he had always wanted to feel this way, but had never allowed himself to expand like this before. Yet now he was letting himself be infused by the fullness that had been missing in his life—the fullness of his own being. To his surprise, he found it a tremendous relief and release to allow this expansion at last.

As Paul got over his surprise, he laughed and said, "Who would have thought that letting myself become inflated could be so liberating?" Of course, he wasn't acting out a state of ego inflation, but rather feeling what it was like to let the energy of desire, fullness, and spontaneous self-valuing flow through his body. In this moment, because he was according himself the recognition he had secretly sought from others, he did not care about how others saw him. Nor was there any desire to lord his newfound strength over anyone. He was enjoying the pure radiation of his inner richness and warmth—let others respond as they may.

Many spiritual seekers who suffer, like Paul, from a deflated sense of self interpret spiritual teachings about selflessness to mean that they should keep a lid on themselves and not let themselves shine. Yet instead of overzealously guarding against ego inflation, Paul needed to let his genie out of the bottle before he could clearly distinguish between genuine expressions of being such as power, joy, or celebration, and ego distortions such as grandiosity and conceit.

Since *need* was such a dirty word in Paul's worldview, he had used his spiritual practice as a way to overcome it. However, trying to leap directly from denial of his need for love to a state of needlessness was only spiritual bypassing—using spiritual teachings to support an unconscious defense. When he stopped fighting his need, he was able to connect with a deeper force within it—a genuine, powerful yes to life and love—which lessened his fixation on outer praise and blame. Paul discovered that this essential yes was quite different from attachment and clinging; it contained a *holy longing* to give birth to himself in a new way. Indeed, as Paul discovered his inner fire, value, and power through unlocking his genuine yes and no, he became less defensive, more open to others and to the flow of love.

Differentiated and Undifferentiated Being

This case example illustrates how unconscious psychological issues can distort someone's understanding of spiritual teachings and interfere with truly embodying them. In addition, Paul's ambivalence, self-denial, and self-blame cut off his access to deeper capacities such as strength, confidence, and the ability to connect with others in a genuinely open way. We could call these capacities *differentiated expressions of being* or *qualities of presence.* If the absolute side of our nature—undifferentiated being—is like clear light, then the relative side—differentiated being—is like a rainbow spectrum of colors contained within that light. *While realizing undifferentiated being is the path of liberation, embodying qualities of differentiated being is the path of individuation* in its deepest sense: the unfolding of our intrinsic human resources, which exist as seed potentials within us, but which are often blocked by psychological conflicts.

While realization can happen at any moment, it does not necessarily lead, as we have seen, to actualization. Although I may have access to the transparency of pure being, I may still not have access to the human capacities that will enable me to actualize that realization in the world. I may not be able to access my generosity, for instance, in situations that require it, if it is obstructed by unconscious beliefs that reinforce an identity of impoverishment and deficiency. If these subconscious beliefs are not brought to light and worked with, generosity is unlikely to manifest in a full and genuine way.

In the Buddhist tradition, differentiated being is often described in terms of "the qualities of a buddha"—wisdom, great clarity, compassion, patience, strength, or generosity. Although some lineages do not emphasize these qualities, others, such as Tibetan Vajrayana, have developed a wide range of transformational practices designed to cultivate various aspects of them.

Since these deeper capacities are often blocked by unresolved psychological issues, working with these conflicts directly can provide another way, particularly suited to Westerners, to gain access to these differentiated qualities of presence and integrate them into our character and functioning. After all, most problems in living are the result of losing access to those capacities—power, love, flexibility, confidence, or trust—that allow us to respond creatively to the challenging situations at hand. In the process of recognizing and working through our psychological conflicts, these missing capacities often become unveiled.

Because Western seekers generally suffer from a painful split between being and functioning, they need careful, specific guidance in bridging the gap between the radical openness of pure being and being in the world. Unfortunately, even in spiritual traditions that emphasize the importance of integrating realization into daily life, special instructions about how to accomplish this integration are often not very fully elaborated. Or else it is not clear how the instructions, formulated for simpler times and a simpler world, apply to handling the complexities of our fast-paced world, navigating the perils of Western-style intimate relationships, or overcoming the apparent gap many people feel between realizing impersonal being and embodying it in personal functioning. By helping people work through specific emotional conflicts that obscure their deeper capacities, psychological work can also help them bring these capacities more fully into their lives. This kind of work is like cultivating the soil in which the seeds of spiritual realization can take root and blossom.[9]

The more we cultivate the full range of human qualities latent in our absolute true nature, the richer our quality of personal presence can become, as we begin to embody our true nature in an individuated way. This type of individuation goes far beyond the secular, humanistic ideal of developing one's uniqueness, being an innovator, or living out one's dreams. Instead, it involves forging a vessel—our capacity for personal presence, nourished by its rootedness in a full spectrum of human qualities—through which we can bring absolute true nature into form: the "form" of our person.

By *person* I do not mean some fixed structure or entity, but the way in which true nature can manifest and express itself in a uniquely personal way, as the ineffable suchness or "youness" of you. How fully the suchness of *you* shines through—in your face, your speech, your actions, your particular quality of presence—is partly grace, but also partly a result of how much you have worked on polishing your vessel, so that it becomes transparent. Thus, individuation, which involves clarifying the psychological dynamics that obscure our capacity to fully shine through, is not opposed to spiritual realization. It is, instead, a way of becoming a more transparent vessel—an authentic person who can bring through what is beyond the person in a uniquely personal way.

In the secular humanistic perspective, individual development is an end in itself. In the view I am proposing here, individuation is not an end but a path or means that can help us give birth to our true form by clearing up the distortions of our old false self. As we learn to be true to our deepest individual imperatives, rather than enslaved to past conditioning, our character structure no longer poses such an obstacle to recognizing absolute true nature or embodying it. Our individuated nature becomes a window opening onto all that is beyond and greater than ourselves.

Conscious and Subconscious Identity

Spiritual traditions generally explain the cause of suffering in global, epistemological terms—as the result of ignorance, misperception, or sin—or in ontological terms—as a disconnection from our essential being. Buddhism, for instance, traces suffering to the mind's tendency to grasp and fixate—on thoughts, self-images, egocentric feelings, and distorted perceptions—as well as to ignore the deeper source of our experience—the luminous, expansive, and creative power of awareness itself. Western psychology, by contrast, offers a more specific *developmental* understanding. It shows how suffering stems from childhood conditioning; in particular, from frozen, distorted images of self and other (object relations) that we carry with us from the past. Since it understands these distorting identities as relational—formed in and through our relationships with others—psychotherapy explores these self/other structures in a relational context—in the healing environment of the client-therapist relationship.

Since the spiritual traditions do not generally recognize how the ego identity forms out of interpersonal relationships, they are unable to address these interpersonal structures directly. Instead, they offer practices—prayer, meditation, mantra, service, devotion to God or guru—that shift the attention to the universal ground of being in which the individual psyche moves, like a wave on the ocean. Thus, it becomes possible to enter luminous states of transpersonal awakening, beyond personal conflicts and limitations, without having to address or work through specific psychological issues and conflicts. Yet while this kind of realization can certainly provide access to greater wisdom and compassion, it often does not touch or alter impaired relational patterns, which, because they pervade everyday functioning, interfere with integrating this realization into the fabric of daily life.

Spiritual practice exerts a powerful global effect on the psyche by undermining the central linchpin of the ego—the identification with a fixed self-concept, which I call the *conscious identity*. The conscious identity is a self-image that allows us to imagine that we are something solid and substantial. From a Buddhist or ontological perspective, this egoic identity also functions as a defense against the reality of emptiness—the open dimension of being, with all its uncertainty, impermanence, and insubstantiality—which the ego interprets as a threat to its existence. Yet if we look at it more psychologically, we can see that the conscious identity also functions as a defense against an underlying sense of inner deficiency, which we originally felt in childhood in response to lack of love, connection, or acceptance. Even though our conscious identity is designed to overcome this sense of deficiency, inadequacy, or unworthiness, we nonetheless tend to identify subconsciously with the very lack we are trying to overcome. This deeply-embedded sense of deficiency—originating in our childhood helplessness in the face of primal fear, anxiety, or pain—is what I call the *subconscious identity*.

The ego structure as a whole thus contains both a deficient, subconscious identity and a compensatory, conscious identity. Because subconscious identities are more hidden and threatening than conscious identities, they are also much harder to acknowledge, dislodge, and transform. If we are to liberate ourselves from the whole compensatory/deficient ego structure, it seems necessary to address the interpersonal dynamics that are embedded in its fabric. The relational context of psychotherapy can often provide a direct, focused, and precise method of working through the subconscious dynamics that keep this whole identity structure intact.[10]

Paul, for example, had developed a conscious identity based on being in control of his life and "not caring what people think." This defensive control structure was a way of compensating for an underlying sense of deficiency that caused him to feel overwhelmed in interpersonal relations. His spiritual practice had partially undermined this compensatory identity by giving him direct access to his larger being. But because he also used spiritual practice as a way to bypass, or not deal with, his subconscious identity—his deeper sense of deficiency, stemming from childhood—it could not totally free him from the grip of his whole identity structure.

Since Paul did not like to feel his deficient identity and its associated feelings of anxiety, frustration, and tension, he was happy to practice spiritual methods that helped him move beyond, and thus avoid, this aspect of his ego structure. Indeed, it was much easier for him to be present with the open, spacious dimension of being than with his anxiety and helplessness when they were triggered. Yet since his capacity for presence did not extend into the totality of his psyche, it was not of much use to him when he was up against his worst demons.

Through the psychological work we did together, Paul was able to acknowledge his underlying sense of deficiency and open to the feelings of vulnerability and helplessness associated with it. Always before, when overwhelmed by obsessive thoughts of praise and blame, he would try to let go of these thoughts as he would in meditation. This was certainly of value in its own way. But our work together also gave him another way to work with this situation. He learned to bring his attention into his belly, feel the sense of deficiency directly, and bring attention to the subconscious belief at its core: "I can't handle this." In this way, he began to work directly with his subconscious identity when it became activated, instead of just trying to move beyond it. In conjunction with his meditative practice, this kind of psychological work helped Paul loosen his larger identity structure, so that he could begin to relax in situations that triggered his deepest fears.

Of course, some might argue that Paul's problem was that he failed to truly understand or apply the spiritual practices and teachings he had received. That may well be. But I don't believe his spiritual practice was a failure. It served him well in many ways. It also brought him to the point where his most primitive, unresolved psychological issues were fully exposed and ready to be worked with. Yet he needed another set of tools to address these issues directly, to penetrate the unconscious roots of his tendency to distort and compartmentalize the spiritual teachings he had received, and to become a more integrated human being.

In the end, Paul felt that both his psychological and spiritual work were of great benefit, in complementary ways. The psychological work also had a clarifying effect on his spiritual practice, by helping him make an important distinction between absolute emptiness—the ultimate reality beyond self—and relative, psychological emptiness—his inner sense of lack and deficiency. Because he had previously conflated these two types of emptiness, his spiritual practice had often served to reinforce his underlying sense of unworthiness.

Toward a Further Dialogue between East and West

The essential difference between Western and Eastern psychology is their differing emphasis on the personal and the impersonal. Unfortunately, contemporary interpretations of the Eastern spiritual teachings often make *personal* a synonym for *egoic*, with the result that the capacity for richly expressive personal presence often becomes lost. Although personal presence may not be as vast and boundless as impersonal presence, it has a mystery and beauty all its own. Martin Buber saw this "personal making-present (*personale Vergegenwärtigung*)" as an integral part of what he considered the primary unit of human experience: the I-Thou relationship. Indeed, to appreciate the power and meaning of personal presence, we only need to look into the face of someone we love. As the Irish priest John O'Donohue once remarked, "In the human face infinity becomes personal." While impersonal presence is the source of an equal concern and compassion for all beings (*agape*, in Western terms), personal presence is the source of *eros*—the intimate resonance between oneself, as this particular person, and another, whose particular suchness we respond to in a very particular way.

We in the West have been exposed to the most profound nondual teachings and practices of the East for only a few short decades. Now that we have begun to digest and assimilate them, it is time for a deeper level of dialogue between East and West, in order to develop greater understanding about the relationship between the impersonal absolute and the human, personal dimension. Indeed, expressing absolute true nature in a thoroughly personal, human form may be one of the most important evolutionary potentials of the cross-fertilization of East and West, of contemplative and psychological understanding. Bringing these two approaches into closer dialogue may help us discover how to transform our personality in a more complete way—developing it into an instrument of higher purposes—thus redeeming the whole personal realm, instead of just seeking liberation from it.

Buddhism for one has always grown by absorbing methods and understandings indigenous to the cultures to which it spread. If psychotherapy is our modern way of dealing with the psyche and its demons, analogous to the early Tibetan shamanic practices that Vajrayana Buddhism integrated into its larger framework, then the meditative traditions may find a firmer footing in our culture through recognizing and relating to Western psychology more fully. A more open and penetrating dialogue between practitioners of meditative and psychological disciplines could help the ancient spiritual traditions find new and more powerful ways of addressing the Western situation and thus have a greater impact on the direction our world is taking.

In sum, we need a new framework of understanding that can help us appreciate how psychological and spiritual work might be mutually supportive allies in the liberation and complete embodiment of the human spirit. We need to re-envision both paths for our time, so that psychological work can function in the service of spiritual development, while spiritual work can also take account of psychological development. These two convergent streams would then recognize each other as two vitally important limbs of an evolving humanity that is still moving toward realizing its potential as

—the being that can open, and know itself as belonging to the universal mystery and presence that surrounds and inhabits all things, and

—the being that can embody that larger openness as human presence in the world, through its capacity to manifest all the deeper resources implicit in its nature, thus serving as a crucial link between heaven and earth.

PART THREE

The Awakening Power *of* Relationship

Introduction

✤ THE THIRD AND FINAL PART of this book draws on understandings developed in the previous sections to illuminate what is undoubtedly the most challenging area of many people's lives—personal relationships, intimacy, love, and passion. One of the most painful ways in which the spiritual crisis of our time affects each of us is in the alienated quality of our relationships with others. In this time of wide-scale dehumanization, all kinds of relations—between friends, lovers, colleagues at work, parents and children, teachers and students—need to be revitalized and revisioned.

It is unusual to include the topic of intimate relationship in a book of this kind. Most books on spirituality, meditation, and psychospiritual issues focus on the transpersonal dimension of our nature, our spiritual essence. While the literature on meditation is vast, nowhere, East or West, do we find a richly articulated tradition that addresses how to remain conscious and awake in an intimate personal relationship. Tibetan Buddhist Tantra perhaps comes the closest, with its teachings on the union of consorts. Yet Tantric principles are quite esoteric and do not address the personal interaction that is the hallmark of modern intimacy. Aside from general recommendations about compassion, generosity, and kindness, spiritual teachings rarely address what comes up between two people who are intimately involved with each other, or how to work with it. Few works in the spiritual literature, and hardly any writing before I first published *Journey of the Heart*, have even considered interpersonal intimacy to be an important or valid vehicle on the path of awakening. To help correct that oversight, I considered it important to include these chapters on relationship in this book.

The truth is that many spiritual seekers find it much easier to feel balanced, conscious, and centered in themselves when living alone than when living with another person. When we live alone, it is easy to avoid looking closely at our habitual patterns because we live inside them. In a relationship, however, since our partner inevitably mirrors back to us how our conditioned personality affects him or her, we cannot avoid having to face all our rough edges. Intimate person-to-person contact also stirs up a whole range of unsettling feelings, along with all our fears, going back to childhood, about love, power, abandonment, betrayal, engulfment, and a host of other interpersonal threats.

Thus it is not surprising that the search for spiritual awakening has for centuries been mostly a solitary affair, often pursued in monastic, celibate, or otherworldly situations. Nor is it surprising that spiritual communities usually suffer from the same kinds of interpersonal neurosis as any other group, and often even more so. The growing consciousness that develops through spiritual practice is often not fully tested or refined in the crucible of interpersonal engagement and dialogue.

The chapters in this part focus primarily on intimate relationship as a sacred path, but also include two that address the relationship to a spiritual teacher, which in many ways resembles the connection between lover and beloved. No doubt other kinds of relationship could have been addressed here as well, since the principles essential for a conscious relationship between lovers—openness, presence, willingness to examine one's emotional reactions, communicating in a truthful and self-revealing manner—certainly hold true for all relationships. Yet I have limited my focus to intimate relationship because it is such a provocative and powerful meeting place, where the psychological and the spiritual come together in a particularly potent way.

As the Russian mystic Vladimir Solovyev wrote, erotic love "differs from other kinds of love by its greater intensity, greater absorption, and the possibility of a more complete and comprehensive reciprocity." While inspiring us to open ourselves fully to another, it stirs up all the most reactive patterns of the conditioned personality at the same time. This is precisely why it can be such a potent transformative force: It forces us to face and work on our most deeply entrenched personality patterns, in the light of our love for another. Intimacy as a transformative path calls on us to become real persons—capable of real meeting and engagement—and at the same time, to root the personal in the larger ground of being, which stretches far beyond the person. It requires us to grow up *and* wake up.

My approach to relationship as a sacred path has been largely shaped by my study of meditation and Tibetan Tantric Buddhism. The Tantric perspective, as distinct from many other Buddhist and Eastern approaches, is based on an appreciation of the love affair between absolute and relative truth, heaven and earth, emptiness and form, realization and embodiment. This love affair is graphically portrayed as the erotic union of male and female deities—eyes wide open, arms waving, and smiling fiercely—surrounded by a radiant halo of energy. These lovers are obviously not just enjoying each other but also waking each other up!

This is one of the most powerful symbolic representations of the human condition that I know. Over the years I discovered that Tantric Buddhism also contained most of the principles necessary for living—and loving another being as well—in a sane, wide awake, spiritually vital way. However, in the Tibetan tradition these principles are often articulated in esoteric ways that are not always clearly applicable to personal relationships. Since I was in desperate need for guidance in the area of relationship myself, I took it upon myself to tease out and interpret some of these principles in a new way, interweave them with certain psychological understandings, and apply them to the interpersonal arena. So while my writings on relationship only fleetingly refer to meditation or Tantric Buddhism, that tradition was a main source of inspiration for the approach I developed in *Journey of the Heart* and *Love and Awakening*. The challenge of bringing meditative principles to bear on the issues of relationship also impressed on me the importance, especially for Westerners, of integrating the impersonal realization of buddha-nature into the whole fabric of our personal embodiment.

Chapter 15 is a concise overview of my vision of intimate relationship as a path of awakening, along with its evolutionary, personal, and sacred significance.

Chapter 16 looks at relationship as a dance of polarities, which requires the capacity to move flexibly between different positions without hardening into a fixed stance. I also suggest some ways in which meditation is excellent practice for learning this kind of flexibility.

Chapter 17 looks at how the psychological obstacles in an intimate relationship can become spiritual opportunities, enabling us to gain access to deeper powers and resources of our being. This then becomes an alchemical process—refining the ore of personality in order to recover the gold of our true nature.

Chapter 18 addresses certain widespread confusions about the nature of unconditional love. It also shows how unconditional love can be a path in its own right, starting out with the first spontaneous flash of falling in love and ripening into an ongoing practice of expanding our capacity to accept all that is human in ourselves and others.

Chapter 19 sets out a new appreciation of the nature of passion that goes beyond the historical Western ambivalence toward it, which has oscillated between fascination/idealization and repulsion/condemnation. Distinguishing between conditional and unconditional passion, I try to show how passion is an awakening force in its own right. Particularly interesting are the parallels between romantic passion and the devotion of a student toward a spiritual teacher.

Chapter 20 considers the great pitfalls and the great promise of the relationship between spiritual master and student—another area of tremendous confusion in our culture. Growing out of a yearlong research project, this chapter explores characteristics of pathological cults and the nature of spiritual authority. It also discusses the important differences between problematic teacher-student relationships and beneficial ones.

Chapter 21, a concluding conversation with writer Paul Shippee, brings together many themes of the book. Here I propose that the work of conscious relationship between two individuals is a powerful force that can help not only to awaken two individuals but also to regenerate greater heart and soulfulness, along with a renewed sense of community, in the world.

15

Intimate Relationship as Transformative Path

All genuine love . . . is based on the possibility the beloved offers to the lover for a fuller unfolding of his own being by being-in-the-world with her.

—MEDARD BOSS

TWO PEOPLE SEEKING to fashion a life together today face a unique set of challenges and difficulties. Never before have couples had so little help or guidance from elders, society, or religion. Most of the old social and economic rationales for marriage as a life-long relationship have broken down. Even the old incentives for having children—to carry on the family name or trade, or to contribute to family work, providing an economic asset—are mostly gone. For the first time in history, the relations between men and women lack clear guidelines, supportive family networks, a religious context, and a compelling social meaning.

Until recently, the form and function of the male/female relationship, and marriage in particular, were carefully prescribed by family, society, and religion. One's family always chose or at least had veto power over one's choice of a marriage partner. Every couple had a set of defined roles within an extended family, which in turn had a place in a close-knit community or village where people shared similar social, moral, and religious values and customs. Marriage had a central place in the community, providing a stabilizing influence and supporting the social order. And society supported it in turn: if a marriage was unhappy, community pressure held it together.

Only in the last few generations has this situation changed. Now that marriage has lost most of its traditional supports and couples are increasingly cut off from family, community, and widely shared values, there are few convincing *extrinsic* reasons for a man and a woman to sustain a life's journey together. Only the *intrinsic* quality of their personal connection can keep them going. For the first time in history, every couple is on their own—to discover how to build a healthy relationship, and to forge their own vision of how and why to be together.

Those of us who are struggling with questions of love and commitment today are pioneers in territory that has never before been consciously explored. It is important to realize just how new this situation is, so we do not blame ourselves for the difficulties we face in our relationships. In former times, if people wanted to explore the deeper mysteries of life, they would often enter a monastery or hermitage far away from conventional family ties. For many of us today, however, intimate relationship has become the new wilderness that brings us face to face with all our gods and demons. It is calling on us to free ourselves from old habits and blind spots, and to develop the full range of our powers, sensitivities, and depths as human beings—right in the middle of everyday life.

Toward a New Vision of Relationship

Traditional marriage achieved stability by serving a prescribed societal function. Modern marriage, by contrast, is based on *feeling* rather than *function*. No wonder it is so unstable. Romantic feelings, while inspiring, are notoriously fickle. Long-term relationships clearly need a new foundation, beyond social duty and romantic intensity. We need a whole new vision and context that can help couples find fresh direction and inspiration.

If we are to cultivate a new spirit of engagement in our intimate relationships, I suggest that we need to recognize and welcome the powerful opportunity that intimate relationships provide—to awaken to our true nature. If relationships are to flourish, they need to reflect and promote who we really are, beyond any limited image of ourselves concocted by family, society, or our own minds. They need to be based on the whole of who we are, rather than on any single form, function, or feeling. This presents a tremendous challenge, for it means undertaking a journey in search of our deepest nature. Our connection with someone we love can in fact be one of the best vehicles for that journey. When we approach it in this way, intimacy becomes a path—an unfolding process of personal and spiritual development.

If form and feeling, duty and romance, have been thesis and antithesis in the historical dialectic of marriage, the new synthesis we can now begin to contemplate is *marriage as a conscious relationship*, which joins together heaven and earth. Since men and women have only rarely looked at each other eye to eye, as equals, as whole human beings, apart from roles, stereotypes, and inherited prescriptions of all kinds, conscious relationship between the sexes is a radical new departure.

The Greek myth of Eros and Psyche suggests what the journey of conscious relationship may entail. Eros becomes Psyche's lover by night on the condition that she must never attempt to see his face. Things go smoothly between them for a while. But never having seen her lover, Psyche begins to wonder who he really is. When she lights a lamp to see his face, he flies away, and she must undergo a series of trials to find him again. When she finally overcomes these trials, she is united with him again, only this time in a much fuller way, and their love can proceed in the light of day.

This myth points to the age-old tension between consciousness (Psyche) and erotic love (Eros). Traditional Western marriages have been like love in the dark. Yet now that relationships no longer function smoothly in the old unconscious grooves, they require a new kind of awareness. Like Psyche, we are presently undergoing the trials that every advance in consciousness entails.

The Nature of Path

Path is a term that points to the great challenge of our existence: the need to awaken, each in our own way, to the greater possibilities that life presents, and to become fully human. The nature of a path is to take us on this journey.

Becoming fully human involves working with the totality of what we are—both our conditioned nature (earth) and our unconditioned nature (heaven). On the one hand, we have developed a number of habitual personality patterns that cloud our awareness, distort our feelings, and restrict our capacity to open to life and to love. We originally fashioned our personality patterns to shield us from pain, but now they have become a dead weight keeping us from living as fully as we could. Still, underneath all our conditioned behavior, the basic nature of the human heart is an unconditioned awake presence, a caring, inquisitive intelligence, an openness to reality. Each of us has these two forces at work inside us: an embryonic wisdom that wants to blossom from the depths of our being, and the imprisoning weight of our karmic patterns. From birth to death, these two forces are always at work, and our lives hang in the balance. Since human nature always contains these two sides, our journey involves working with both.

Intimate relationships are ideally suited as a path because they touch both these sides of us and bring them into forceful contact. When we connect deeply with another person, our heart naturally opens toward a whole new world of possibilities. Yet this breath of fresh air also makes us more aware of how we are stuck. Relationship inevitably brings us up against our most painful unresolved emotional conflicts from the past, continually stirring us up against things in ourselves that we cannot stand—all our worst fears, neuroses, and fixations—in living technicolor.

If we focus on only one side of our nature at the expense of the other, we have no path, and therefore cannot find a way forward. This also limits the possibilities of our relationships as well. If we emphasize only the wonderful aspects of relationship, we become caught in the "bliss trap"—imagining that love is a stairway to heaven that will allow us to rise above the nitty-gritty of our personality and leave behind all fear and limitation: "Love is so fantastic! I feel so high! Let's get married; won't everything be wonderful!" Of course these expansive feelings are wonderful. But the potential distortion here is to imagine that love by itself can solve all our problems, provide endless comfort and pleasure, or save us from facing ourselves, our aloneness, our pain, or ultimately, our death. Becoming too attached to the heavenly side of love leads to rude shocks and disappointments when we inevitably have to deal with the real-life challenges of making a relationship work.

The other distortion is to make relationship into something totally familiar and totally safe, to treat it as a finished product, rather than a living process. This is the security trap. When we try to make a relationship serve our needs for security, we lose a sense of greater vision and adventure. Relationship becomes a business deal, or else totally monotonous. A life devoted to everyday routines and security concerns eventually becomes too stale and predictable to satisfy the deeper longings of the heart.

Once a couple loses a sense of larger vision, they often try to fill the void that remains by creating a cozy materialistic lifestyle—watching television, acquiring upscale possessions, or climbing the social ladder. Curling up in their habitual patterns, they may fall entirely asleep. After twenty years of marriage, one of them may wake up wondering, "What have I done with my life?" and suddenly disappear in search of what has been lost.

Neither of these approaches leads very far or provides a path. The illusion of heavenly bliss may allow us to ascend for a while, until we finally crash when the relationship inevitably comes back down to earth. The illusion of security keeps us glued to the earth, so that we never venture to reach beyond ourselves at all.

Love is a transformative power precisely because it brings the two different sides of ourselves—the expansive and the contracted, the awake and the asleep—into direct contact. Our heart can start to work on our karma: rigid places in us that we have hidden from view suddenly come out in the open and soften in love's blazing warmth. And our karma starts to work on our heart: coming up against difficult places in ourselves and our partner forces our heart to open and expand in new ways. Love challenges us to keep expanding in exactly those places where we imagine we can't possibly open any further.

From the perspective of bliss or security, it seems terrible that relationships confront us with so many things in ourselves we would rather not look at. But from the perspective of *path*, this is a great opportunity. Intimate relationships can help free us from our karmic entanglements by showing us exactly how and where we are stuck. When someone we love reacts to our unconscious patterns, these patterns bounce back on us and can no longer be ignored. When we see and feel the ways that we are stuck, in the context of a loving relationship, a desire to move in a new direction naturally begins to stir in us. Then our path begins to unfold.

So even though the current upheavals going on between men and women may seem daunting and perplexing, they are also forcing us to become more conscious in our relationships. In looking beyond comfort and security needs, we can begin to appreciate the pure essence of relationship, its capacity to bring together the polarities of our existence—our buddha-nature and our karmic tendencies, heaven and earth, unconditioned mind and conditioned mind, vision and practicality, male and female, self and other—and heal our divisions, both inner and outer.

Tapping Larger Qualities of Being

If our heart is like a flame, our karma or conditioned habits are the fuel this fire needs in order to blaze brightly. Although the burning of old karma creates great turbulence, it also releases powerful resources within us that have been locked up in our habitual patterns. As these patterns start to break down, we gain access to a wider spectrum of our human qualities.

All the most universally valued qualities—such as generosity, tenderness, humor, strength, courage, or patience—allow us to be more fully human by enabling us to meet whatever life presents. Each of these resources allows us to engage with a different facet of reality. The more of them we have access to, the more we can embrace the whole of life—in its joys and delights, as well as in its difficulties and sorrows.

We each have access to a whole spectrum of these human qualities, at least as seed potentials. Yet most of us have developed one type of quality, such as strength, at the expense of its opposite, such as tenderness. In this way, we are lopsided and incomplete. This sense of incompleteness is part of what draws us to relationship. We often feel most strongly attracted to people who manifest qualities we lack and who challenge us to develop a greater fullness and depth of being than we have yet discovered.

As our habitual patterns burn in the fire of intimate relationship, our genuine human qualities become released. For instance, when we can no longer maintain our old guardedness with someone we love, we may feel quite naked and vulnerable without this old shield to hide behind. Yet this nakedness also makes us more transparent to our true nature. The less we need to hide, the more we can come forward as we really are. And this deeper connection to ourselves also provides access to the inner resource we most need in letting down our guard: true strength, which comes from within, rather than from having the upper hand. This is how love's alchemy works.

Three Levels of the Path: Evolutionary, Personal, and Sacred

The path of conscious love has three different, interrelated dimensions. At the collective level, it has evolutionary significance. Centuries of imbalance between the masculine and feminine ways of being have left a deep scar in the human psyche. No one can escape the effects of this wound—which pervade both our inner and outer lives. Inwardly we experience it as a split between heart and mind, feeling and thinking, tenderness and strength; outwardly it manifests in the war between the sexes and in the mindless ravaging of nature that is endangering our planet. Until human consciousness can transform the ancient antagonism between masculine and feminine into a creative alliance, we will remain fragmented and at war with ourselves, as individuals, as couples, as societies, and as a race.

Developing a new depth and quality of intimacy in our relationships today is an important step in healing this age-old rift and bringing together the two halves of our humanity. As we begin to move in this direction, the man/woman relationship takes on a larger purpose, beyond just survival or security. It becomes an *evolutionary path*—an instrument for the evolution of human consciousness.

Secondly, as a *personal path* relationship involves moving through our individual barriers to openness and intimacy, contacting deeper levels of our being, and gaining access to the full range of our human resources. By helping us become more fully available to the creative possibilities of our life, intimate relationship refines us as individuals and can transform us into more awake, fully developed human beings.

Beyond that, the love between man and woman presents a sacred challenge—to go beyond the single-minded pursuit of purely personal gratifications, to overcome the war between self and other, and to discover what is most essential and real—the depths and heights of life as a whole. Through helping us heal our alienation from life, from other people, and from ourselves, relationship becomes a *sacred path*. I don't mean to suggest that a relationship in and of itself is a complete path that can substitute for other spiritual practices. But if we have some aspiration and dedication to wake up to our true nature, along with a practice that helps us do that, then in that context, relationship can be a particularly potent vehicle to help us contact a deeper level of truth.

In this light, the difficult challenges that men and women encounter in joining their energies together are not just personal travails. They are also invitations to open ourselves to the sacred play of the known and the unknown, the seen and the unseen, and the larger truths born out of intimate contact with the great mystery of life itself.

16

Dancing on the Razor's Edge

✤ INTIMATE RELATIONSHIP is a dynamic, often dizzying dance of contradictions that is sometimes delightful and seductive, sometimes fierce and combative, sometimes energizing, sometimes exhausting. This dance requires being able to flow continuously back and forth between polar opposites—between coming together and moving apart, taking hold and letting go, engaging and allowing space, yielding and taking the lead, surrendering and standing firm, being soft and being strong. This is not an easy dance to learn. Many couples quickly lose the flow, fall out of step, and wind up deadlocked in antagonistic positions, struggling for supremacy, pushing and pulling, attacking or withdrawing. Teachers of the dance are few, and as the years go by the conventional dance steps we learned from the culture seem increasingly stiff and outmoded. How, we may wonder, can we learn to dance with grace and power?

The back and forth begins as soon as we find ourselves attracted to another person who moves us. On one hand, we long to break out of our separateness and go out to meet this person who represents a whole new, unexplored world. Yet at the same time, we also experience trepidation. Going out to another entails some big risks, and we find ourselves hanging on for dear life to the very separateness we long to overcome. In our attraction to another, we seem to be expanding and contracting at the same time, or at least in rapid alternation.

Meditation practice can teach us a great deal about how to flow with the dance of relationship, because it is designed to overcome the split between self and other—within ourselves, first of all. Sitting quietly, following the breath while letting thoughts and feelings arise and pass away, we start to overcome our separation from our own experience, which we often keep at arm's length. We see how the struggle of grasping experiences we like and rejecting experiences we don't like keeps us stuck in reactive mind and prevents us from being fully present. In releasing ourselves from this struggle with our experience, we discover our larger nature, which is able to be with what is, free of reactivity.

Meditation also helps us work with the basic polar tension of human life—between heaven and earth, emptiness and form—which all relationships intensify. By learning to keep our seat regardless of what is going on in our mind, we come down to earth. We find that we cannot escape this form, this body, these needs and feelings, this karma, these characteristics and traits, this personal history. Following the breath, letting go of mental fixations, and resting again and again in the present moment, we also connect with openness and space—the heaven principle (for a fuller discussion of the heaven and earth principles, see chapter 1). And as we keep our seat and let go with the breath, the whole soft front of the body, through which we let the world and other people in, starts to open up. This soft, open front represents our humanness, which joins together heaven and earth.

In a relationship, keeping our seat might mean maintaining our own sense of integrity in the face of outer demands and manipulations, or inner fears and compulsions. And the meditative practice of letting go of mental fixations might correspond in a relationship to not becoming locked into any fixed position, not making our ego a solid fortress, but being willing to soften our heart, let down our guard, and risk ourselves in love.

The Buddha likened meditative awareness to tuning a musical instrument—the strings must be neither too tight nor too loose. If we hold on too tight or let go too much, we lose our balance. This kind of balancing act is crucial in relationships. While it is important to respect our own needs (the earth principle), we must also be able to let go of being too identified with them (the heaven principle). While we must be able to meet another with engagement and commitment (form), we must also be able to let go of the relationship, drop all our agendas and ideas about it, and give the connection room to ebb and flow as it may (emptiness). And though we must loosen our boundaries to unite with another person, if we simply merge with the other, we may lose ourselves in the relationship—which usually spells disaster. Relationship is full of these contradictions. We want freedom, yet we also want stability and commitment. Can we have both? Can we remain loving when anger and critical feelings arise? How can we surrender in a relationship without losing our power and being controlled by the other person? How can we come to know another yet continue to see him or her with fresh eyes?

It would be so much easier if we could just maintain a safe distance and a clear set of boundaries to protect us from risking too much, or if we could simply merge with the other person and lose ourselves in the relationship. But neither of these alternatives is possible or satisfactory. In learning to swing back and forth between too tight and too loose, our movements become more fluid, and the dance begins to develop grace and vigor.

The path of working with the polarities and contradictions of being human—in classical Buddhist terms, "the middle way"—involves not identifying with anything: either pleasure or pain, separateness or togetherness, attachment or detachment. The middle way is not some bland middle ground. Rather, it requires us to be alert and awake at all times, so that we do not harden into any position, no matter how righteous it may seem. Not solidifying a position keeps us sensitive to what is needed at each moment, so that the dance of relationship can continue to flow fluidly. When two people become too invested in their positions (for example, "I need more closeness" versus "I need more space"), they become polarized and the dance grinds to a halt.

The middle way is not about weighing one thing against another so that the scales even out. It is a much more dynamic and immediate process, which involves becoming aware of how we lose our balance. In losing our seat, the very act of falling out of it wakes us up; and in waking up, we regain our seat. Regaining our seat means coming back to the present, letting go of identifying with this or that position, and taking a fresh look at what is going on and what the situation needs right now. Not that we should never take a stand; indeed, right now the situation may require me to stand up for what is important to me, even fight for it if I have to. But tomorrow, circumstances may call on me to let go of this stand, give in, and let my partner's needs take precedence over mine.

The paradox of relationship is that it calls on us to be ourselves fully, to express who we are without hesitation, to take a stand on this earth, and at the same time, to let go of fixed positions and our attachment to them. Nonattachment in relationship doesn't mean not having needs or paying no attention to them. If we ignore or deny our needs, we cut off part of ourselves and therefore have less of ourselves to offer our partner. Nonattachment in the best sense means not being identified with our needs, our likes and dislikes. We recognize certain needs, yet we also have a connection with our larger being, where those needs do not have a hold over us. Then we can either assert our desire or let it go, according to the dictates of the moment.

Tantric Buddhism describes the middle way—living in the present without fixed strategy or agenda—in sharper terms, as a razor's edge. Whenever we solidify or identify with any position—exclusively arguing for closeness or space, separateness or togetherness, freedom or commitment—we fall off this edge and can harm ourselves because we lose touch with the whole of what we are, in favor of one isolated part. We need to keep coming back again and again to the open-ended quality of the present moment, which is as sharp and thin as a razor's edge.

Finding our way back to fresh, unpredictable nowness is a dynamic rebalancing act, which gives us a slight jolt that wakes us up from our daydreams and imaginings. These little moments of waking up to the present—of beginner's mind—are pulsing with uncertainty. In the split second of nowness I realize that I really don't know what's going on. How could I? I only just arrived here! When I wake up from my fantasy of the relationship and look freshly into my partner's eyes, I suddenly realize, "I don't know who you are." And further, I don't know who I am, I don't know what this relationship is. In such moments there is freedom to start fresh all over again. We don't have to become stuck in our hopes or images about who we are or where this relationship is going. At the same time, we can't make not knowing into a fixed position either.

Dancing on the razor's edge involves living from the ground of our larger being, which enables us to welcome and allow all of what we are as human beings. After a fight with my partner, part of me wants to nurse my anger, and another part of me wants to drop it and show my love instead. This uncertainty brings me once again to the knife's edge of the present. Feeling all that I feel at this moment—I am angry, and I also love you intensely—can be quite unsettling. Yet in such moments we also taste what it means to be human: we have these emotions, and we do not have to deny or transcend them. Nor do we have to get stuck in our angry thoughts, using them to build a solid case that allows us to justify ourselves or attack the other person. Here on the edge of uncertainty, where we are simply present with what is, we can only respond freshly to what is happening. The challenge of feeling all that we are, expanding to include it all, and not settling into a fixed position stretches the heart and allows a larger love to flow, free from confinement to any viewpoint.

Some people would rather meditate in solitude than relate to other people, while others would rather relate than meditate. Personally, I consider meditation and relationship both indispensable for developing the full range of our human capacities. And meditation is the most powerful practice I have found for learning how to handle the challenges of relationship—practice for the further practice of loving another. Both of these practices are equally challenging.

17

Refining the Gold

✤ THE POET RILKE once wrote, "For one human being to love another, this is the most difficult of all our tasks, the work for which all other work is but preparation. It is a great, exacting claim upon us, something that chooses us out and calls us to vast things." In these few words Rilke addresses the totality of what an intimate relationship presents us with: the most difficult work of all, and at the same time, a calling to vast things. A deep, loving connection with another being always leads in both directions—bringing up tremendous challenges, while also inspiring us to expand in new, unforeseen directions. We cannot separate the difficulties from the vast things—they go hand in hand.

Now that the traditional rationales for marriage have withered away, and the modern dream of living happily ever after in romantic bliss has not borne fruit, we need to re-envision the purpose of intimate relationship from the ground up. It is time for couple's consciousness-raising, starting with the most basic questions: What is a couple? What is the purpose and meaning of intimate relationship? What are two people actually meant to do together?

One way to approach these questions is by considering what makes being in love such a powerful experience. When I ask people what they most value about falling in love, they mention qualities such as joy, truth, passion, acceptance, vitality, surrender, innocence, power, magic, openness, curiosity, aliveness, creativity, awakeness, purpose, genuineness, trust, appreciation, and expansiveness. When we recognize that these qualities are facets of our true nature, it becomes clear that falling in love can provide a powerful glimpse of who we really are. Opening to another in love gives us a taste of what it is like to be fully present and awake, with access to a rainbow spectrum of human resources emanating from deep within. Falling in love is an act of grace that stirs our dormant seed potentials. Though some people regard falling in love as an illusion or temporary psychosis, that is true only when we imagine our partner to be the source of these larger qualities, and then grasp at the other to give us what is already ours.

For most of us, our deepest potentials are like seeds that have gone dormant or become deformed in the course of our development. To the extent that we were not received with unconditional love, or never felt truly seen or encouraged to be ourselves, we had to shut down as children to protect ourselves from the enormity of that pain, which threatened to overwhelm us. Emily Dickinson wrote of this in one of her poems:

> *There is a pain so utter*
> *It swallows Being up.*
> *Then covers the abyss with trance,*
> *So memory can step*
> *Around, across, upon it.*

As children, the pain of not being truly seen or loved is so *utter* that we contract and thus disconnect from the original openness of our being. This loss of being leaves behind an abyss, a gaping hole, which we cover up with trance—with beliefs, imaginings, and stories about who we are. Our ego structure develops as a survival strategy, as a way of getting by in a world that does not see or support who we really are. It is a protective shell, which diverts our attention from the abyss of loss of being, so that our mind can "step around, across, upon it" without falling in. Yet the shell of our self-constructed identity also blocks access to the deeper seed potentials—for passion, vitality, joy, power, wisdom, presence—contained in our basic nature.

Later in life when we experience a deep loving connection with someone, it is like letting in the warmth of the sun, which stirs the dormant seed within the shell. This might happen with a lover, a spiritual teacher, or a friend. Yet as the seed starts to swell, this expansion brings us up against the hard shell in which we are encased—our conditioned ego structure, which now functions as a soul cage.

Thus, at the outset of a relationship, we expand, until we hit the imprisoning shell of our self-concepts, based on our early transactions with adults in childhood: "I'm a bad boy . . . I'm a good girl . . . I'm special . . . I don't need anyone . . . I'm helpless . . . I'm inadequate . . . I need to maintain control . . . I need to please."

As the expansive force of love threatens these outmoded identities from the past, this brings us to the razor's edge. Here in this zone of uncertainty that emerges when we move from the known into the unknown, we can no longer bear to continue playing out our old patterns, yet nothing new has emerged to take their place. This provides an opportunity to experience what it is like to simply be, without knowing who we are. It can be a scary place to be. At this point people often start to feel, "I don't know if I can handle this relationship. This isn't what I bargained for—not knowing who I am!"

A Hasidic master quoted by Martin Buber describes this in-between zone: "Nothing in the world can change from one reality into another unless it first turns into nothing, that is, into the reality of the between-stage. And then it is made into a new creature, from the egg to the chick. The moment when the egg is no more and the chick is not yet, is nothingness. This is the primal state which no one can grasp because it is a force which precedes creation. It is called chaos." We all experience these moments of chaos when an old identity, with its sense of safety and security, is threatened. This is one of the most creative moments in a relationship, since it is where something really new can happen. As Chögyam Trungpa once said, "Chaos should be regarded as extremely good news."

The deeper a relationship goes, the more it brings old darkness and pain to light. A genuine soul connection between two people always challenges any identity that interferes with the free flow of love, such as "I can't really have this" or "I don't deserve it." Even if we are discovering a depth of connection we've never known before, if we have a subconscious belief that we don't deserve to feel this good, it's not going to last. The undeserving identity will cut it off. Therefore, true love calls for the death of this false self. As the Sufi poet Ibn Al Faradh wrote:

Dying through love is living;
I give thanks to my beloved that she has held this out for me.
For whoever does not die of his love
Is unable to live by it.

Of course, the prospect of letting go of our old, cherished identities inevitably brings up tremendous fear and resistance. Yet if we can let our resistances—which are signs of where we are attached to an old identity—come up and be worked with, this will allow us to take real steps forward on this path. Just as all forward movement—foot against ground, wheel against pavement—requires resistance, so too love advances through encountering and overcoming resistance. In this sense, every psychological difficulty in a relationship provides a spiritual opportunity—to work through the obstacles presented by our conditioned patterns and gain greater access to essential inner resources.

The Sufis make an interesting distinction between what they call "states" and "stations." A state is a temporary moment of access to an essential human quality—such as aliveness, joy, strength, kindness—that arises and passes away spontaneously, beyond our power to call it up or hold on to it. A station is the same essential quality when we have fully integrated it, so that we have permanent access to it whenever it is called for.

In love's early grace period, we experience the *state* of love and presence, but we are not yet installed in the *station* of love and presence. We glimpse the gold of our true nature, but soon discover that we don't have full access to that gold. It is still embedded in the iron ore of our conditioned patterns. If love or any other quality of our being is to become a station in our lives, rather than just a passing state, we must go through a refining process, in which the gold is extracted from the ore. This refining is the journey of conscious love.

18

Love, Conditional and Unconditional

❖ EVERY HUMAN BEING INTUITIVELY recognizes at their core the value of unconditional love. We experience the greatest joy in loving when we can open to another without reservation, suspending judgments and fully appreciating the other just for who he or she is. And we feel most loved when others recognize and respond to us this way as well. Unconditional love has tremendous power, awakening a larger presence within us that allows us to feel the vastness and profundity of what it is to be human. This is the presence of the heart.

We often experience flashes of unconditional love most vividly in beginnings and endings—at birth, at death, or when first falling in love—when another person's pure suchness shines through and touches us directly. Tough, frozen places inside begin to melt and soften as love's spontaneous arising warms us like spring sun. Yet soon enough, especially in intimate relationships, we come up against inner fears, restraints, or cautions about letting our love flow too freely. Will we get swept away? Can we let ourselves feel this open? Will we get hurt? Can we trust this person? Will we be able to get our needs met in this relationship? Can we live with the things that irritate us in the other? These cautions lead us to place conditions on our openness: "I can only be this open and vulnerable with you *if* . . . I get my needs met; you love me as much as I love you; you don't hurt me . . ."

This pull between loving unconditionally and loving with conditions heightens the tension between two different sides of our nature—the unconditional openness of the heart and the conditional wants and needs that are part of our personality. Yet this very tension between conditional and unconditional love, if clearly seen and worked with, can actually help us learn to love more deeply. The friction between these two sides of our nature can ignite a refining fire that awakens the heart to the real challenge, the outrageous risk, and the tremendous gift of human love.

Unconditional Love and Conditional Love

It is the heart's nature to want to circulate love freely back and forth, without putting limiting conditions on that exchange. The heart looks right past things that may offend our personal tastes, often rejoicing in another's being despite all our reasonable intentions to maintain a safe distance, play it cool, or break off contact if the relationship is too painful. Love in its deepest essence knows nothing of conditions and is quite unreasonable. Once the heart has opened to someone who has deeply touched us, we will most likely still feel some connection with that person for the rest of our lives, whatever form the relationship takes. Unconditional love has its reasons, which reason cannot know.

Unconditional love does not imply that a relationship must take a particular form. We may love someone deeply, yet still be unable to live with that person. Inasmuch as we are not just pure heart, but also have conditioned likes and dislikes, certain conditions will always determine how fully we become involved with another. This is inevitable. As soon as we consider the *form* of relationship we want with someone, we are in the realm of conditions. Because we are of this earth, we exist within certain forms and structures (body, temperament, personality characteristics, emotional needs, likes and dislikes, sexual preferences, styles of communication, lifestyles, beliefs and values) that fit with someone else's patterns more or less well. For an ongoing relationship to work, certain kinds of "chemistry," compatibility, or communication must be possible.

Conditional love is a feeling of pleasure and attraction based on how fully someone matches our needs, desires, and personal considerations. It is a response to a person's looks, style, personal presence, emotional availability—what he or she does for us. This is not something bad, but it is a lesser form of love, because it can easily be negated by a reversal of the conditions under which it formed. If someone we love starts acting in ways we don't like, we may not like him as much anymore. Conditional liking inevitably gives way to opposite feelings of fear, anger, or hatred when our personality is in conflict with another's personality.

Still, love in its deepest essence knows nothing of these conditions. Beyond both conditional yes and conditional no lies the larger unconditional yes of the heart.

Confusing the Two Orders of Love

We often feel most strongly attracted to another when the two orders of love are in accord: this person not only touches our heart but also fulfills certain conditions for what we want from an intimate partner. It can be extremely confusing when these two orders are in conflict. Perhaps this person meets our conditions but somehow does not move us very deeply. Or else he or she touches our heart, so that we want to open and say yes, yet our personal considerations and criteria lead us to say no.

A common mistake at this point is to try to impose our conditional no on the yes of the heart. For instance, if we have to end a relationship because the other cannot meet certain essential needs of ours, our heart may still want to keep right on loving this person just the same. To deny or cut off the love that is still flowing can be quite damaging, for this would constrict the very source of joy and aliveness inside us. Whenever we forcibly try to close our heart to someone we love, even in times of separation, we only create greater suffering for ourselves and make it harder to open up again the next time we fall in love.

Similarly, whenever someone we love hurts us, and we feel disappointment, anger, or hatred toward that person, we may try to stop loving, to shut down the heart, as punishment or revenge. But the truth is, because we still love this person, denying it by trying to close the heart hurts us just as much as it hurts the other. Unconditional love means being able to recognize our love for another even in the midst of our hate.

In fact, it is not really possible to close the heart. What we can do is to *close off* the heart, by building a barrier around it. The danger here lies in closing ourselves off from people in general and shutting ourselves in. Damming up the natural outflow of the heart creates a pool of stagnant energy that breeds psychological dis-ease.

I am not suggesting that we should stay in a relationship that doesn't work just because our heart is open to the other person. We may indeed have to break off contact and communication with someone in order to recover from the pain of a separation. But this does not mean that we have to constrict the love that still flows from the heart. Even if we feel hatred for the other, this is possible only because the heart has been so open, because we have felt so vulnerable with this person. Understanding this can help prevent our feelings of hatred from freezing solid and allow them to pass through us without turning into a weapon or doing real harm.

The other common way of confusing the two orders of love is by trying to impose the yes of the heart on the no of our personal considerations. A common misconception of unconditional love is that it requires putting up with everything someone does. An article in *Scientific American* illustrated this misconception when it stated, "Unconditional love and support can be damaging to the development of a child's self-esteem. . . . Most parents are too concerned with making life easy for their children."[1] The confusion here lies in equating unconditional love with undiscriminating acclaim, permissiveness, or indulgence.

Imagining that we should tolerate unconditionally that which is conditioned—another's personality, behavior, or lifestyle—can have very painful or destructive consequences. Unconditional love does not mean having to like something we in fact dislike or saying yes when we need to say no. Unconditional love arises from an entirely different place within us than conditional like and dislike, attraction and resistance. It is a being-to-being acknowledgment. And it responds to that which is itself unconditional—the intrinsic goodness of another person's heart, beyond all their defenses and pretenses. Arising from our own basic goodness, unconditional love resonates with and reveals the unconditional goodness in others as well.

The parent-child relationship provides our first experience of the confusing ways in which conditional and unconditional love become mixed up. Although most parents originally feel a vast, choiceless love for their newborn child, they eventually place overt or covert conditions on their love, using it as a way of controlling the child, turning it into a reward for desired behaviors. The result is that as children we rarely grow up feeling loved for ourselves, just as we are. We internalize the conditions our parents put on their love, and this internalized parent (the "superego" or "inner critic") often rules our lives. We keep trying to placate this inner voice, which continually judges us as never good enough.

In this way we become conditional toward ourselves as well. We think we have to earn love, as a reward for being good. We like ourselves only *if*—if we live up to some standard, if we don't have this fear, if we're firmly in control, if we prove ourselves, if we are a good boy or girl, a good achiever, a good lover, and so on. We come to distrust that we could be lovable just as we are, just for being ourselves. Internalizing the restrictions placed on love in our family, we create an elaborate system of dams, checks, and blockages, armoring and tensions in the body that constrict the free flow of love. And so we perpetuate and pass on to our children the pain and confusion that results from putting conditions on the love whose nature is to flow freely from the heart.

Nonetheless, underneath these distortions of love, and all the disappointment or anger that may exist between children and parents, most of us can find at the core of this connection a larger, choiceless caring and concern that has no why or wherefore—it simply is, and it never entirely disappears, no matter what happens. No matter how their love gets distorted, parents and children cannot entirely cut off the unconditional openness of their hearts toward each other.

Trusting in the Goodness of the Heart

As a spontaneous outflow of the heart, unconditional love is often most obvious in the early stages of an intimate relationship. But it often becomes obscured by two partners' struggle to see if they can fit, communicate, meet each other's needs, or create a working partnership. It may also get buried beneath preoccupations with the stresses of everyday life, family responsibilities, and work demands. How then can we stay in touch with the revitalizing presence of unconditional love in an ongoing way?

The most obvious answer is to learn to trust in the heart. Yet how do we do this? We need an actual way to develop this trust, not as an article of belief or hope, but as a living experience.

The best way I have found to develop this trust is through the practice of awareness and inquiry, both through meditation and focused self-reflection. At first, we need to become conscious of the mind's desperate attempts to *prove* that we are good by fulfilling certain conditions, and to see our tendency to beat ourselves up when we fail to live up to those conditions. All the things we dislike about ourselves—the tight, constricted, shut-down parts of us that give us the most trouble—are like children in need of our attention, whom we have cut off from our unconditional caring. Seeing all of this also helps us feel the tremendous suffering that whole project causes us. Out of that, it becomes possible to recognize the importance of opening our heart to ourselves without conditions.

We have to start with ourselves. As long as we are conditional in accepting ourselves, we will inevitably be conditional with others in a similar way.

Breaking Open the Heart

Through activating the flow of unconditional love within us, intimate relationship can be profoundly healing, as we learn to open our heart to parts of ourselves and others that have been wounded, cut off, or deprived of caring. Yet the heavenly perfection of unconditional love, which we may know in our heart, rarely translates into perfect love or union with another on the worldly plane. Human relationships are always a work in progress. They are like clay we are continually reworking, so that it embodies and expresses the perfect love that is our very essence. Because two people live in space and time, with different experiences, temperaments, timing and rhythms, likes and dislikes, they can never actualize absolute unconditional union in any conclusive, uninterrupted way.

In fact, the very openness two lovers feel with each other also stirs up all the obstacles to that openness within them: conditioned fears, unrealistic hopes and needs, unconscious identities and shadow elements, and unresolved issues from the past. So while intimacy awakens a deep longing for perfect love, the conditions of our earthly natures conspire to frustrate its perfect expression and realization. Although we may experience moments, glimpses, waves of total openness and union with another, we can never expect a human relationship to give us the total fulfillment we seek.

The pain of this contradiction between the perfect love in our hearts and the imperfections we encounter on the path of relationship breaks the heart—wide open. The pain of love, in Sufi master Hazrat Inayat Khan's words, is "the dynamite that breaks open the heart, even if it be as hard as a rock." It reveals the essential rawness of being human, of reaching for heavenly perfection while forever having to grapple with earthly limitations. Yet the heart itself cannot break, or break open, in that its essential nature is already soft and receptive. What *can* actually break is the wall around the heart, the defensive shield we have constructed to try to protect our soft spot, where we feel most deeply affected by life and other people.

Though encountering the obstacles to love may bring sorrow and anger, the only way to move through these disappointments without doing harm to ourselves or others is to let the heart open up *further* in those moments we would most like to shut it down. Just as rocks in a stream accentuate the force of the water rushing against them, so the obstacles to perfect love can help us feel the full force of our love more strongly.

How can we keep the heart open in those moments when the pain of loving makes us want to withdraw or shut down? It is important not to deny the pain or try to be artificially loving. That only pushes the hurt and anger deeper inside. Instead, we have to start where we are—which involves *being with* our hurt or anger and *letting that be,* without having to fix it. In opening to the pain of loving we bleed, yet this bleeding itself, when met with warmth and caring, helps awaken the heart, allowing the larger force of love to keep flowing.

So in encountering the obstacles to love, we discover what is most alive in us—the rawness and tenderness of the broken-open heart. The painful fact is that no one else can ever give us all the love we need in just the way we want. But when we can hold our own pain and rawness with compassionate awareness, then the unconditional love we most long for becomes available.

Letting the heart break open awakens us to the mystery of love— that we can't help loving others, in spite of what we may dislike about them, for no other reason than that they move and touch us in ways we can never fully comprehend. What we love is not just their pure heart but also their heart's struggle with all the obstacles in the way of its full, radiant expression. It's as though our heart wants to ally itself with their heart and lend them strength in their struggle to realize the magnificence of their being, beyond all their perceived shortcomings.

Indeed, if those we love perfectly matched our ideal, they might not touch us so deeply. Their imperfections give our love a purchase, a foothold, something to work with. Thus, the obstacles in a relationship are what force our heart to stretch and expand to embrace all of what we are. In this way, unconditional love can ripen further, beyond its spontaneous arising in the first flash of falling in love. It becomes an ongoing practice of courage and humility, of learning to be fully human.

Breaking open the heart is the transmuting force in the alchemy of love that allows us to see the unconditional goodness of people in and through all the limitations of their conditioned self. It helps us recover the beauty in the beast and realize how the unconditioned and conditioned sides of human nature are always intertwined, making up one whole cloth. The overflow of the broken-open heart starts with kindness toward ourselves, then radiates out as compassion toward all other beings who hide their tenderness out of fear of being hurt, and who need our unconditional love to help awaken their heart as well.

19

Passion as Path

No better love than love with no object.

—RUMI

If man fails to recognize his true nature, the true object of his love, the confusion is vast and irremediable. Bent on assuaging a passion for the All on an object too small to satisfy it, his efforts will be fruitless, a terrible waste. How much energy do you think the spirit of the earth [thus] loses in a single night?

—TEILHARD DE CHARDIN

ALTHOUGH THE DANISH PHILOSOPHER Kierkegaard claimed that the modern age was lacking in passion, perhaps we are not so much lacking passion as squandering it, by failing to understand its true nature and thus failing to channel it in a direction that can bring true satisfaction.

Passion can take two very different forms. In its initial upsurge it radiates energy and fire, lifting us out of ourselves and generating powerful, fresh inspiration. Yet it can also be a force that leads us down into addiction and delusion. We can easily become obsessed and emotionally enslaved by the object of our passion. This can happen both with worldly passion—a temporal love affair—or with spiritual passion—attachment to a spiritual teacher or teaching. Passion can either uplift us or drag us down into obsession or self-destruction.

So it is not surprising that our culture is ambivalent toward passion, alternately viewing it as a stairway to heaven or a pathway to hell. During most of Western history, passion has been regarded with suspicion and fear, as an animal drive, a base, irrational impulse that pulls you down into your lower nature, down into hell. This has led to repression, the attempt to hide it underneath a civilized veneer.[1]

In trying to break away from this repressive attitude, the modern temperament has gone to the other extreme, glorifying romantic passion as life's ultimate experience. Absent a sense of the sacred, a love affair or a sexy evening is the closest many people come to an experience of transcendence. Most of our advertising and pop music is geared toward filling people's spiritual hunger with fantasies of salvation through passion: if you just use the right shampoo, Mr. or Ms. Right will come along and sweep you away; you won't be lonely anymore and your life will finally have meaning. Advertising agencies are all too cognizant of passion's addictive lure.

These divergent views of passion reflect an inner division between the two sides of our nature; between heaven—the expansive, visionary side—and earth—the sensuous, concrete, grounded side. Glorifying and inflating passion is a way of trying to rise above our earthly nature and the sorrows and limitations of worldly life. Yet this emphasis on heaven at the expense of earth makes passion manic, ungrounded. On the other hand, denigrating passion, condemning it as a primitive instinct that will deplete or destroy us, leads to depression. For when we deny or suppress our passion, we lose touch with our expansive, heavenly nature as well. Our spirit can no longer soar, and we lose our inspiration.

We clearly need a more balanced understanding of passion, one that can lead beyond the manic/depressive attitudes in which our culture is caught. For passion is, at its core, the experience of life energy in its raw, naked state. The question is how to relate to this energy. If passion is like electricity, how can we draw on it for light and warmth without being electrocuted? What can we use this energy for? Will we use it just to run our domestic appliances—our hair dryers and toasters—and thus fritter it away? Or will we utilize it for larger purposes—to nurture greater aliveness, awakening, wisdom? How can passion become fuel on the path of becoming more fully human, more fully who we are?

Unconditional Passion: Pure Resonance with Life

Passion often awakens in response to someone—for some a teacher, for some a lover, for some a distant movie star—who stirs our desire to feel more fully alive. Often we make the mistake of seeing the one we fall in love with as the source of our passion. Yet the real source of our passion is our basic nature—our openness to reality. We can fall in love only because our nature is so permeable to begin with. Inherent in this basic openness is a desire to reach out and connect with the world, with other people, with nature, and with life in all its wild beauty. Our nature is an opening through which what is out there can come in here and penetrate us, pierce our usual armory of defenses and facades, and stir our heart.

This is why passion is such a central human experience. Usually we protect all our doors and windows with heavy padlocks and alarms. When passion strikes, however, reality can slip right past all our defenses, get to us, and shake us to the core.

Passion is, in essence, unconditional, because it is an immediate, unfabricated resonance with life, the life inside us connecting with the life outside. This resonance with reality is an essential constituent of our being. We come upon a spring meadow carpeted with wildflowers, and out of our mouths springs the primordial sound: "Ahhh!" We exchange glances with someone who is beautiful: ahhh! We hear the words of a spiritual teacher that strike us to the core: ahhh! When something pierces us like this, passion arises and takes our breath away.

Conditional Passion: Obsession and Enslavement

Passion is *energized presence*. We feel it as a richness, a wealth of feeling that fills us up and overflows. Since we don't normally feel so fully alive, our ordinary life seems impoverished by contrast. And so we readily imagine that the object of our passion is the cause of this richness. "Yesterday I was lonely and unhappy. Today I have met this person and suddenly feel so full and alive. It must be because of her."

It is easy to fall into seeing things this way, to imagine that we need this person, this job, this sport, this drug, this house in the country to feel fully alive. This is the first step in converting passion into delusion.

We don't realize that our passion is the life within us radiating out and illuminating the life all around. All we see is the object illuminated, not the illuminating power itself. This distorts our perception. Our unconditional passion becomes converted into a conditional attachment to the object on which our light is shining. Fixating on the object leads to obsession and addiction. We can't stop thinking about how to securely possess the object of our passion.

If passion is our life energy naturally radiating outward, then fixating narrowly on the object of passion is like filtering the energy of the sun through a magnifying glass. The situation becomes too hot and soon goes up in smoke.

So it's important to realize that when our passion fixates on another person, we are projecting our own radiance, which the other reflects back and helps us to experience. Usually we don't see how this radiance is coming from us. Of course, we may also be recognizing the radiant beauty in the one we love. But when we start to idolize or become addicted to those we love, it is because we're giving them so much of our juice. As a result, they appear larger than life, while we feel poverty-stricken. And the more obsessed and addicted we become, the more impoverished we feel. In this way, passion becomes destructive when we fail to understand its true nature and origin.

This fall into impoverishment is also common in corrupt spiritual communities, such as Jonestown or Rajneeshpuram. The corrupt spiritual leader sets himself up to take advantage of his followers' projection and idealization tendencies. He practices black magic, transforming something potentially positive (the student's capacity for devotion) into something destructive (enslavement). He derives his power from inducing his followers to give him their juice, while making himself appear to be the one who is dispensing the juice. (Interestingly, Jonestown ended with the leader dispensing poison juice, as though he were saying to his followers: "I am giving you back the juice you gave me. When you give away your juice, it turns to poison.") Clever charlatans enslave people by reinforcing their followers' dependency and sense of poverty. (Rajneesh would daily parade by a lineup of his devotees in one of the many Rolls Royces he purchased with their donations.) As the followers become more depleted, the only way to feel good about themselves is by basking in the leader's reflected glory. Eventually they wind up acting in strangely destructive ways just to stay connected to this imagined source of their feeling good.

Ordinary love affairs can also have bizarre, destructive consequences. How many times have we compromised our integrity or bent ourselves out of shape so that the object of our desire would approve of us? How many a jilted lover has killed himself or his beloved "because he loved her so much"?

Passion and Transformation

Despite its dangers, passion can also be a tremendously creative, transformative force. This was true in twelfth-century France, the birthplace of romantic love. Suddenly, in the midst of a dark medieval world, a new kind of sentiment appeared in the love songs of the troubadours and quickly spread through the courts of Provence. One of the main influences behind courtly love was the Sufi tradition of devotional love songs to the Beloved. The Beloved in Sufi poetry is the divine, in the form of God, the soul, or the spiritual master. The troubadour songs secularized this devotional passion, addressing it to a worldly beloved—the Lady—instead of to the divine.

Courtly love in its pure form was governed by strict rules. A knight would fall in love with a lady who was already married to another noble, and they would have a clandestine love affair. Since their love was not supposed to be sexually consummated, the passion that was generated could be used for personal transformation. The knight would undergo for his lady tests and trials that refined his character. Courtly love had an enormous civilizing influence on medieval culture. Women were appreciated and honored for the first time, while many a brutish male became transformed into the era's new ideal: the *gentle man.*

Passion can lead in this kind of creative direction only when its spiritual potential is recognized. Although courtly love was a secularized version of the Sufis' devotion to the divine Beloved, it nonetheless retained a spiritual cast because it provided a path of purification and character development. Since the knight could never fully possess his lady, his unrequited passion became transformative. Instead of degenerating into addiction, it ripened into pure devotion.

Wholehearted devotion, whether directed toward a loved one, a spiritual master, or ultimate truth, is a powerful refining fire that can work magic on the human soul. Recognizing this, many religious traditions have developed devotional practices that harness this energy for spiritual purposes. Since we cannot possess the object of devotion—God or the spiritual master—devotional practice requires us to relinquish fixation, so that we may discover the fullness of love as *the treasure of our own heart.* This awakens us from the poverty of depending on others to the richness of celebrating our true nature, which we can then begin to share more fully with the world at large.

Devotion to a genuine spiritual master—a central feature of many sacred traditions—is like courtly love in that it is, in some sense, unrequited. Although genuine teachers have their own kind of devotion toward their students, nonetheless students cannot expect to have their teacher respond to them in the way they want, give them the validation and approval they would like, or make them feel good. Genuine spiritual masters neither hold out promises and rewards nor encourage projection and idealization. They continually throw you back on yourself. This cuts through the student's tendency to conditionalize passion, to be a good student in order to win the teacher's praise, affection, or approval. In this sense, the student comes to experience the brokenhearted quality of unrequited love.

The Brokenhearted Love Affair

Experiencing a broken heart brings a choice. We can shut down, out of pain and resentment about not getting what we want. Or if we pay attention to what our heart truly desires, we find it wanting to break open, despite the pain we feel. When we let our heart break open, a sweetness starts to flow from us like nectar. As the Sufi teacher Hazrat Inayat Khan put it, "The warmth of the lover's atmosphere, the piercing effect of his voice, the appeal of his words, all come from the pain of his heart." This is one of the great secrets of love. Instead of trying to ward off this pain, which is futile anyway, the lover can use it to transform himself, to develop invincible tenderness and compassion, and as the troubadours discovered, to become a heroic warrior in the service of love.

This brokenhearted quality of pure devotion has a particular poignancy, like the sadness that is often present in the most moving love poems and songs. This is what Chögyam Trungpa called "the genuine heart of sadness." It is a fullness of feeling that arises in response to loving someone we can never finally possess. The one we love is going to die; we ourselves are going to die; it's all going to pass away. Even if we marry, the marriage will change and finally pass as well. There's nothing to hold on to. Nothing can save us from our aloneness. The more we love our life, our sweetheart, our spiritual teacher, the more brokenhearted we will feel, sooner or later.

The sweet quality of this sadness is interesting. The word *sad*, being related to *satisfied* and *sated*, reveals that genuine sadness is a fullness, a fullness of heart that wants to overflow. As Trungpa puts it, "This kind of sadness is unconditioned. It occurs because your heart is completely exposed. You would like to spill your heart's blood, give your heart to others." From this arises a desire to melt all the barriers between oneself and others, the life in here and the life out there.

All our ideas about romantic love grow out of the discovery of the power of devotional passion by the courtly lovers of Provence. Unfortunately, our culture no longer understands the devotional dimension of passion; instead we look at passion as a vehicle for "getting ours." We have lost the original sacred meaning of passionate love.

We have also lost the original sacred meaning of the spiritual path, which involves surrendering to a transcendent principle that is greater than ourselves and that guides our lives. When you meet a teacher who really strikes to your core, when you fall in love with a teacher and a teaching, this pulls you out of yourself, draws you out of your cozy little world of habitual patterns. Although you may be drawn to that teacher and teaching, you can't possess them in any conventional way. So meeting a genuine teacher brings up all your conditional grasping along with your unconditional passion. This allows you to work with passion as part of your path.

As you learn to distinguish between grasping and devotion, you begin to understand the deeper nature of passion—as a doorway into the experience of surrender. The spiritual path is a brokenhearted love affair because the ultimate teaching, which is no other than life itself, is about relinquishing, not acquiring. The spiritual path is about "losing it." From the perspective of ego, this seems shocking or threatening. Yet for our being, which feels encumbered by the weight of our self-centered compulsions, it is a relief. That's what makes passion so intriguing: Losing it—dropping old, confining personality patterns— is totally frightening and exciting at the same time.

Just as the flame of the courtly lover's unconsummated passion purified his heart, so our unrequited love for a spiritual teacher can intensify our desire to be one with the greater life that he or she represents. The only way we can do that is by joining the teacher in the awakened state that he or she inhabits. And the only way to do that is by devoting ourselves to that greater life, and to removing our inner barriers to greater openness, awareness, and genuineness. Once we stop trying so hard to get the spiritual goods, the warmth of unconditional passion can begin to illuminate every aspect of our lives.

Passion and Surrender

The ultimate goal of passion is surrender. This is the heart's true desire. The fruition of sexual pursuit is the moment of orgasm, a moment of total letting go. The French call it "the little death" *(la petite mort)*. Similarly, the fruition of the spiritual path is to realize complete openness, beyond all grasping. This brings unconditional joy, arising out of experiencing the intrinsic richness of our being.

Passion is a stream of life energy passing through us, like a river that must finally empty into the sea. It is a passage between two worlds, leading from the world of the known self to a greater world that lies beyond—as represented by a lover, a guru, a teaching, or by life itself. Arising as inspiration and culminating in surrender, the path of passion reveals the essence of life as well as death.

In one of his poems (as translated by Robert Bly), Goethe recognizes the transformative impulse contained in passion as a "holy longing":

> *I praise what is truly alive,*
> *what longs to be burned to death.*

He describes how, like a moth drawn out of the darkness toward the flame of a glowing taper,

> *a strange feeling comes over you*
> *when you see the silent candle burning.*

Carried along by your longing to connect with what is truly alive,

> *a desire for higher love-making*
> *sweeps you upward.*

Then, as your hesitation falls away, the current of passion carries you into the act of surrender:

> *and, finally, insane for the light,*
> *you are the butterfly and you are gone.*

The conclusion Goethe draws is simple and unequivocal:

> *And so long as you haven't experienced*
> *this: to die and so to grow,*
> *you are only a troubled guest*
> *on this dark earth.*

20

Spiritual Authority, Genuine and Counterfeit

Just as a goldsmith gets his gold
First testing by melting, cutting, and rubbing,
Sages accept my teachings after full examination
And not just out of devotion to me.

—SHAKYAMUNI BUDDHA

Counterfeiters exist because there is such a thing as real gold.

—RUMI

✤ IN THE PRESENT AGE of cultural upheaval, declining morality, family instability, and global chaos, the world's great spiritual masters may be among humanity's most precious resources, serving as beacons of illumination in a darkening world. Yet at the same time, the intense spiritual hunger of our times has set the stage on which countless false prophets have appeared, issuing self-important proclamations and commands that often wind up damaging their followers and leading them astray. Thousands of well-meaning seekers, from a wide range of educational, social class, and ethnic backgrounds, have been attracted to disreputable teachers, only to end up with their lives in ruins. At the extreme end, widely publicized cult meltdowns, such as Jonestown, Waco, or Heaven's Gate, enacted everyone's worst fears of what could happen when a self-styled religious zealot gains control over people's lives. And this has led to widespread debunking of spiritual teachers and communities that fall outside mainstream Western religion.

It is important to distinguish intelligently between misguided and authentic spiritual teachers, between unhealthy groups and genuinely transformative spiritual communities. The false prophet and the genuine master both undermine the habitual patterns of self. Yet one does so in a way that creates bondage, while the other does so in a way that promotes liberation. What is this important difference? How does genuine spiritual authority operate?

Characteristics of Pathological Spiritual Groups

A number of years ago I participated in a study group on authority patterns in nonmainstream religious movements, sponsored by the Center for the Study of New Religious Movements and funded by the National Endowment for the Humanities. As a group of psychologists, philosophers, and sociologists, we interviewed participants in many different spiritual groups, covering a wide spectrum ranging from the totally pathological, such as Jim Jones's People's Temple, to the mildly deluded, to communities that seemed genuinely wholesome, sane, and beneficial. From these interviews, as well as from my own personal observations of spiritual groups over the years, I found that groups with the greatest potential for pathological or destructive behavior had a clearly recognizable set of characteristics in common.

1. *The leader assumes total power to validate or negate the self-worth of the devotees, and uses this power extensively.* The leader in pathological groups is usually a magnetic, charismatic person who exudes, in the words of Eric Hoffer, "boundless self-confidence. What counts is the arrogant gesture, the complete disregard of the opinion of others, the single-handed defiance of the world." Something about this unflappable self-assurance especially appeals to those lacking in self-esteem, who often become mesmerized by the self-proclaimed cult leader's grandiose displays. As Hoffer points out, "Faith in a holy cause is . . . a substitute for lost faith in ourselves." The false prophet and the true believer are made for each other; they are two sides of the same coin. Through their mutual collusion, the leader gains power and control,

while the followers gain reassurance and security from his guidance and approval, as well as vicarious power through identification with him.

Corrupt leaders prey deliberately on their followers' sense of personal inadequacy. For example, meetings at the People's Temple often included degradation rituals where members' flaws and failings were paraded and ridiculed in front of the whole group. After thoroughly degrading a follower in this way, Jim Jones would often build the person back up, as one survivor of Jonestown describes:

> First you become nobody. They tear you down and strip your mind, you don't know anything. And after that, whatever he do, then you have to thank him for what he did. And then you'd become totally dependent on him, because you don't have anything else yourself. Everything you had was bad. I mean, he said, "You will listen to me and I will instruct you of things that was good," and most people actually believed that. . . . He made everybody think like they was somebody.

Chuck Dederich, founder of the cultlike group Synanon, had a similar way of operating, according to a former member's description: "You get a group of people around you, and you say to them, '*I* am very happy. *My* life is wonderful. I have done an enormous number of good things, and I love it. How are *you?* Now you ain't so good. Now who would you rather be, you or me?' We have just established that you feel lousy, and I feel fantastic, so you answer, 'You.'" At first Dederich impressed this member with his boundless self-confidence: "He was charismatic, he was funny, he was bright, he was involved, his instincts were unbelievable. And I really fell in love." In admitting he would rather be Dederich than himself, he handed Dederich power over him. Dederich then tightened his control by confirming the follower's value: "And because Chuck Dederich said that I was fantastic, now it's wonderful. Because he said it, I believed it. And it changed my life, no question about it. And I would say to people, 'Who would you rather be, you or me?' And they would say, 'You.' And I would think that was just fine."

In this way leaders such as Jones and Dederich take away a person's

old (already weak) ego supports, replacing these with their own attention and approval, which makes their followers feel important and
special—"like you was somebody." Instead of an adult, eye-to-eye relationship built on a respect for human dignity, the relations between
cultic leader and follower are those of parent and child. (The members
of Jonestown even called Jim Jones "Dad.") The follower takes on a
new identity as a satellite of this larger-than-life parent figure. And
the more the followers give the leader power to validate the worth of
their existence, the more he can up the ante and force them to do
anything he wants in order to maintain his approval. As one ex-
member put it: "If you have that experience of love [from the leader],
and then you're cut off from it, it's like being put in quarantine—
there's a tremendous motivation to get back to it, tremendous desire
to reconnect with that love. And you'll do anything to get back to that
love. Because it makes you feel good and makes you feel like you're a
good person."

2. *The central focus of the group is a cause, a mission, an ideology that is
not subject to question.* The leader lays out the ideology, while the followers accept without question the beliefs handed down to them. The
leader often maintains his position by claiming to have special access
to God or a source of authority that is not accessible to the followers.
This increases their dependence on the leader for "The Word"—for
interpreting events and telling them what to do. Because they depend
on the leader to tell them what is so, their own intelligence begins to
atrophy. Groupthink prevails.

The central ideology is treated with such deadly seriousness that
the members are unable to have any humor about themselves or their
leader. They are caught in what one ex-member called "an airtight
worldview, an intellectual maze." As Eric Hoffer describes this:

> All active mass movements strive . . . to interpose a fact-proof screen
> between the faithful and the realities of the world. They do this by
> claiming that the ultimate and absolute truth is already embodied in
> their doctrine and that there is no truth or certitude outside it. The
> facts on which the true believer bases his conclusions must not be de-

rived from his experience or observation but from holy writ. . . . It is startling to realize how much unbelief is necessary to make belief possible.

The effectiveness of such an ideology derives from its absolute certitude, as the one and only Truth, rather than its inherent truth or meaning. For a doctrine to have such certitude, it must be believed in, rather than understood or tested out. If the followers were to try to understand the doctrine or test it out, they would have to trust in the validity of their own experience; but inasmuch as they join the group out of low self-esteem to begin with, they have little inclination to appeal to the truth of their own experience. The more that self-trust is broken down, the more the followers try to model themselves on the prevailing image of the ideal group member, often imitating the actions, mannerisms, and thought of the leadership.

In this environment, a high level of suspicion exists among the members, lest any of them betray the Cause. Any independent frame of reference is interpreted as heresy, disloyalty, or betrayal of the group's mission. And spy networks may exist to report members who dissent from the central mission. Members who have given up their own intelligence and autonomy resent and feel threatened by independent thinking from fellow members, and so become willing informers. As Hoffer points out, "Strict orthodoxy is as much the result of mutual suspicion as of ardent faith." One ex-member described this situation:

> If you were in a group with me, I couldn't say to you, "Boy, that was really an awful meeting," because I couldn't be sure that you wouldn't call [the leader] as soon as you left and say, "Betty just said that was an awful meeting." And these were good friends. But you couldn't be sure, even between husbands and wives, that you wouldn't get turned in. That was a really important dynamic of control. For good friends, we did some terrible things to each other, I would say.

In a group where self-esteem depends on the Cause, doubt is a deadly sin.

And because allegiance to the Cause is based primarily on belief, as well as on emotional needs for belonging and approval, rather than on a genuine search for truth or a discipline of self-knowledge, the ideology is easily used to justify morally questionable behavior. The Cause takes precedence over common decency and respect for human dignity.

3. *The leader keeps his followers in line by manipulating emotions of hope and fear.* The coin of the realm governed by the cultic leader is the promise. The leader promises his followers rewards—that they will reach salvation or attain a special status above the rest of the world if they remain true to the Cause. This "carrot approach" appeals to the greed, vanity, and impoverished self-esteem of the followers. The future rewards of allegiance to the Cause take precedence over any appreciation or enjoyment of present experience.

To insure that the flock stays in line, the cultic leader also uses the "stick method," intimidating members with threats of doom, vengeance, or damnation if they stray from the Cause. A wall of terror surrounds the group. Members who try to leave may even be threatened with persecution or death. A survivor of Jonestown describes this tactic of Jim Jones: "He'd say, if you leave the Temple, he had connections with the Mafia, he had connections with the CIA. He said, 'If you leave, forget it, 'cause they'll find you in a hole somewhere.'" An ex-member of another pathological group observed, "The 'transpersonal carrot in the sky' was: this is the way to salvation. If you deviate in any way, you're going toward your evil part, you're making it bigger. So that became very frightening. And another thing that became frightening was that if you thought about leaving the group, you had to face the fact that in the system you'd be spiritually damned."

Absurd as these fears may seem, we must remember that cult members have given up any connection with their own intelligence, leaving them prey to this kind of emotional manipulation. As Hoffer puts it: "The estrangement from the self, which is a precondition for both plasticity and conversion, almost always proceeds in an atmosphere of intense passion. . . . Once the harmony with the self is upset . . . a man . . . hungers to combine with whatever comes within his reach. He cannot stand apart, poised and self-sufficient, but has to attach himself wholeheartedly to one side or another."

4. *There is a strict, rigid boundary drawn between the group and the world outside.* Being in the group is defined as good; being outside the group is seen as debased or corrupt. Such groups often maintain a notion of absolute evil, defined as the world outside its boundaries. As Hoffer points out, "Usually the strength of a . . . movement is proportionate to the vividness and tangibility of its devil."

To discourage independence, members of the group are often prevented from spending much time alone or with their families. Pair bonding between couples may also be deliberately undermined to foster greater dependence on the leader, as happened at Synanon.

5. *Corrupt cult leaders are usually self-styled prophets who have not undergone lengthy training or discipline under the guidance of great teachers.* Many religious traditions have clear lineages of spiritual transmission. Those who are to teach others are usually tested by their own teachers before they are allowed to represent themselves as masters. This is especially true in Buddhism and other Asian traditions. The process of testing and transmission serves as a form of quality control to ensure that given teachers do not distort the teachings for their own personal gain. But most of the dangerous cultic figures of our times are self-proclaimed gurus who sway their followers through their charismatic talents, outside the stabilizing context of tradition, lineage, or transmission. They may make ridiculous, spurious claims to authenticity, as did one leader, for instance, who recruited new followers by advertising a list of his past lives as an enlightened being in the great traditions.

Relative Spiritual Authority

The above analysis addresses only the most extreme, unhealthy dynamics that occur in spiritual groups. Beyond this, however, many spiritual teachers and communities function in more of a gray zone, often mixing genuine teachings with questionable practices and behavior. In truth, there is often a very thin line between a brilliant teacher and an unscrupulous one. So it is not enough to make lists of problematic features, for this only shows what false teachers do wrong, without telling us what genuine teachers do right. To take this discussion further, we need to consider what true spiritual authority is and where it comes from.

Great teachers manifest in a wide range of different ways. Some are saintly and pure, others are wild and provocative, and still others are so completely ordinary that they would barely stand out in a crowd. It is impossible to set up an ideal model for what a true spiritual teacher should look like, any more than we could elevate one style of therapy as the model that all others should follow. Carl Rogers, Fritz Perls, and Milton Erickson, for instance, achieved therapeutic results in strikingly different ways. Each had a different personality type, style of working, and probably a different type of client with whom he might be most effective. Spiritual teachers also come in many different forms and guises, and it is fruitless to try to spell out exactly how a good guru will behave.

Instead we need a more subtle analysis that looks at what goes on between teacher and student. Two questions are particularly important here: How does spiritual authority operate in the relationship between teacher and student? And what is the source from which a teacher derives that authority?

Spiritual authority is, in part, interrelational; that is, a given teacher has such authority only for those who respond to his or her presence and teachings. A disciple—literally, a "learner"—is one who recognizes that he or she has something important to learn from this particular teacher. Often the choice of a teacher is as unpredictable and mysterious as the attraction to a potential lover. You sense that you have something essential to learn here, something that no one else has ever imparted to you before. And this recognition is what allows the teacher to take on a certain authority for you.

Many people today question the need for spiritual teachers at all, claiming, in the spirit of democracy, that everyone should be his or her own master. Many traditions do in fact assert that the true teacher is found only within. Yet in the early stages of one's development one does not know how to find or listen to the inner master, or to distinguish genuine inner guidance from more superficial wishes and preferences. Just as one would turn to an acknowledged master in any field one wanted to pursue in depth, so a person who seeks to overcome the limitations of egocentricity will naturally be drawn to someone who has actually mastered that work. The role of effective teachers is to instruct, encourage, and correct the student, as well as to provide an example of what is possible. Effective teachers also try to see what individual students most need at each step of their development, rather than trying to fit the student into a preprogrammed agenda.

Thus spiritual teachers derive a certain *relative authority* through the actual help they offer their students. This is not unlike the authority that clients grant therapists in their work together. Although I may feel uneasy with the authority clients grant me as a therapist, I am willing to accept it, especially in the early stages of the work. I understand that clients can more readily enter into the process of shedding old patterns if they grant me the authority to guide them. Beyond the conventional authority granted by professional training and certification, or by transference idealizations, the real source of my authority is my focus on clients' well-being and my capacity to help them find a deeper relationship with themselves. Granting me this authority can be a step toward recognizing their own authority—that they are indeed the "authors" of their own experience, rather than passive victims of circumstance.

In a parallel, though far more profound way, a genuine spiritual master's presence may serve as a mirror that reflects back to students qualities of their awakened being: openness, generosity, discernment, humor, gentleness, acceptance, compassion, straightforwardness, strength, and courage.

Absolute Authority

Beyond the relative authority that teachers assume through the help they give their students, true masters also have access to an absolute, unconditional source of authority—awakened being. Since this is a universal source of wisdom that is available to everyone, the genuine spiritual teacher is more than willing to help others find it themselves, if they are ready.

The genuine teacher is one who has realized the essential nature of human consciousness, usually through practicing a self-knowledge discipline such as meditation for many years. In contrast to false teachers, who often create a condition of dependency in the student by claiming special access to truth, authentic teachers delight in sharing the source of their own realization with the student. This often involves giving students an awareness practice, along with instructions that help them directly recognize their own nature. This kind of guidance sharpens students' perceptions so they can better discern whether the teacher's words are true. Without a practice or method that gives them direct knowledge of what is true, students are totally dependent on the teacher to define their reality for them.

The more the students' discrimination and discernment grow, the more they can recognize and appreciate the teacher's mastery, just as when we study and practice any art, we come to recognize the skill of an accomplished master much more than we could have before. When the teaching leads to a deeper connection to one's own being, this appreciation often grows into natural feelings of love, respect, and devotion.

Such devotion may look like slavishness to the secular eye. Yet true devotion does not aggrandize the teacher or debase the student. Rather, it is a way of recognizing and honoring wisdom, awareness, and truth as higher realities than the egoic realm of confusion, ignorance, and self-deception. Devotion is a sign of a shift in allegiance—away from the petty tyrant of egocentricity toward the call of our larger being, whose wisdom the teacher embodies in fully developed form. Yet devotion can have its own kind of dangers, especially in our culture, and can lead to certain pitfalls on the path unless it is grounded in an awareness practice that cuts through self-deception and sharpens the student's discernment.

Surrender and Submission

To appreciate the potential value of commitment to a spiritual teacher and teaching, it is essential to distinguish between mindful surrender, which is an opening to a deeper dimension of truth, and mindless submission, which is a deadening flight from freedom. The notion of surrender is widely misunderstood in our culture. It often conjures up images of "come out with your hands up"—waving a white flag, admitting defeat, being humiliated. For many people today, the idea of surrender implies giving up one's intelligence or individuality and adopting a weak, dependent, submissive, "one-down" position. True surrender, however, is never an enslavement, but rather a step toward the discovery of real power. It is the act of yielding to a larger intelligence, without trying to control the outcome.

True surrender is not blind. It requires real discrimination—the capacity to recognize the necessity of completely opening oneself and letting go. Surrender does not have a finite object; one does not give oneself to something limited and bounded. If one does, then it is most likely submission—to the teacher's personality or the Cause.

Submission is a handing over of power to a person one idealizes, based on the hope of gaining something in return. One seeks approval from an idealized other in order to feel good about oneself. This is a symptom of weakness rather than strength—"I give myself to my guru because he is so great and I am so small." The more one depends on another for validation, the more one is likely to act in ways that compromise one's integrity. And the more one's integrity becomes compromised, the less one trusts oneself, which increases one's dependency on the leader.

Critics of gurus see all involvements with spiritual masters in this light, failing to distinguish between submission as a developmentally *regressive* retreat from maturity, and genuine surrender, which is a *progressive* step beyond egocentricity toward a fuller connection with being. They fail to distinguish between the giving of surrender, which brings increase—of love, intelligence, wisdom—and the giving of submission, which results in decrease and loss.

With a genuine spiritual master, surrendering means presenting oneself in a completely honest, naked way, without trying to hold anything back or maintain any facade. How rarely we let anyone see us as we are, without hiding behind a mask of some kind. Being in the presence of a true master is a rare opportunity to let down all our pretenses, to unmask and reveal all of what we are, our egocentric failings as well as our strengths. This is quite different from submissively trying to be "good" or "devoted," to please someone in order to feel worthy.

Submission has a narcissistic quality, in that followers seek to bask in the reflected glory of their leader as a way to inflate their self-importance. The authentic teacher-student relationship leads beyond narcissism by teaching students how to devote themselves to a greater power that lies within yet beyond themselves.

The acid test is not how well the students please the master but how fully they meet and respond to life's challenges. Through becoming more responsive, transparent, and open with their teacher, they learn to approach all people and situations in the same way. Devotion to a spiritual teacher serves a much larger purpose than just creating a beautiful relationship between two human beings. It is a way in which spiritual aspirants can learn to develop devotion to what is greater, more intelligent, and more authoritative—within themselves—than their own ego. The essential surrender is the ego's yielding to this larger wisdom. In opening to this higher wisdom within, the student becomes more pliable and available to others. In this way, genuine surrender helps one open toward all beings, instead of enslaving one to the parochial perspectives of an in-group.

In Search of a Genuine Master

How then does one recognize a master one can trust? Certainly no single teacher or teaching could be expected to appeal to all people, any more than any single psychotherapist or school of therapy could be effective for all potential clients. The ultimate criterion for judging teachers is whether they guide their students toward a more authentic, transparent quality of human presence and being-in-the-world.

Genuine teachers encourage self-respect as the basis for self-transcendence. And they are willing to reveal the source of their authority and wisdom to their students, so that the student's path is based on experiential realization rather than on ideology or belief. They also recognize ambiguity and paradox, rather than insisting on absolute certitude in the One and Only Truth. They do not give their disciples any privileged status above the uninitiated. They do not manipulate the emotions of their students but appeal to their innate intelligence. Instead of promoting herd behavior, they recognize the importance of solitude and inner inquiry. And their own realization is based not just on dramatic revelations but on extensive testing and practice.

A teacher's embodiment of love, truth, and living presence is a much more reliable gauge than whether his or her lifestyle, appearance, or personal quirks fit our image of what a spiritual person should look like. The annals of all spiritual traditions include examples of masters whose behavior and lifestyle challenged the prevailing conventions.

Great teachers also have their share of human foibles. Often they are effective precisely because they are so human, because they are so deeply in touch with the nature of the human sickness in themselves. The Buddhist sage Vimalakirti, to whom many bodhisattvas came for teachings, was always sick in bed, and when asked about this, said, "I am sick because all beings are sick." If the spiritual path is about transforming our core sickness and neurosis, then we can hardly expect spiritual teachers and communities to manifest in a totally pure, spotless way. Human development being the complex tapestry that it is, islands of unfinished business may remain intact even within a genuine teacher's stream of spiritual realization (as discussed in chapter 14). If we expect total perfection from spiritual teachers, this can also lead us astray, as the American Zen teacher Philip Kapleau points out: "In the West a roshi is expected to [have] flawless conduct. . . . But this idealistic view can blind one to the merits of a teacher. . . . A Japanese long experienced in Zen once told me, 'My roshi does have character flaws, yet of the teachers I have had he is the only one who has taught me real Zen and I am exceedingly grateful to him.' "

Undoubtedly the most important guideline in evaluating a teacher is the effect he or she has upon us. In replying to a question about whether a master should be "a man of self-control who lives a righteous life," the Vedanta teacher Nisargadatta Maharaj replied: "Such you will find many of—and no use to you. A guru can show the way back home to your Self. What has this to do with the character or temperament of the person he appears to be? . . . The only way you can judge is by the change in yourself when you are in his company. . . . If you understand yourself with more than usual clarity and depth, it means you have met with the right man."

The Buddha responded in a similar vein when approached by a group of villagers, the Kalamas, who had been visited by various monks expounding their different doctrines. They asked the Buddha, "Venerable sir, there is doubt, there is uncertainty in us concerning them. Which of these reverend monks spoke the truth and which falsehood?" To which the Buddha replied:

> It is proper for you to doubt, to be uncertain. . . . Do not go upon what has been acquired by repeated hearing; nor upon tradition; nor upon rumor; nor upon what is in a scripture; nor upon surmise; nor upon specious reasoning; nor upon a bias toward a notion that has been pondered over; nor upon another's seeming ability; nor upon the consideration, "The monk is our teacher." Kalamas, when you yourselves know, "These things are good, these things are not blamable; undertaken and observed, these things lead to benefit and happiness."

The Buddha specifically advised the Kalamas that they could recognize a worthy teaching by how much it helped them reduce the afflictions of attachment, aversion, and delusion.

In sum, the question of spiritual authority is a subtle and difficult matter that permits no easy answers or hasty conclusions. Although I have focused on the extremes of true and false teachers, these are but two ends of a broader spectrum of more or less spiritually mature human beings. Some teachers may have genuine realization that is not fully integrated, so that their teaching remains incomplete. Some start out with good intentions but are not ripe enough to avoid leading their followers astray. Others may be quite wise but lacking in the skillful means necessary to communicate their wisdom in a way that truly helps their students.

The tendency commonly found in mainstream Western media to discount nonmainstream spiritual teachers because of the acts of those who are unripe or unfit is as unprofitable as refusing to handle money because there are counterfeit bills in circulation. As Nevitt Sanford stressed in the classic study *The Authoritarian Personality*, the abuse of authority is hardly any reason to reject authority where it is useful and legitimate. Failing to recognize important distinctions between true and false teachers only contributes to the confusion of our age and retards the growth and transformation that are required for humanity to survive and prosper in the times to come.

21

Conscious Love and Sacred Community

A Conversation with Paul Shippee

PS: In your books *Journey of the Heart* and *Love and Awakening* you say that it's important to realize how new it is to consider the possibility of conscious relationship. What is so new?

JW: While we might imagine that the capacity to create a close, loving relationship is programmed into our genes, and that we should instinctively know how to go about it, personal intimacy is actually quite a new idea in human history. Being genuinely intimate in a personal way has never been part of the marriage ideal until recently; in fact, most couples throughout history have managed to live together their whole lives without engaging in personal conversations about what was going on within and between them. As long as family and society prescribed the rules and roles of marriage, individuals never had to develop much consciousness in this area. Although marriage has often been regarded as sacred, it still wasn't personal.

We are only now beginning to understand what goes on between two intimate partners, and can only now begin to talk or think clearly about it.

PS: What about the great lovers of history and legend, such as those of the courtly love era, or the Tantrics?

JW: The romantic love ideal of the twelfth century was mostly about burning in your passion for someone you worshiped at a distance—which served as a kind of spiritual purification and refinement.

PS: Like Dante and Beatrice.

JW: Yes. This was a fabulous invention, but it was still not intimacy as we know it. The beloved served as a vehicle for the lover's projections. Courtly love did not involve a day-to-day relationship that went on between two real human beings. Romantic love was originally regarded as a heavenly delight that was incompatible with marriage and its earthly demands.

PS: So romantic love is not necessarily about real intimacy.

JW: No. Nor was Tantra, which focused on spiritual ritual and realization, rather than personal intimacy. To reveal yourself personally to your beloved—rather than just falling in love with a beautiful face—this is something quite new in history.

For thousands of years couple consciousness remained in an undeveloped, childlike state, in that couples lived at home, in the extended family, and did what they were told. This changed with the Industrial Revolution, as the family started to disintegrate and children sought more freedom—which led to a radical new invention: dating.

With this new freedom, couple consciousness grew from childhood into adolescence, which was marked by rebellion against tradition and by romantic idealism. This development reached its peak in the 1960s with the sexual revolution and the soaring divorce rate. Yet two important developments in the sixties laid the groundwork for a more adult stage of couple consciousness, which is becoming possible only now. The women's movement cast off old stereotypes and made relationships more egalitarian. And the dissemination of psychological ideas into the culture—mostly through popular psychology books—started to give people a new set of language and concepts, unavailable to previous generations, to talk about what actually goes on in relationships.

So it is only now that we can begin to envision the transformational potential of conscious relationship, in which two partners value their connection as a vehicle for cultivating their deeper capacities and awakening from the prison of their past.

 PS: So this new development is a shift from being guided by external form to basing relationships on inner, spiritual values?

JW: Yes. While the early stage of the couple was characterized by duty, and the adolescent stage was characterized by freedom and rebellion, the mature, adult stage is marked by consciousness and responsibility.

PS: And that's why relationships are so difficult today?

JW: There's no reason in the world that we should know how to have a conscious intimate relationship with another person, because it's never been done before! We have no history, no guidance, no models. Our families and schools never taught us anything about this. We're the pioneers of a whole new possibility.

PS: The subtitle of your book *Love and Awakening* is *Discovering the Sacred Path of Intimate Relationship*. It sounds like you're offering a vision of how the sacred can enter daily life and find expression in relationships.

JW: For thousands of years institutional religion held the sacred at the center of human life. Now that the sacred is no longer at the center of our lives, humanity has lost its bearings. Although we can no longer rely on religion, the new possibility is that individuals could develop a more conscious relationship to the sacred in their own lives.

PS: Individuals, rather than institutions, are now being called upon to be holders of the sacred.

JW: Yes. And one way we can start to rebuild our connection to the sacred and integrate the sacred into the community is through conscious relationship. Since the culture at large no longer nurtures soul, one place we can start regenerating soul is in our connection with those we love.

PS: How do you define *soul*?

JW: Different traditions have used this term in different ways. In my understanding, soul is not some kind of metaphysical entity that inhabits the body. It's not a reified *thing*.

Soul is a way of speaking about the individual way that our larger being manifests in us, through us, *as* us. Soul is the human element in us, an intermediate element between the absolute or divine, which is our ultimate nature, and our conditioned ego, which spiritual traditions regard as the source of delusion. It is our individual consciousness, in contrast to our divine nature, which is universal, the same in everyone. Soul is true nature as it unfolds and develops in time and space, during the course of a lifetime. It is the principle of *becoming*, unlike the absolute, which is timeless: "as it was in the beginning, is now, and ever shall be."

Soul has a double yearning. It has one eye on the absolute, like the drop that wants to dissolve into the ocean. Yet as Rumi wrote, "the ocean too becomes the drop." The individual is also a vehicle of the highest truth. There is a line from another Sufi poet, Yunus Emre, that describes this individuated quality of soul: "I am the drop that contains the sea. How beautiful to be an ocean hidden within an infinite drop."

Our absolute nature is what allows us to have universal compassion and love everyone equally, as many sacred traditions urge us to do. But on a personal level, on a soul level, we do not love everyone in exactly the same way. When we have a deep soul connection with someone, we love *this* person in a way that we love no other person in the whole universe. There's a particularity to it. This is *eros*.

PS: Christianity describes the universal "love everybody the same" as *agape*. Do spiritual traditions tend to undervalue the individual love of another individual—the *eros?*

JW: Some spiritual traditions discount or discredit individual experience. They regard what you go through as an individual as a dream, of no particular significance. One of the unique contributions of modern Western culture, and this is especially true in America, is the appreciation of personal experience. And this is what intimacy is about—the genuine, personal meeting of I and Thou. Then intimate relationship becomes a vehicle for the sacred, a crucible in which to forge soul.

PS: What is the relation between eros and sex?

JW: Eros is the whole of the dynamic interplay between two lovers, of which sex is but one expression. Sex is naturally sacred, for it is an expression of the subtle life force that animates the whole body and the whole universe. When we make love, our subtle energies interpenetrate in a way that is much finer than our contact at the gross body level. Only human beings make *love* through sex because only human beings lie and linger face to face, with the softest parts of our bodies—belly and heart—fully exposed and in contact.

When the modern mind reduces sex to a gross bodily function or animal instinct subordinated to the rational ego, it engages in a form of sacrilege. The more we try to capture or manipulate sexual experience, the more we lose touch with its capacity to unveil the mystery of human experience. As D. H. Lawrence wrote of this mystery: "The sexual act is not for the depositing of seed. It is for leaping off into the unknown, as from a cliff's edge, like Sappho into the sea."

PS: Can you talk about the roots of your vision of the sacred psychology of love? Where did it come from and how did you draw on the spiritual traditions?

JW: I started out, like most of us, coming from unconscious relationship. My first marriage was based on love, but I didn't have much understanding of the dynamics going on between us. When it ended, I felt a strong need to understand what relationships were really about. I explored various traditions, East and West, but couldn't find any teachings about the sacred psychology of the couple. There was mundane psychology—how to have sex, how to communicate, how to fight—but nothing about the subtle, multidimensional play between two individuals as a mysterious blend of body, mind, soul, and spirit. And there were spiritual teachings, containing universal principles such as compassion, loving-kindness, and putting others first, but not saying much about the sacred dimension of eros or the nitty-gritty work of becoming genuinely intimate with another person.

In crafting a sacred psychology of the couple, I have tried to draw on, adapt, and bring together principles from the sacred traditions as well as from Western psychology.

PS: The title of your book, *Love and Awakening*, seems like a tautology. One could say that love *is* awakening.

JW: No, not entirely. Although we might like to believe, with the Beatles, that "love is all you need, it's easy," love is not all you need, and it's not easy. By forcing us to see the ways we continually play out our unconscious patterns with those we love, intimate relationship offers us the opportunity to wake up from these patterns.

PS: Is this spiritual work?

JW: In the broad sense. But I make a distinction between spiritual work in its purest sense—which involves realizing our absolute nature—and soulwork, which involves embodying this larger nature in our personal lives, bringing it through this body-mind vehicle. Relationship is a kind of soulwork, which is also sacred.

PS: We've defined soul and spirit; can you define *sacred?*

JW: What is sacred is the movement toward deeper truth, deeper connection, deeper understanding, and whatever helps us move in that direction. It is the meeting of the human and the divine. In this sense, intimate relationship is full of sacred possibilities.

PS: So when the divine shows up in here-and-now personal experience, that's what is sacred. Connecting with the sacred means acknowledging that flow from something larger than you into you.

JW: Yes. If you're just resting in pure, absolute being, the issue of the sacred doesn't come up, because self and other are not operating there at all. You are just "That." It's only when we take up our lives and have relationships with our wife or husband or children, that this question arises. In relationship, the sacred manifests as I-Thou communion.

To find the sacred in personal relationships requires working with our interpersonal conditioning from the past—what I call *self/other setups*—which obstruct and distort the deeper I-Thou communion. When two people bring love and awareness to bear on these conditioned patterns blocking their love, their relationship can truly be a vehicle for embodying the sacred in their lives.

PS: Bringing together heaven and earth?

JW: Yes. That's where the sacred enters, right at that meeting point.

PS: So love by itself does not necessarily bring awakening?

JW: Love is an awakening power, but it doesn't always dissolve our defenses. Love is like the light and warmth of the sun that starts to wake up a dormant seed within us. Soul is that seed, which wants to grow, blossom, and bear fruit, to become all that it can be. But often the shell around the seed is so thick that it blocks those expansive possibilities.

These deeper potentials often start to come alive through a soul connection—a loving relationship that kindles a recognition of what is truly possible in this lifetime—whether this is with a lover, teacher, or friend.

PS: So one of the ways we can wake up from the trance of ego, that sleep, that wound, is through love.

JW: Yes, through relationship, since it was in our relations with others that we first learned to shut down. As we expand in love, we inevitably come up against our old tendencies to shut down and play it safe.

PS: And that's the obstacle?

JW: To be stuck in these conditioned self/other setups is a prison, a soul cage. Perhaps you learned to be tough in order to survive in your family, or to gain respect or approval. So you come to think of yourself as "someone who's in command"—and that becomes your soul cage. When you find a good, loving relationship, it will confront you with how this identity obstructs an open, direct meeting between you and the one you love. Your compulsion to be in control also cuts you off from a whole range of inner resources—spontaneity, trust, receptivity to love, letting go, facing the unknown, and genuine strength. If you want to be fully present to life and to another person, this identity has to dissolve.

But of course, you're likely to feel tremendous resistance at that point, because your whole sense of self—your survival, strength, and self-approval—is so tied up with being tough and in control.

PS: When you hit the walls of your prison, and your resistance comes up, what can you do then?

JW: The operative principle is to start where you are. We need to feel and open to the pain of being stuck inside the prison of our old self-concepts. And we need to recognize that our love is calling on us to break out of this prison and become the vast being we truly are.

We often feel tremendous resistance to letting love all the way into us, because love is a power that can break open the shell of the false self. We start to think, "I didn't get into a relationship to have my most precious strategy for security and survival threatened like this!" At this point, we imagine something is desperately wrong—with ourselves, with our partner, or with the relationship. Yet this is actually a tremendous opportunity to break through to a larger and truer sense of who we are.

PS: What you're saying is that the suffering is actually the key that can open the door of your prison.

JW: Not just suffering—because everyone suffers anyway—but *conscious* suffering. Making your suffering conscious. Having to maintain control is suffering, but you may not realize that until your love for another shows you how trapped you are in that identity. Because love makes you want to expand and connect, it also lets you see what's keeping you contracted and isolated.

PS: Everyone suffers; *conscious* suffering is the difference.

JW: Normally you act out your conditioned patterns unconsciously. But now you have a chance to feel what it's like to be a control freak, and see how that cuts off your openness to love, the sunlight that will help you develop into a genuine human being.

PS: How do you do that?

JW: We need to develop the capacity to see and open completely to where we actually are—through *unconditional presence*. The two limbs of unconditional presence are awareness and loving-kindness. In this case, awareness involves becoming conscious of our unconscious setups and the conditioned beliefs that keep us stuck.

PS: So you're saying that identity structures are made of beliefs. This is important. A lot of people don't make this connection.

JW: When we put an identity structure under the microscope of awareness, we find that it is made of a number of little beliefs linked together. Each of those beliefs needs to be exposed. If you always have to be in control, for instance, what beliefs are behind that? Maybe you imagine that if you're not in control, others will control you. Or maybe you think that being in command is the only way you can get respect. It helps to understand what purpose this control identity serves—because it *did* serve a useful function at some point in the past. Becoming free of that structure requires this kind of inquiry.

PS: In *Love and Awakening* you say that when you're up against the walls of your conditioned identity, you're likely to encounter threatening feelings, such as helplessness. And you say that's an essential part of the process: If helplessness starts to come up, let go of your bias against helplessness.

JW: Yes. Now we're talking about loving-kindness. If you're starting to feel helpless, the challenge is to actively allow that and bring your presence to bear on it. That also starts to dissolve the control structure, which was built as a defense against feeling helpless.

PS: You're saying that loving-kindness involves being able to fully experience negative or difficult feelings.

JW: Yes. Fully, directly. It's an absolutely essential element of this work.

PS: Of soulwork.

JW: Yes, and of conscious relationship. This kind of compassion is essential for developing a more conscious relationship with yourself, with the whole range of your experience. This means opening our heart to ourselves—which helps us overcome self-hatred and connect with ourselves more deeply. As Rilke wrote, "Perhaps all the dragons in our lives are only princesses who are waiting to see us act just once with beauty and courage. Perhaps everything terrible is, in its deepest essence, something helpless that needs our love." When we relate to our inner dragons with beauty and courage—by being fully present with our experience—something wakes up inside, and we gain access to hidden resources.

PS: Doing battle with your inner demons—is that the spadework for conscious, intimate, sacred relationships?

JW: Yes, our conditioned patterns are the demons and dragons we need to slay.

PS: So we're recovering the chivalry of romantic love, but making it much more conscious.

JW: Conscious romantic love. Absolutely, that's it. Romance, in its original meaning, was an adventure. *Roman*, the French word for novel, was originally a tale of heroic deeds the lover performed for his beloved. In this case, the heroic deeds involve breaking out of our soul cage and becoming who we are. That's conscious romantic love. Men and women can relate to that equally. It's a warrior's path.

PS: So we have to be really courageous to do this work on ourselves. Then not only will we blossom, but our relationships will blossom too.

JW: Yes. And if couples do this work together, it could help our whole world blossom. This is where we can start to regenerate our world—between one person and another. How can we hope to create a better world if we can't even relate to our partner when we come home at night?

Conscious relationship can be a vehicle for regenerating soul in our culture, for rediscovering community and sacredness in daily life. Through learning to speak truthfully and listen respectfully to one other person, we start to practice genuine meeting and dialogue—which is exactly what our world most needs on the collective level.

PS: So conscious relationship provides a vision of our larger possibilities and a path toward realizing them. In that way, people can become more awake through the secular form of conscious relationships—

JW: The *sacred* form of conscious relationships.

PS: Sacred, but in a secular setting. And that is what could help re-build community and create a saner society.

JW: Yes. Community is born in the relationship between I and Thou. If large numbers of couples and families start relating in that way, it could spread from there.

PS: Can you say more about this larger social significance of conscious relationship?

JW: Conscious love could play an important part in regenerating the planet and awakening humanity from its collective trance. As two partners become devoted to the growth of awareness and spirit in each other, they will naturally want to share their love with others. The larger arc of a couple's love reaches out toward a feeling of kinship with all of life, what Teilhard de Chardin calls "a love of the universe."

As two lovers break open their hearts and cultivate greater soulfulness through their connection, they will also experience the soullessness of the modern world more keenly. Here is where they as a couple can give something back to this world: by extending the heart and soul they kindle in each other to all beings. They might start by making their home a sacred environment, nurtur-ing the deeper potentials in their children, or cultivating a com-munity of caring friends. They might extend further by bringing greater humanness into their everyday dealings with people, by helping others wake up from the numbing and soullessness taking over the world, by caring for the place on earth they inhabit, by turning away from soul-depleting influences like television and devoting more time to real conversation, meditation, spiritual practice, or creativity, or by dedicating their lives to serving the forces of awakening and renewal in our society at large. These are but a few of countless ways that lovers could start to expand their vision and their love. Sharing with others what they discover as they heal their own inner divisions is the greatest gift they could offer our fractured world.

Notes

INTRODUCTION

1. "Therapy and meditation have their own proper domains, which should not be confused. People often ask me if I teach my therapy clients to meditate. I generally do not try to mix these two paths. Since meditation is the most powerful method I know for dissolving ego-clinging, introducing it as a purely therapeutic technique for feeling better would be to risk making it into a mental health gimmick. As the British psychologist Robin Skynner points out, 'The more powerful a technique is, the more dangerous it can be in preventing real change if it is misused.'

It is important not to blur the distinction between therapy and meditation, for this may lead to confusing self-integration and self-transcendence. This confusion could weaken the effectiveness of therapy to help us find ourselves, by trying to make it achieve something more than it is designed for. And it could dilute the power of meditation, diminishing its unique potential to open our eyes to a radically fresh vision of who we are and what we are capable of." (Welwood 1980, pp. 138–39).

PART I INTRODUCTION

1. Although I use the term *Eastern psychology* in this book, strictly speaking, there is no Eastern *psychology* in the Western sense of this term: the objective study of psyche, self, and behavior as they develop through time. The Eastern understanding of the mind is arrived at mostly through intuitive knowledge, based on direct, nonconceptual recognition of different states and dimensions of consciousness.
2. Of course, these three levels could be further differentiated into further sublevels, as Ken Wilber, for one, has done in his work. I limit my investigation here to just these three levels because they are the most readily demarcated in our ongoing experience.
3. The Buddhist teaching of the three *kaya*s is much vaster and more profound than my description here. The three levels of mind, as I articulate them here, are but one way of looking at the three *kaya*s.

4. For a further discussion of this, see Welwood 1979a.
5. There are many schools in Western psychology that have also focused on the body-mind; for example, the existential/humanistic tradition, which has given special attention to prereflective felt experience and its meaning. The Jungian tradition has also illuminated this level of mind by studying its archetypal patternings.

   Eastern psychology focuses on the body-mind through energy practices such as tai chi chuan, hatha yoga, dream yoga, and inner yogas that work with chakras and subtle energy flow. However, the special focus of Eastern psychology is on the still deeper level of unconditioned, nonconceptual awareness, which is accessed through meditation. To study this level of mind, Western psychologists would also have to engage in contemplative disciplines—which is in fact finally beginning to happen.

Chapter 3   Ego Strength and Egolessness

1. This description of the *skandha*s is not the traditional formulation found in Abhidharma psychology, but grows out of a more Vajrayana-style interpretation that was set forth by Chögyam Trungpa (1973).
2. These three strategies correspond to Karen Horney's analysis of the three basic styles of defense mechanism: moving toward, moving against, and moving away from.
3. Of course, this is true only for those who already have an intact ego.

Chapter 4   The Play of the Mind

1. In terms of the Buddhist teaching of the three *kaya*s, we could say that the contents of consciousness belong to the *nirmanakaya*, the realm of manifest form. The pulsation of the mindstream, with its alternation between movement and stillness, belongs to the *sambhogakaya*, the realm of energetic flow. And the larger open ground of awareness, first discovered in moments of stillness, is the *dharmakaya*, the realm of pure being itself, eternally present, spontaneous, and free of entrapment in any form whatsoever.

Chapter 5   Meditation and the Unconscious

1. Of course, the essence of meditation can never be grasped through conceptual understanding alone, precisely because its very nature transcends the conceptual mind, which functions through dualistic constructs based on the self/other split. Meditation is not a particular delimited experience, but rather a way of *seeing through* experience. For this reason, no psychology of meditation could ever be a substitute for the personal understanding derived from actually engaging in the practice.

2. The id remained an unconscious region separate from the ego, and Freud continually fell back into the topographic language whose implications he himself repudiated.

3. Freud, for instance, conceived of mind as a psychical "apparatus to which we ascribe the characteristics of being extended in space" (1949, p.14).

4. Jung admits the separation between mind and universe as a basic feature of Western thought: "The development of Western philosophy during the last two centuries has succeeded in isolating the mind in its own sphere and in severing it from its primordial oneness with the universe" (1958, p. 476).

CHAPTER 6   PSYCHOLOGICAL SPACE

1. A couple of exceptions to this are James 1890 and Matte Blanco 1975.

2. Strictly speaking, all three types of space should not be called *psychological*. Inner, feeling space is psychological in the proper sense of the term, while outer, orientational is *somatic*, and the space of being is *ontological* (prior to felt experience). I use the term *psychological space* loosely in this chapter, as a synonym for *lived space*, space as experienced.

3. This kind of limitless openness is different from the relative openness of "self-actualization," which is often taken as the goal of psychotherapy and personality-based psychologies. While self-actualizing individuals may be able to move fluidly from one feeling space to another, they still move in a world of limits, boundaries, and self-referentiality. While they may have some mastery in the area of feeling space, the fully awake being is a master of open space.

CHAPTER 14   EMBODYING YOUR REALIZATION

1. Certainly under the right circumstances spiritual practice by itself can totally transform the personality—for instance, under the close personal tutelage of a great teacher, or in a person with strong innate aptitudes, or in spiritual retreat of many years' duration. (In Tibet, certain kinds of transformation were said to require a twelve-year retreat.)

2. Although living an otherworldly life was a common and accepted lifestyle in traditional Asia, I am not suggesting that all or even most Asian spiritual adepts display this otherworldly strain. Many have lived in the world with a high level of personal integration. What is true in general is that the essential Eastern teachings focus on realizing absolute true nature, rather than on cultivating an individuated, personal expression of that nature. Of course, different Asian cultures and traditions, and even different schools within a single tradition, such as Buddhism, differ greatly in how much they stress the impersonal element. I have chosen not to

address these distinctions here, which would require a much longer, more scholarly treatment.

3. This is of course a generalization. I am speaking here of most Tibetans who have grown up in a traditional family/community context. I do know some modern Tibetans, even teachers, who suffer from personal, psychological wounding, for whom psychotherapy might be of benefit. I have also spoken with one Tibetan who has a sophisticated understanding of Western psychology and recognizes its benefits for Tibetans who live in the West. In his words:

> Tibetans will need more psychological care as they come into the modern world, even in India. We are seeing more disruptive behavior as well as cognitive problems in children coming out of Tibet.
>
> For myself, since I've chosen to live in the West, rather than in a monastery, I find that Buddhist teachings alone are not adequate to meet my own needs to function effectively in this world. I have to turn to Western psychology for basic things like interpersonal skills, learning to communicate well, and having meaningful relationships.
>
> Considering how some Tibetan monks who come to the West deal with emotional and relationship problems they encounter here, we can infer that the traditional spiritual practices alone are not enough for helping them deal with these problems. In many ways Buddhism does not have the specificity that is required to handle the emotional and relational situations that they encounter in a Western cultural context.

4. One telling sign of the difference between child-rearing influences East and West: Tibetan teachers, who traditionally begin compassion practices by instructing students to regard all sentient beings as their mothers, have been surprised and dismayed by the difficulty many American students have in using their mothers as a starting point for developing compassion.

5. Roland reports an interesting case of two Indian women married to American men with whom he worked, for whom "it took many years of psychoanalysis with a warm, supportive analyst gradually to be able to have a more individualized self" and thus function normally in American society (1988, p. 198).

6. This is not to say that most Westerners are truly individuated or even interested in this. Unfortunately, individualism—which is a lower-level approximation—is the closest most modern Westerners come to individuation. Nevertheless, genuine individuation is a real possibility here, and often the most alienated are those who feel most called in this direction.

7. As Karlfried Graf Dürckheim points out, for most Eastern teachers, "the individual form acquired in the process [of spiritual awakening] is not taken seriously as such. . . . This, however, is the very thing that counts

for Western masters . . . [freedom] *to become* the person that one individually is. For us in the West, it is more important that a new worldly form should emerge *from* true nature and witness to Being . . . than that the ego should dissolve *in* true nature and *in* Being" (1992, p.100).

Speaking of the Japanese Zen masters he studied with, Dürckheim notes: "As masters, they appear in a supreme form in which every personal element has been converted into something suprapersonal, almost remote from the world, or at least not involved in it. One rarely, if ever, meets the happy or suffering individual, through whose joy-filled, sorrow-filled eye the otherworldly glimmers in a unique personal sense. . . . Is such a master a person in our sense of the term?" (p. 101).

8. Teachers from the Far East—often from China, Japan, or Korea, who work with the body-mind, emphasizing the connection to the earth in their teaching—are one major exception to this. For example, teachers of tai chi, chi kung, and aikido always stress the importance of the belly center and good grounding. Many Zen teachers also rarely speak of spiritual realization, but instead have their students attend to the earthy details of chopping wood and carrying water.

9. Of course, personal psychological work is not in itself sufficient for spiritual transformation or for the integration of our larger being into our personal functioning. In addition to finding a spiritual teacher or practice that strips away egocentricity, particular individuals may also need to work on their body, their livelihood, their intimate relationships, or their relation to community. But psychological work can help people recognize the areas where they need work and clear away some obstacles in these areas.

10. The relationship with a spiritual master can also address these dynamics, especially for those rare students who have a close, personal connection with a teacher who carefully supervises them.

CHAPTER 18   LOVE, CONDITIONAL AND UNCONDITIONAL

1. This was quoted in *Brain/Mind Bulletin* 9, no. 10 (May 1984).

CHAPTER 19   PASSION AS PATH

1. Many of the great cathedrals of Europe were built on pagan power spots and dedicated to St. Michael, the slayer of dragons, which represent this "lower" nature.

Glossary

Included here are short definitions of Buddhist terms as well as some of my own terminology, as used in this book. All non-English terms are in Sanskrit, except where noted.

AWAKENING   The process of (a) waking up *from* unconscious tendencies, beliefs, reactions, and self-concepts that function automatically and keep us imprisoned in a narrow view of who we are and what life is about; and (b) waking up *to* our true nature as the free and spontaneous, transparent presence of being.

AWARENESS   As used in this book, this term points to something much larger than the ordinary meaning of "I am aware that . . ." *Awareness* here indicates the very essence of the mind—a larger, direct knowing that is not dependent on concepts. This *nonconceptual awareness* is the larger, fluid, dynamic, expansive ocean that both underlies and constitutes all the various mind waves of thought and feeling.

    Awareness in this larger sense is self-existing, for it is always present as the very core of our experience and thus cannot be fabricated. It also has its own experiential qualities of clarity, presence, energy, responsiveness, alertness, fluidity, spaciousness, and warmth.

BASIC GOODNESS   The translation of a Tibetan term that refers to the wholesome nature of our being, as well as the intrinsic wonder and delight of reality when things are seen in their suchness. This is not a Pollyanna term meant to gloss over the evil, greed, and aggression in human behavior; instead, it signifies the unconditional awakeness and responsiveness that constitute our very essence. Basic goodness is nonconceptual and unconditional, having nothing to do with concepts of good versus bad. It is what we perceive when the doors of our perception are cleansed of egocentric fixation, bias, and grasping.

BEING   A Western term that indicates our fundamental, essential nature, which is a living presence within us. As the Indian teacher Poonja said, "Being is presence. To recognize this is wisdom and freedom." As a noun, the word *being* can sound static or abstract. But if we consider it as a verb form—*be-ing*—it denotes the living process that we are, an immediate coming-into-presence and engaging with what is. This nameless, formless presence—in, around, behind, and between all our particular thoughts and experiences—is what the Eastern traditions regard as our true nature, or home ground, and the Western traditions regard as the essential self or holy spirit. Because being is present in all things, our being is also, in Thich Nhat Hanh's words, *interbeing*. (In this book I avoid capitalizing *being* except in cases where the syntax could otherwise be confusing.)

BODHICHITTA   Although this term has different specific meanings in different Buddhist contexts and traditions, it generally refers to the mind that is turned toward awakening. Sometimes translated as "the mind of enlightenment" or "awakened heart," this term is also usually associated with compassion and the genuine desire to help others. In many contexts it means the aspiration to awaken fully to our true nature, so that one can help others also awaken in this way.

BODY-MIND   *See* MIND.

BUDDHA-NATURE   Literally, our awake nature, embryonically present in all human beings. Although most people do not recognize their fundamentally awake nature, it nonetheless remains active and alive behind the scenes.

COEMERGENCE   A term from the Mahamudra tradition that indicates the tendency of absolute and relative, clarity and confusion, true nature and ego to arise together as two inseparable aspects of human experience. From this perspective, the self-referential ego is not some separate principle, but only a limited version of true nature. Therefore, it need not be rejected, but can instead be transmuted into its essence, which is buddhanature.

DHARMA   The way reality works, the basic law of the universe. It also refers to the teachings about the nature of reality, as in the term *Buddhadharma*.

DZOGCHEN (Tibetan)   Literally, the great completion or perfection. The ultimate nondual teaching found in the Tibetan tradition, oriented toward the pure nature of nonconceptual awareness. Dzogchen is often known as the path of self-liberation because it emphasizes allowing whatever arises in one's experience to arise just as it is without reacting to it in any way; when one can meet one's experience in this fresh, nonreactive way, it spontaneously releases any fixation or tension, revealing itself as none other than pure awareness itself.

EGO   In this book I use this term broadly, to refer to the habitual activity of grasping onto images and concepts of oneself, an activity that separates us from our true nature. In Western psychology, *ego* has many different meanings, but generally refers to (a) the managerial capacity of the psyche that balances different impulses and demands and governs worldly functioning, and/or (b) the self-representational capacity that maintains a stable self-image and thus a consistent, continuous sense of self. Eastern and Western psychology could probably agree on a broad definition of *ego* as a fabricated or constructed sense of self, which provides a sense of control that we seem to need in our early development for survival and protection (see chapter 3).

EGOLESSNESS   A translation of the Buddhist term *anatman*, which literally means no-self. This term is not meant to deny the conventional existence of a functional, working ego or self, but rather to point beyond it to our larger being, which is inherently free of egoic self-concern. Egolessness, then, is the ground of ego, just as an open hand is the basis for making a fist. In this analogy, the hand is more basic, more fundamental, more real than the fist, which is only a transitory contraction that arises out of the open hand (see chapter 3).

EMPTINESS   This term, which has many levels of meaning in different Buddhist contexts and traditions, does not refer to some *thing* that can be pinned down, or to a definite attribute of things, like hot or cold, large or small. *Emptiness* is a word that points to what is beyond all words and concepts—the dimension of reality that cannot be pinned down as something definite, solid, fixed, unchanging, or graspable. It is the spacious boundlessness of being, or in Herbert Guenther's term, "the open dimension of being." It is being experienced as spaciousness, which is both pregnant with possibilities and intrinsically free of conceptual obscurations. Because it is what allows things to be, to manifest as what they are, it is also a fullness. And because of this spacious quality of being, no mental fixation or emotional compulsion can finally stick to us. Therefore, it forms the basis for spiritual liberation and awakening.

Other terms that approximate the meaning of emptiness: *fathomlessness, expansiveness, the undefinable, the unknown* or *unknowable, ever-changingness, potentiality.*

HEART   Our basic openness and responsiveness to reality, which expresses itself in human tenderness and warmth. *Heart* is one possible way to translate the Buddhist term BODHICHITTA. In contrast to soul, which unfolds in time and space, like a seed developing its potential, heart is like the sun—already full and radiant.

IDENTITY   A self-concept fashioned out of our childhood relations with others, which we identify with, imagining that it accurately represents who we are. This is like looking in a mirror and taking the image we see there as an accurate and complete picture of who we are, instead of recognizing that it is only a partial, superficial image of our bodily form. The identity structure is generally comprised of two halves: the *conscious identity*—a positive image of self that we actively try to promote in order to compensate for an underlying *subconscious identity*—a sense of deficiency that we try to cover up because it threatens our security and self-esteem.

IDENTITY PROJECT   The continual attempt to establish our conscious identity as something solid, definite, and worthwhile. This is an endless project because identity is only a mental concept and can thus never be finally established. Part of the driving force behind the identity project is our need to establish and prove our conscious identity in order to counteract a subconscious, deficient identity that is threatening. For example, "I am in control" covers up the underlying fear that "I am helpless"; "I am independent" covers up "I am too needy"; and so on.

INDIVIDUATION   The path of embodying our absolute true nature in an individual way that expresses our unique calling and unique gifts. Becoming a fully developed individual involves cultivating a whole range of our basic human resources, which exist as seed potentials within us, but which are often blocked by unconscious psychological patterns. Individuation in this sense has nothing to do with individualism—compulsively defending and reinforcing our separate individuality. Instead, it involves forging a vessel—the authentic individual—through which we can bring absolute true nature into form—the "form" of our person. The authentic individual is fully transparent to the larger ground of being.

KARMA   The chain of cause and effect, conditioned responses, and habitual patterns. More specifically, the transmission of tendencies from one mind-moment to the next, the process of one thing leading to another, usually without much consciousness on our part. The path of awakening is often seen as a process of bringing consciousness to bear on this unconscious functioning of habitual patterns from the past, so that they no longer rule our life.

KAYA   Literally, body; used in Buddhism to refer to the three bodies of the Buddha, the three ways in which reality manifests: as form *(nirmanakaya)*, energy *(samboghakaya)*, and space *(dharmakaya)* (see introduction to part 1).

KLESHA   Emotional fixations that accompany the activity of ego clinging, namely, pride, aggression, greed, jealousy, and indifference.

MAHAMUDRA   Literally, the great gesture. The complete, spontaneous opening to reality as it is through recognizing reality as no different from oneself, no different from the awareness that is opening to it, so that there is complete interpenetration of self and world. *Mahamudra* also refers to the Vajrayana tradition that practices this teaching.

MAITRI   Loving-kindness, unconditional friendliness; the willingness to allow ourselves to feel what we feel and have the experience we are having, without judging ourselves for it. This is the basis for real growth and change, for as long as we stand in judgment of ourselves, we remain divided and cannot move forward in any wholesome, unified way.

MIND   As generally used in this book, this term refers to the whole of our experiencing, not just mental functioning. What we usually call *mind* in the West refers to the surface level of conceptual activity. Yet beyond the *conceptual mind* we also can find two larger levels of mind always operating. *Body-mind* is a more subtle, holistic way of sensing, knowing, and interacting with reality that usually operates outside the range of normal consciousness. At this level, I am not just my fleshly body, not just my thoughts, not just my feelings, and not just my bounded ego, but a larger field of energy, which is intimately interconnected with the whole of reality and can therefore tap into subtler ways of knowing and being. Body-mind is a bridge between the form-oriented functioning of surface mind and the deeper, formless dimension of *big mind*, nonconceptual awareness. Nonconceptual awareness is the larger essence of mind itself, an eternal, living presence that gives rise to all the mind activity at the other two levels. These three levels of mind correspond to the gross, subtle, and causal bodies in certain esoteric systems and to the three KAYAS in Buddhist psychology (see part 1 introduction, and chapter 4).

MINDFULNESS   Clear attention to what is happening in one's MINDSTREAM, in one's activity, or in the environment. This involves noticing what is happening without reacting to it or becoming identified with it. Mindfulness meditation is a practice that deliberately cultivates this kind of nonreactive witnessing.

MINDSTREAM   The ongoing stream of mind activity, whose dynamic is an alternation between movement and stillness, between differentiated mind-moments (thought, feeling, sensation, and perception) and undifferentiated mind-moments (open spaces, gaps, silence, and nondoing) that point to the larger, unconditional stillness of the ground of being, which lies behind the mindstream altogether.

NONDUAL   Refers to the highest level of the Eastern spiritual teachings, which emphasize that our relative self is not essentially different or separate from the absolute ground of being, the true nature of all things. Nondual teachings take the absolute perspective, where individual differences are recognized but not regarded as fundamental. For example, there are countless forms of gold jewelry in existence, yet they are all fundamentally gold. Whether we judge their particular shapes and forms beautiful or ugly does not alter the fact that they are all equally gold.

Thus, from a nondual perspective, personal and suprapersonal, body and mind, individual and universal, matter and spirit, are only different expressions of a more primary, fundamental reality, which, strictly speaking, cannot even be named. Because this fundamental reality is our very nature, we cannot stand back from it and objectify it.

NONMEDITATION   A term from the DZOGCHEN tradition that refers to completely resting, without meditation technique, in the pure, transparent presence of self-existing awareness. From this perspective, formal meditation methods still remain within the sphere of conceptual mind because they involve some directed intention or method. Nonmeditation is the fruition of meditation practice and goes beyond the conceptual mind altogether.

OBJECT RELATIONS   A technical term that refers to the self/other imprints that form in the course of our development and shape our sense of identity. To say that our identity is based on object relations means that it is constructed out of our reaction to how significant others saw us, treated us, and responded to us.

Every object relation consists of three elements: a view of other, a view of self in relation to other, and a feeling that accompanies this particular relation. For example, if we see our parents as caring and supportive, we may develop a view of ourselves as worthwhile, and the corresponding feeling might be confidence or self-respect. If our parents are abusive, we may come to see others as threatening and ourselves as a victim, and our life may be permeated by a mood of fear, distrust, or paranoia. From this perspective, every view of other implies a view of self, and every view of self implies a view of other. A less technical term I use for object relations is *self/other setups*.

ONTOLOGY   The study of being. An ontological approach looks at things in light of our essential being, rather than in light of more contingent conditions that have shaped us. Psychology, by contrast, is the study of developmental, environmental, temperamental, and organic conditions that shape human life, in contrast to the more fundamental perspective of ontology, the study of being itself and how it infuses our life.

OPEN GROUND, OPEN SPACE   The fundamentally open nature of awareness underlying all conditioned states of mind. This open background awareness—somewhat analogous to the screen on which a film is projected—can be glimpsed in the spaces between thoughts and moments of mind fixation. Meditation provides a more formal way of noticing these gaps in the MINDSTREAM.

PERSON   When I use the term *true* or *authentic person*, I am referring to the way in which absolute true nature can manifest and express itself in a uniquely personal way. The person in this sense is the uniquely human vehicle through which true nature shines. It is not a solid, substantial structure, but rather a particular quality of presence. The true person develops through inner work, through stripping away the dross—the conditioning and obscurations that prevent us from embodying our individual seed potentials. The true person is the fruition of the process of individuation. Person is the outer manifestation of this fruition—how we manifest. SOUL is the inner manifestation—how we are. The true person is the capacity for personal presence, personal contact, and personal love—which makes it possible for personal intimacy to become a transformative path.

PERSONALITY   The whole complex of our conditioned nature, including the managerial ego, the ego identity, and all the habitual patterns that arise out of taking ourselves to be this identity. Conditioned personality is thus quite different from the true person.

PHENOMENOLOGY   Literally, the study of phenomena; the study of the structure of experience and how it works. Thus, a phenomenological psychology does not start with theories or hypotheses but stays very close to experience. Its concepts are experience-near. For example, defining ego as the synthesizing activity of the psyche is not phenomenological, because we cannot actually experience this synthesizing activity. Ego in this definition is merely a theoretical construct, what the philosopher F. S. C. Northrup calls a *concept by postulation*. Defining ego as the activity of grasping, by contrast, *is* phenomenological because we can actually experience this grasping activity as a tension in the mind and in the body. This is what Northrup calls a *concept by intuition*.

Of course, concepts by postulation have their place and their usefulness. But in the realm of psychology they can become problematic, especially when they are jumbled together with experiential realities. The psychoanalytic concept of ego, for example, is often confusing because it mixes hypothetical and experiential elements together.

SAMSARA   The way that the mind creates a deluded view of reality through mistaken or false ideas. In Tibetan, this terms implies "going around in circles." Samsara is the confusion and suffering that results from not recognizing our true nature, but instead basing our life on the fiction of the constructed self, imagining that our thoughts about who we are represent reality.

SKANDHAS   Literally, aggregates of tendencies that form the building blocks of EGO. These five constituents of ego activity include: *form* (the tendency to contract against the open ground and solidify self as separate from other, as well as separate from Being itself), *feeling* (taking positions for or against, based on that initial split), *impulse* (grasping, rejecting, ignoring), *conceptualization* (developing elaborate story lines and beliefs about self and other), and *consciousness* (the ongoing stream of mind activity, the busy mind).

SOUL   Our true nature as it unfolds and individuates in time and space, soul is, in Rumi's words, "a growing consciousness." In Aurobindo's words it is a "spark of the divine" that contains a double yearning: (a) to connect with our ground, to realize our deeper essence as pure, open presence; and (b) to embody our larger nature *in this world*, to know ourselves *in this human form*. Thus, soul is an intermediate principle or bridge, which allows a living integration between the two sides of our nature: the individual and the universal, the embodied realm of personal experience and the formless presence of pure being.

Soul is like a seed, an embryonic potential of authentic humanness that may or may not sprout and develop in a given individual. In this sense, soul needs to be cultivated if it is to reach its full potential. Soul is the inner side of the authentic person.

SUCHNESS   The pure, ineffable isness of things, which can only be known directly and wordlessly. For example, how could anyone ever put into words the particular youness of you, the quality of your unique presence, which no one else manifests in just the same way? Suchness means *as it is in itself, just so.*

TANTRA, TANTRIC BUDDHISM   *Tantra* literally means *continuity,* referring to the continuity and coemergence of absolute and relative truth, heaven and earth, spirit and matter, emptiness and form, awakening and SAMSARA. From the Tantric perspective, samsara and awakening are woven together as two sides of one cloth. That is why confused emotions and mind-states can suddenly transform into awakened consciousness, and why Tantra is known as the path of transformation. Therefore, one does not have to try to escape or avoid impurity, confusion, pain, darkness, aggression, fear, and all the other difficult states. In fact, the more one flees these states or tries to fix them, the more one distances oneself from the potential awakening hidden within them. *See also* VAJRAYANA.

TRANSMUTATION   A process of psychological transformation that involves dissolving negative, harmful states of mind back into their true nature as pure, awake AWARENESS.

TRUE NATURE　That which is intrinsic and unconditioned; roughly synonymous with BUDDHA-NATURE and *ground of being*. This term is an attempt to name the unnamable. Our essential nature is a presence that we can directly experience but cannot capture in words, any more than we can really describe what a peach tastes like. For this reason, some Eastern teachers prefer not to use any word to name our fundamental nature, using only the term *That*.

UNCONDITIONAL PRESENCE　The capacity to fully acknowledge, allow, and open to our immediate experience just as it is, without agenda, judgment, or manipulation of any kind. Here we are at one with our experience, without the subject/object barrier. This is an innate capacity of our being, yet we usually have to learn to cultivate it at first, because the habitual tendency of EGO always involves grasping and rejecting, which reinforce separation and counteract authentic presence.

UNDERSTANDING　In the context of psychological work, this term is meant to indicate empathic knowing, rather than purely intellectual comprehension. For example, if your child is crying, you can be understanding without having to know the exact cause of the tears: "I can see you're hurting. I understand you're having a hard time." That type of kind understanding is what we need to extend to ourselves when we are caught up in our various conditioned mind-states. As a blend of both wisdom and compassion, it has a clarifying and liberating effect.

VAJRAYANA　Literally, the indestructible path; this term is roughly synonymous with TANTRA in the Buddhist tradition. This path is considered indestructible because it works directly with all the energies of the psyche and the phenomenal world, transmuting negative forces and emotions into qualities of awakened AWARENESS. Vajrayana Buddhism developed mainly in Northern India and Tibet, though it can also be found in all the Himalayan countries, as well as in Japan.

Sources

Chapter 3. Ego Strength and Egolessness

P. 39   James 1890, p. 339.
P. 40   Ramana Maharshi, in Godman 1985, p. 53.
P. 40   Becker 1973, p. 55.
P. 41   Masterson 1988, pp. 23–24.
P. 41   Ramana Maharshi, in Godman 1985, p. 52.
P. 41   Jung 1958, p. 484.
Pp. 44–45   James 1890, p. 299.
P. 45   Cox 1977, p. 139.
P. 46   Freud 1959, p. 57.

Chapter 4. The Play of the Mind

P. 49   James 1890, p. 255.
P. 51   James 1890, pp. 243–44.
P. 51   James 1890, p. 244.
P. 52   James 1890, p. 240.
P. 54   James 1890, p. 253.
P. 54   James 1890, p. 252.
P. 54   Mozart quoted in James 1890, p. 255n.
P. 55   Trungpa and Hookham 1974, p. 8.
P. 55   Tarthang Tulku 1974, pp. 9–10.
P. 56   Capra 1975, p. 210.
P. 57   Guenther 1959, p. 54.
P. 57   Wangyal 1997, p. 29.
P. 57   quoted in Guenther 1956, p. 269.

Chapter 5. Meditation and the Unconscious

P. 58   Kretschmer 1969, p. 224.
P. 59   Jung 1958, pp. 501, 508.
P. 59   *in at least sixteen different senses:* see Miller 1942.
P. 60   Jung 1933, p. 185.
P. 60   *a place or a realm that can be inhabited by such entities as ideas:* MacIntyre 1958, p. 45.
P. 61   *to the state of unconsciousness with its qualities of oneness, indefiniteness, and timelessness:* Jung 1958, p. 496.
P. 61   *I cannot imagine a conscious mental state that does not relate to an ego:* Jung 1958, p. 484.
P. 62   Trungpa 1969, p. 55.
P. 62   Jung 1958, p. 485.
P. 62   *The practice of meditation:* Trungpa 1969, p. 52.
P. 63   *You are not distracted because you see everything as it is:* Dhiravamsa 1974, p. 32.
P. 63   *like using a stone to sharpen a knife, the situation being the stone:* Guenther and Trungpa 1975, p. 22.
P. 63   Jung 1958, p. 502.
P. 64   For more about diffuse attention, see Ehrenzweig 1965.
P. 67   Gendlin 1973, p. 370.
Pp. 67–68   *systems of condensed experience (COEX):* Grof 1975.

P. 69   Dhiravamsa 1974, pp. 13, 31.
P. 69   Wilber 1975, p. 108.
P. 70   Traherne quoted in Huxley 1944, p. 67.
P. 71   *The alaya is the first phenomenalization of the Absolute:* Chaterjee 1971, pp. 18, 19, 22.
P. 71   Suzuki 1930, p. 197.
P. 71   Trungpa 1973, p. 122; 1976, p. 58.
P. 72   Matte Blanco 1975, p. 230.
P. 72   Trungpa 1973, p.122.
P. 73   *as though a veil had been removed from our eyes:* Trungpa, 1973, pp. 223, 219.
P. 74   *"an extraordinarily significant and numinous content [that] enters consciousness," resulting in a "new viewpoint":* Kirsch 1960, p. 85.
P. 74   Guenther 1975, p. 27.
P. 74   *the disintegrating powers of the unconscious:* Horsch 1961, p. 148.
P. 74   Hisamatsu 1968, p. 31.
P. 75   Van Dusen 1958 p. 254.
P. 76   *the whole universe with absolute simplicity and nakedness of mind:* Trungpa and Hookham 1974, p. 6.

CHAPTER 6. PSYCHOLOGICAL SPACE

P. 78   Minkowski 1970, p. 400.
P. 79   Rilke, as quoted in Bachelard 1964, p. 203.
P. 80   Govinda 1959, p. 117.
P. 81   *One Zen text suggests:* "Records Mirroring the Original Source," as cited in Hisamatsu, 1960.
P. 82   Trungpa 1976, pp. 153, 145.
P. 82   Jung 1959, pp. 356–57.
P. 83   Van Dusen 1958, p. 254.
P. 85   Rilke 1975, p. 28.

CHAPTER 7. THE UNFOLDING OF EXPERIENCE

P. 88   James 1967, pp. 295–96.
P. 89   For a fuller discussion of my holographic analogy, see Welwood 1982.
P. 89   Pribram 1971, p. 150.
P. 90   For Gendlin's work on Focusing and its philosophical underpinnings, see Gendlin 1962, 1964, 1978; for the research background of Focusing, see Gendlin et al. 1968; Rogers 1967; Walker et al. 1969.
P. 92   Levinson 1975, p. 12.
P. 92   Picard 1952, pp. 173, 36.
P. 93   Bohm 1973, p. 146.
P. 94   Gendlin 1978, p. 76.
P. 95   Levinson 1975, p. 18.
P. 96   Hillman 1972, p. 290.

CHAPTER 8. REFLECTION AND PRESENCE

P. 100   Poonja 1993, p. 33.
P. 102   Koestenbaum 1978, pp. 35, 70.
P. 102   Krishnamurti 1976, p. 214.
P. 103   *As the great Dzogchen yogi:* Kunsang 1993, p. 114.
P. 103   Nishitani 1982, p. 128.
P. 104   *Zen Master Dogen:* quoted in Izutsu 1977, p. 140.
P. 107   Marcel 1950, p. 101.
P. 108   Lodro Thaye quote in Nalanda 1980, p. 84.
P. 110   Nyima 1991, p. 129.
P. 111   Koestenbaum 1978, pp. 73, 82, 100, 101.
P. 112   Heidegger 1977, p. 127.
P. 112   Merleau-Ponty 1968, pp. 38–39, 139.
P. 112   Merrill-Wolff 1994.
P. 113   Nishitani 1982, p. 124.
P. 113   *Instead of seeking mind by mind, let be:* Guenther 1977, p. 244.

P. 114   Lodro Thaye quote in Nalanda 1980, p. 84.

P. 115   Trungpa 1973, pp. 218–19, 221, 222, 234, 235–36.

P. 115   Trungpa 1976, pp. 70–71.

P. 120   the "content mutation" that Gendlin describes: Gendlin 1964.

P. 122   Paltrul Rinpoche quote in Kunsang 1993, p. 120.

P. 122   Nishitani 1982, pp. 165-6.

P. 123   the standpoint of the subject that knows things objectively, and like-wise knows itself objectively as a thing called the self, is broken down: Nishitani 1982, p. 154.

P. 123   It can never be the "straight heart" of which the ancients speak: Nishitani 1982, pp. 154–55.

P. 123   Norbu 1986, p. 144.

P. 124   Tarthang Tulku 1974, pp. 9–10, 18.

P. 125   when we leap from the circumfer-ence to the center, into their very [suchness]: Nishitani 1982, p. 130.

CHAPTER 10. VULNERABILITY, POWER, AND THE HEALING RELATIONSHIP

P. 154   Hume 1888, p. 252.

P. 155   Sartre 1957, pp. 100–101.

CHAPTER 11. PSYCHOTHERAPY AS A PRACTICE OF LOVE

P. 166   It helps you make friends with the whole range of your experience. see Welwood 1986.

P. 169   Thurman 1987.

P. 169   the love that is imperturbable be-cause totally ultimate: Thurman 1976, pp. 56–57.

CHAPTER 13. MAKING FRIENDS WITH EMOTION

P. 182   Hillman 1961, p. 289.

P. 183   You can even be suffering; but just being alive is a quality per se: René Dubos in Needleman 1979, p. 59.

P. 188   Trungpa 1973, pp. 68–69.

P. 188   Trungpa 1976, p. 69.

P. 189   Tarthang Tulku 1978, pp. 54, 52; 1975, pp. 160–61.

P. 190   Benoit 1959, p. 143.

P. 191   Trungpa 1969, p. 23.

P. 191   Suzuki Roshi 1970, p. 36.

P. 192   Trungpa 1976, pp. 69–72.

CHAPTER 14. EMBODYING YOUR REALIZATION

P. 195   Aurobindo n.d., p. 98.

P. 201   Roland 1988, p. 250.

P. 202   Roland 1988, p. 226.

P. 202   pediatrician and psychoanalyst D. W. Winnicott: see Winnicott 1965.

P. 203   Dürckheim 1977.

P. 203   a state of "going-on-being" out of which . . . spontaneous gestures emerge: Greenberg and Mitchell 1983, p. 193.

P. 206   Klein 1995, p. 26.

P. 218   it contained a holy longing: for a further discussion of holy longing, see Welwood 1996, p. 100

P. 222   which I call the conscious identity: for a further discussion of con-scious and subconscious iden-tity, see Welwood 1996, chapter 3.

P. 224   an integral part of what he con-sidered the primary unit of human experience: the I-Thou relationship: see Schilpp and Friedman, 1967, p. 117.

Bibliography

Aurobindo. n.d. *Letters on Yoga.* Vol. 1. Pondicherry: Sri Aurobindo Ashram Birth Centenary Library.

Bachelard, G. 1964. *The poetics of space.* Trans. M. Jolas. New York: Orion Press.

Becker, E. 1973. *The denial of death.* New York: Free Press.

Benoit, H. 1955. *The supreme doctrine.* New York: Viking Press.

Bly, R., ed. 1980. *News of the universe.* San Francisco: Sierra Club Books.

Bohm, D. 1973. Quantum theory as an indication of a new order in physics. Part B. Implicate and explicate order in physical law. *Foundations of Physics* 3:139–68.

Boss, M. 1963. *Psychoanalysis and daseinsanalysis.* New York: Basic Books.

———. 1965. *A psychiatrist discovers India.* London: Oswald Wolff.

Buber, M. 1947. *Tales of the Hasidim.* New York: Schocken Books.

Capra, F. 1975. *The Tao of physics.* Boston: Shambhala Publications.

Casper, M. 1979. Space therapy and the Maitri project. *J. Transpersonal Psychol.* 6, no. 1. Reprint in J. Welwood, ed., *The meeting of the ways: Explorations in East/West psychology.* New York: Schocken Books.

Chaterjee, A. 1971. *Readings on Yogacara Buddhism.* Banaras: Hindu University Press.

Cox, H. 1977. *Turning East: The promise and peril of the new orientalism.* New York: Simon & Schuster.

Dhiravamsa. 1974. *The middle path of life.* Surrey, England: Unwin.

Dürckheim, K. G. 1977. *Hara: The vital center of man.* London: Unwin.

———. 1992. *Absolute living: The otherworldly in the world and the path to maturity.* New York: Arkana.

Ehrenzweig, A. 1965. *The psychoanalysis of artistic vision and hearing.* New York: Braziller.

Freud, S. 1933. *New introductory lectures on psychoanalysis.* London: Hogarth Press.

———. 1949. *An outline of psychoanalysis.* New York: Norton.

———. 1961. *Collected papers.* Vol. 4. New York: Norton.

Gendlin, E. T. 1962. *Experiencing and the creation of meaning*. New York: Free Press.

———. 1964. A theory of personality change. In P. Worchel & D. Byrne, eds., *Personality change*. New York: Wiley.

———. 1973. A phenomenology of emotions: Anger. In D. Carr and E. Casey, eds., *Explorations in phenomenology*. The Hague: Nijhoff.

———. 1981. *Focusing*. New York: Bantam Books.

———. 1996. *Focusing-oriented psychotherapy*. New York: Guilford Press.

Gendlin, E. T., J. Beebe, J. Cassens, M. Klein, and M. Oberlander. 1968. Focusing ability in psychotherapy, personality, and creativity. In J. Schlien, ed., *Research in psychotherapy*. Vol. 3. Washington, D.C.: American Psychological Association.

Godman, D., ed. 1985. *Be as you are: The teachings of Sri Ramana Maharshi*. New York: Arkana.

Govinda, Lama. 1959. *Foundations of Tibetan mysticism*. London: Rider.

Grof, S. 1975. *Realms of the human unconscious*. New York: Viking Press.

Greenberg, S., and S. Mitchell. 1983. *Object relations in psychoanalytic theory*. Cambridge, Mass.: Harvard University Press.

Guenther, H. V. 1956. Tibetan Buddhism in western perspective: The concept of mind in Buddhist Tantrism. *J. Oriental Studies* 3, no. 2: 261–77.

———. 1959. The philosophical background of Buddhist Tantrism. *J. Oriental Studies* 5:45–64.

———. 1977. *Tibetan Buddhism in western perspective*. Berkeley, Calif.: Dharma.

Guenther, H. V., and C. Trungpa. 1975. *The dawn of Tantra*. Boston: Shambhala Publications.

Heidegger, M. 1977. On the essence of truth. In D. F. Kreel, ed., *Martin Heidegger: Basic writings*. New York: Harper.

Hillman, J. 1961. *Emotion*. Evanston, Ill.: Northwestern University Press.

———. 1972. *The myth of analysis*. Evanston, Ill.: Northwestern University Press.

Hisamatsu, S. 1960. The characteristics of Oriental nothingness. In *Philosophical Studies of Japan*. Vol. 2. Tokyo: Maruzen.

———. 1968. Additional note to: On the unconscious, the self, and therapy. *Psychologia* 11:25–32.

Hoffer, E. 1951. *The true believer*. New York: Harper.

Horsch, J. 1961. The self in analytical psychology. *Psychologia* 4:147–55.

Hume, D. 1888. *A treatise on human nature*. Oxford: Clarendon Press.

Huxley, A. 1944. *The perennial philosophy*. New York: Harper & Row.

Izutsu, T. 1977. *Toward a philosophy of Zen Buddhism*. Teheran: Imperial Iranian Academy of Philosophy.

James, W. 1890. *The principles of psychology*. New York: Holt.

————. 1967. *The writings of William James.* Ed. J. McDermott. New York: Random House.

————. 1976. *Essays in radical empiricism.* Cambridge, Mass.: Harvard University Press.

Jung, C. G. 1933. *Modern man in search of a soul.* New York: Harcourt Brace.

————. 1958. Psychological commentary on the *Tibetan book of the great liberation.* In *Collected works.* Vol. 11. *Psychology and religion.* New York: Pantheon Books.

————. 1959. *The archetypes and the collective unconscious.* Vol. 9 of *Collected works.* New York: Pantheon Books.

Kapleau, P. 1979. *Zen: Dawn in the West.* New York: Doubleday.

Khan, H. I. 1962. *The Sufi message of Hazrat Inayat Khan.* Vol. 5. London: Barrie & Rockliff.

Kirsch, J. 1960. Affinities between Zen and analytical psychology. *Psychologia* 3:85–91.

Klein, A. 1995. *Meeting the great bliss queen: Buddhists, feminists, and the art of the self.* Boston: Beacon Press.

Koestenbaum, P. 1978. *The new image of the person.* Westwood, Conn.: Greenwood Press.

Kretschmer, W. 1969. Meditative techniques in psychotherapy. In C. T. Tart, ed., *Altered states of consciousness.* New York: Wiley.

Kunsang, E. P., trans. 1993. *The flight of the garuda: Five texts from the practice lineage.* Kathmandu: Rangjung Yeshe.

Levinson, E. 1975. A holographic model of psychoanalytic change. *Contemporary Psychoanalysis* 12, no. 1:1–20.

MacIntyre, A. 1958. *The unconscious: A conceptual analysis.* London: Routledge & Kegan Paul.

Marcel, G. 1950. *The mystery of being.* Vol. 1. *Reflection and mystery.* Chicago: Regnery.

Masterson, J. F. 1988. *The search for the real self.* New York: Free Press.

Matte Blanco, I. 1975. *The unconscious as infinite sets.* London: Duckworth.

Maupin, E. 1969. On meditation. In C. T. Tart, ed., *Altered states of consciousness.* New York: Wiley.

Merleau-Ponty, M. 1968. *The visible and the invisible.* Evanston, Ill.: Northwestern University Press.

Merrill-Wolff, F. 1994. *Experience and Philosophy.* Albany: State University of New York Press.

Miller, J. 1942. *Unconsciousness.* New York: Wiley.

Minkowski, E. 1970. *Lived time.* Evanston, Ill.: Northwestern University Press.

Nalanda Translation Committee, trans. 1980. *The rain of wisdom.* Boston: Shambhala Publications.

Needleman, J., ed. 1979. *Speaking of my life: The art of living in the cultural revolution.* San Francisco: Harper.

Nisargadatta 1973. *I am That.* Vol. 2. Bombay: Chetana.

Nishitani, K. 1982. *Religion and nothingness.* Berkeley and Los Angeles: University of California Press.

Norbu, N. 1986. *The crystal and the way of light.* New York: Routledge & Kegan Paul.

Northrop, F. S. C. 1946. *The meeting of east and west.* New York. Macmillan.

Nyima, C. 1991. *The bardo guidebook.* Kathmandu: Rangjung Yeshe.

Picard, M. 1952. *The world of silence.* Chicago: Regnery.

Poonja, H. L. 1993. *Wake up and roar.* Vol. 2. Maui, Hawaii: Pacific Center.

Pribram, K. 1971. *Languages of the brain.* Englewood Cliffs, N.J.: Prentice-Hall.

Rilke, R. M. 1975. *On love and other difficulties.* Ed. J. L. Mood. New York: Norton.

Rogers, C. R. 1959. A theory of therapy, personality, and interpersonal relationships. In S. Koch, ed., *Psychology: A study of a science.* Vol. 3. New York: McGraw-Hill.

———. 1967. *The therapeutic relationship and its impact: A program of research in psychotherapy with schizophrenics.* Madison: University of Wisconsin Press.

Roland, A. 1988. *In search of self in India and Japan: Toward a cross-cultural psychology.* Princeton, N.J.: Princeton University Press.

Sartre, J. P. 1957. *The transcendence of the ego.* New York: Noonday Press.

Schilpp, P., and M. Friedman, eds. 1967. *The philosophy of Martin Buber.* La-Salle, Ill: Open Court.

Solovyev, V. 1985. Love evolving. In J. Welwood, ed., *Challenge of the Heart: Love, sex, and intimacy in changing times.* Boston: Shambhala Publications.

Suzuki, D. T. 1930. *Studies in the Lankavatara Sutra.* London: Routledge & Kegan Paul.

Suzuki, S. 1970. *Zen mind, beginner's mind.* New York: Walker, Weatherhill.

Tarthang Tulku. 1974. On thoughts. *Crystal Mirror* 3:7–20.

———. 1975. Watching the watcher. *Crystal Mirror* 4:157–61.

———. 1978. *Openness mind.* Emeryville, Calif.: Dharma.

Thera, S., trans. 1963. *Kalama Sutra: The Buddha's charter of free inquiry.* Ceylon: Buddhist Publication Society.

Thurman, R. 1987. Dharma talk. *Wind Bell* 22, no. 2.

Thurman, R., trans. 1976. *The Holy Teaching of Vimalakirti.* University Park: Pennsylvania State University Press.

Trungpa, C. 1969. *Meditation in action.* Boston: Shambhala Publications.

———. 1973. *Cutting through spiritual materialism.* Boston: Shambhala Publications.

———. 1976. *The myth of freedom.* Boston: Shambhala Publications.

———. 1983. *Shambhala: The sacred path of the warrior.* Boston: Shambhala Publications.

Trungpa, C., and M. Hookham, trans. 1974. Maha Ati. *Vajra* 1:6–8.

Tsoknyi Rinpoche. 1998. *Carefree dignity: Discourses on training in the nature of the mind.* Kathmandu: Rangjung Yeshe.

Van Dusen, W. 1958. Wu-Wei, no-mind, and the fertile void in psychotherapy. *Psychologia* 1:253–56.

Walker, A., R. Rablen, and C. R. Rogers. 1959. Development of a scale to measure process change in psychotherapy. *Journal of Clinical Psychology* 16:79–85.

Wangyal, T. 1997. *A-Khrid teachings.* Vol. 2. Berkeley, Calif.: Privately published.

Watts, A. 1961. *Psychotherapy East and West.* New York: Pantheon.

Welwood, J. 1974. A theoretical re-interpretation of the unconscious from a humanistic and phenomenological perspective. Ph.D. diss. University of Chicago.

———. 1979a. Self-knowledge as the basis for an integrative psychology. *Journal of Transpersonal Psychology* 11, no. 2: 23–40.

———, ed. 1979b. *The meeting of the ways: Explorations in East/West psychology.* New York: Schocken Books.

———. 1980. Reflections on focusing, psychotherapy, and meditation. *Journal of Transpersonal Psychology* 12, no. 2: 127–142.

———. 1982. The holographic paradigm and the structure of experience. *Re-Vision* 1, nos. 3–4 (1978): 92-96. Reprint in K. Wilber, ed., *The holographic paradigm and other paradoxes.* Boston: Shambhala Publications.

———. 1983. *Awakening the heart: East/West approaches to psychotherapy and the healing relationship.* Boston: Shambhala Publications.

———. 1985. *Challenge of the heart: Love, sex, and intimacy in changing times.* Boston: Shambhala Publications.

———. 1986. On compassion and human growth. *The American Theosophist* 74, no. 9.

———. 1990. *Journey of the heart: The path of conscious love.* New York: HarperCollins.

———. 1992. *Ordinary Magic: Everyday life as spiritual path.* Boston: Shambhala Publications.

———. 1996. *Love and awakening: Discovering the sacred path of intimate relationship.* New York: HarperCollins.

Wilber, K. 1975. Psychologia perennis: The spectrum of consciousness. *Journal of Transpersonal Psychology* 7, no. 2:105–32.

Winnicott, D. 1965. *Maturational process and the facilitating environment: Studies in the theory of emotional development.* Madison, Wis.: International Universities Press.

Acknowledgments and Credits

I would like to thank my wife, Jennifer, as well as my editor, Joel Segel, for carefully reading the manuscript and giving me helpful feedback. Thanks also to all the friends and editors who read and commented on the original versions of the material in this book, and in particular, Barbara Green and Miles Vich. Finally, I would like to express my deep gratitude to all the great Dharma teachers who have imparted to me their wisdom, understanding, and blessings along my path.

The original sources of the material in this book are as follows:

Chapter 1 is a revised version of "Principles of Inner Work: Psychological and Spiritual," which originally appeared in *Journal of Transpersonal Psychology* 16, no. 1 (1984).

Chapter 2 is a revised version of "Personality Structure: Path or Pathology?," which originally appeared in *Journal of Transpersonal Psychology* 18, no. 2 (1986).

Chapter 3 is a completely new chapter based on some material that originally appeared in "On Ego Strength and Egolessness," a chapter that was co-written with Ken Wilber and published in my first book, *The Meeting of the Ways: Explorations in East/West Psychology* (New York: Schocken Books, 1979).

Chapter 4 is a substantial revision of "Exploring Mind: Form, Emptiness, and Beyond," which originally appeared in *Journal of Transpersonal Psychology* 8, no. 2 (1976).

Chapter 5 is a condensed and revised version of "Meditation and the Unconscious: A New Perspective," which originally appeared in *Journal of Transpersonal Psychology* 9, no. 1 (1977), and which grew out of my doctoral dissertation at the University of Chicago.

Chapter 6 is a substantial condensation and revision of "On Psychological Space," which originally appeared in *Journal of Transpersonal Psychology* 9, no. 2 (1977).

Chapter 7 is a substantial revision of "The Unfolding of Experience: Psychotherapy and Beyond," which originally appeared in *Journal of Humanistic Psychology* 22, no. 1 (1982).

Chapter 8 is a revised version of "Reflection and Presence: The Dialectic of Self-Knowledge," which originally appeared in *Journal of Transpersonal Psychology* 28, no. 2 (1997). Copyright © 1997 by The Transpersonal Institute.

Chapter 9 is a revised version of "The Healing Power of Unconditional Presence," which originally appeared in *Quest,* winter 1992.

Chapter 10 is a revised version of "Vulnerability and Power in the Therapeutic Process," which originally appeared in *Journal of Transpersonal Psychology* 14, no. 2 (1982).

Chapter 11 is a revised version of "Psychotherapy as a Practice of Love," which originally appeared in *Pilgrimage,* June 1988.

Chapter 12 is a revised version of "Depression as a Loss of Heart," which originally appeared in *Journal of Contemplative Psychotherapy* 3, no. 1 (1987).

Chapter 13 is a revised version of "Befriending Emotion: Self-Knowledge and Transformation," which originally appeared in *Journal of Transpersonal Psychology* 11, no. 1 (1979).

Chapter 14 is a completely new chapter.

Chapter 15 is a revised version of "Intimate Relationship as Path," which originally appeared in *Journal of Transpersonal Psychology* 22, no. 1 (1990).

Chapter 16 is a revised version of "Dancing on the Razor's Edge," which originally appeared in *Yoga Journal,* September 1984.

Chapter 17 is a revised version of "The Path of Conscious Relationship," which originally appeared in *Shambhala Sun,* January 1997.

Chapter 18 is a revised version of "On Love: Conditional and Unconditional," which originally appeared in *Journal of Transpersonal Psychology* 17, no. 1 (1985).

Chapter 19 is a revised version of "Passion as Path," which originally appeared in *Pilgrimage,* March 1993.

Chapter 20 is a revised version of "On Spiritual Authority: Genuine and Counterfeit," which originally appeared in *Journal of Humanistic Psychology* 23, no. 3 (1983).

Chapter 21 is a revised version of "Love and Awakening," which originally appeared in *Gnosis,* April 1997.

Index

About the Author

John Welwood, Ph.D., is a psychotherapist in San Francisco and associate editor of the *Journal of Transpersonal Psychology*. He received his Ph.D. in clinical psychology from the University of Chicago, where he studied existential psychology with Eugene Gendlin, and has been a student of Tibetan Buddhism and other Eastern spiritual traditions for more than thirty years. He has published more than fifty articles on relationship, psychotherapy, consciousness, and personal change, as well as several books including the best-selling *Journey of the Heart: The Path of Conscious Love; Love and Awakening: Discovering the Sacred Path of Intimate Relationship; Awakening the Heart: East/West Approaches to Psychotherapy and the Healing Relationship;* and *Ordinary Magic: Everyday Life as Spiritual Path*.

John and his wife Jennifer offer a range of different trainings, workshops, and meditative retreats on the integration of psychological and spiritual transformative work, as well as on conscious relationship. If you would like to be on their mailing list, please contact:

John and Jennifer Welwood
P. O. Box 2173
Mill Valley, CA 94942
415-381-6077